Alive in Christ

Alive in Christ

THOMAS HOLTON

CFI
An imprint of Cedar Fort, Inc.
Springville, Utah

© 2021 Thomas Holton
All rights reserved.

No part of this book may be reproduced in any form whatsoever, whether by graphic, visual, electronic, film, microfilm, tape recording, or any other means, without prior written permission of the publisher, except in the case of brief passages embodied in critical reviews and articles.

This is not an official publication of The Church of Jesus Christ of Latter-day Saints. The opinions and views expressed herein belong solely to the author and do not necessarily represent the opinions or views of Cedar Fort, Inc. Permission for the use of sources, graphics, and photos is also solely the responsibility of the author.

ISBN 13: 978-1-4621-3700-8

Published by CFI, an imprint of Cedar Fort, Inc.
2373 W. 700 S., Springville, UT, 84663
Distributed by Cedar Fort, Inc., www.cedarfort.com

Library of Congress Control Number: 2021939448

Cover design by Courtney Proby
Cover design © 2021 Cedar Fort, Inc.

Printed in the United States of America

10 9 8 7 6 5 4 3 2 1

Printed on acid-free paper

CONTENTS

Introduction 1

1. The Promise of New Life 5
2. Alive in Christ 11
3. Messianic Messengers 33
4. His Holy Name 51
5. Abounding through Covenants 71
6. Sainthood through Christ's Atonement 83
7. The Light That Shines in Darkness 111
8. The Schoolmaster 123
9. Revelatory Riches 143
10. In the Strength and Power of the Lord 159
11. The King of Kings Returns 181
12. Glorious Resurrection 191
13. The Greatest of All Gifts 201
14. Testifying of This Great Important Truth 209
15. An Eye Single to God's Glory 221

About the Author 247

INTRODUCTION

This book was born from my great admiration for the Lord Jesus Christ and my feelings of love toward my brothers and sisters everywhere. It is out of love—the Savior's profound love for me, and my learning to love Him and others—that I felt moved to write about how I have come to sense that each of us can achieve great and wondrous development in the things of the soul. When I have been touched by love, I have felt to love others. When I have been impacted by inspiration, I have yearned to inspire others. When I have known divine assurance, I have been moved to share such assurances with others so that they also might rejoice. The words that follow are written out of a deep personal desire to bless, serve, uplift, strengthen, comfort, console, beautify, and bring peace to all who read them.

I have long been convinced that there is a dreaded disease that subtly but persistently seeks to lull individuals into a state of spiritual slumber. It is a potent pandemic that easily crosses borders and endeavors to reach into the life of every living soul. It is spiritual apathy. It manifests itself in spiritual boredom, sluggishness, sleepiness, drowsiness, slumbering, casualness, fatigue, reluctance, hesitance, laziness, procrastination, carelessness, indifference, inaction, and ineffectiveness. It might appear to be relatively harmless, but it can be highly insidious and potentially dangerous to us. We are all at possible risk of catching this sickness that has the capacity, if we let it, to rob our lives of deep meaning, purpose, and power.

I have seen this ailment in my own life. I have also seen it in the lives of others. In every case it is disarming and effective at undermining the very principles and powers that have the most power to transform our lives. If we are not careful and decisive, we run the very real risk of nullifying those opportunities that could benefit us most and bring great blessings to others.

Thankfully, there is a tried and tested solution to this pernicious disease. When the Lord Jesus Christ walked the earth, He continually shocked, surprised, astonished, amazed, confronted, confounded, contradicted, disturbed, and breached the thoughts, traditions, expectations, and routines of people. Whether Pharisees, Sadducees, scribes, temple guards, tax collectors, fishermen, Romans, Jews, Gentiles, Samaritans, or even His own apostles, He constantly provided those around Him with different, distinctive, unusual, and altered ways of thinking, speaking, acting, behaving, and becoming. He did not believe, teach, or do what people expected Him to. Rather, He purposefully acted in a way that would be special and original. Consider the following phrases used in connection with his radical mortal ministry:

- "And all the people were amazed, and said, Is not this the son of David?" (Matthew 12:22–23).
- "And they were all amazed, insomuch that they questioned among themselves, saying, What thing is this? what new doctrine is this? for with authority commandeth he even the unclean spirits, and they do obey him" (Mark 1:27).
- "And immediately he arose, took up the bed, and went forth before them all; insomuch that they were all amazed, and glorified God, saying, We never saw it on this fashion" (Mark 2:12).
- "And he went up unto them into the ship; and the wind ceased: and they were sore amazed in themselves beyond measure, and wondered" (Mark 6:51).
- "And all that heard him were astonished at his understanding and answers. And when they saw him, they were amazed" (Luke 2:46–48).

INTRODUCTION

- "And it came to pass, that after three days they found him in the temple, sitting in the midst of the doctors, *and they were hearing him, and asking him* questions" (JST, Luke 2:46).
- "And immediately he rose up before them, and took up that whereon he lay, and departed to his own house, glorifying God. And they were all amazed, and they glorified God, and were filled with fear, saying, We have seen strange things to day" (Luke 5:25–26).
- "Many therefore of his disciples, when they had heard *this*, said, This is an hard saying; who can hear it? When Jesus knew in himself that his disciples murmured at it, he said unto them, Doth this offend you?" (John 6:60–61).

So, if we wish to put off spiritual distraction, boredom, and apathy, our need is to become "alive in Christ." This profound cure is literally what it purports to be. It is to put off the sleepy, slumbering, drowsy, and sluggish effects of apathy by becoming aware, awake, alert, and attentive through the soul-penetrating, pervasive, and lasting life-giving powers of our Lord and Savior Jesus Christ. To become alive in this sense is to become conscious of, and blessed by, the renewing, regenerating, refreshing, and revitalizing power of the living Son of God. This trek rescues us from the constant weariness of spiritual indifference and endows us with a newness of spiritual life. We can overcome spiritual denseness, sluggishness, sleepiness, drowsiness, cloudiness, fogginess, fuzziness, and murkiness. We can become spiritually alert, awake, focused, clear, alive, and full of clarity. How else can we find a new life of wonder, splendor, and majesty save in and through the Fountain of Life—Jesus Christ? This is surely a journey of critical and vital importance.

In this book I discuss some principles of power that allow every one of us, if we are willing, to become alive in Christ. To do so is to be forever transformed. My hope is to give comfort to those who find themselves afflicted by spiritual apathy but who may want to escape from its entangling clutches. To find significant meaning in deep tragedy, to receive consolation when we are disappointed, to discover purpose when we feel aimless, to be washed in excitement when waves of indifference have encompassed us about—these are worthwhile pursuits. Inspiration, amazement, rejoicing—these await us as we perceive the possibilities and opportunities that the Son of God makes available to us.

I am utterly assured that great blessings await each of us as we make this most important journey. The personage Christ should be met with joyful rejoicing on both sides of the veil (see Doctrine and Covenants 76:1; 114–118). His capacities are astonishing by any standard. He is mighty and majestic and cannot be overcome, defeated, or disempowered. He is truly the never failing, ever enduring Son of God. Jehovah is indeed the Good Shepherd of our souls, the great leader in our lives, and the remarkable restorer of our righteousness. Our Messiah is the compassionate comforter, the master of mercy, and the generous giver of grace. Jesus of Nazareth is the Creator, Atoning One, and Lord of the Resurrection. He is the instructor of prophets, the teacher of truth, and the King of Glory. How blessed we are to have His transforming influence come upon us, change us, guide us, and lift us. The praise that we give Him is never enough to truly indicate His impressive greatness. The ongoing revelations that allow us to know Him, love Him, and become more like Him are essential and important; indeed, they are crucial and vital.

1

THE PROMISE OF NEW LIFE

A NEWNESS OF LIFE

"I am ready." These are the words I said to my wife as I prepared to have emergency surgery for a ruptured small intestine just before Christmas in 2010. These words were intended to give comfort and consolation to my wife, who was obviously deeply worried about the state of my health. I had experienced much pain and inconvenience relating to a serious bowel disease in the years preceding this. There were many times of stress, pain, tears, and confusion. There was much soreness, disruption to my daily activities, medical tests, diverse treatments, and plenty of exhaustion.

This culminating experience, however, was much more painful and dangerous than any I had previously had. The pain was on an entirely different level, and I was in serious trouble. The surgery lasted many hours. Thanks to the goodness of the Lord, many prayers on my behalf, and the guided hands of a skilled and caring surgeon, I was blessed to live and recover from my life-threatening condition. When I woke up after surgery, I was completely immobilized. This is the closest I have ever felt to being paralyzed, and it was quite a scary reality. I felt wiped out. I was absolutely parched. I felt extremely sore, as if I had been run over by a bus. The effect of the painkillers I was on was scary, as I had quite severe hallucinations.

In addition, I found myself being depressed about the state I was in. Although I was relieved to be alive, I was also acutely aware of the suffering I had experienced, and it really got me down. I was in intensive care for about a week and then in a surgical ward for another five weeks or so. During that time, I was fed via a feeding tube. I lost a significant amount of weight and found being in the hospital—with all the attendant challenges that go with that—to be a refiner's fire.

At my wife's suggestion, I wrote my life history at that time. It became an insightful experience to me to clearly discern the hand of the Lord in my life up to that point. That was a healing and beneficial opportunity. I was grateful for family and friends to help me through a difficult time. Most of all, I was grateful to the Lord. I remain convinced to this day that were it not for the healing influence of the Savior throughout that time, I would not be here to relate the tale. When we say that the Lord is willing and able to run to us and to provide succoring help, we can be very much assured that this represents a glorious truth.

My recovery progressed quickly, and I healed remarkably. The medical staff were surprised at this. I have no doubt that the principles of the Word of Wisdom were very much in play in blessing me to this end. I became deeply grateful for the opportunity to be made well—not just physically but also emotionally and spiritually. I had further elective surgery in 2011 and have lifetime medication and regular medical check-ups to ensure I remain in remission. I have also found that I have learned to appreciate health and being pain free in a new way. I have a new understanding of what it means to be well because I know what it means to be sick. I comprehend the importance of vigor and energy much more deeply, as I have experienced excessive and persistent tiredness.

Why am I relating this personal incident? It is because of the lesson it teaches. Due to the nature of my medical condition, I have experienced physical fatigue as a recurrent feature of my life for the past twenty-plus years. Of course, there has also been emotional and spiritual fatigue. Nevertheless, I have also found that there are remedies for this weariness. The remedy has been the touch of the physician's hand and the prescribed course of treatment for however long it takes. Whether we are talking about mortal doctors who help heal the body or the Master Healer who can heal both body and spirit, the principle is somewhat the same.

We are all in need of help and healing. We all have ailments and difficulties that test and try us and deplete our energy. Whether the energy we need is to do temporal or spiritual tasks, we are all in need of strength and assistance at various times, in various ways, and from various sources. I am a great believer in getting the appropriate help from a useful source. If we need financial advice, we are wise to consult those who can teach us sound financial principles. If we want to learn a language, we go to those who are trained to teach us. We have doctors for health, lawyers for law, electricians for electrical repairs, pilots for flying, and teachers for teaching.

So, what about when it comes to learning about life? We are far more than just mortal beings. We are the spirit children of God. Is this not the powerful truth that Moses learned when he spoke with the premortal Jehovah who was representing His father: "And God spake unto Moses, saying: Behold, I am the Lord God Almighty. . . . And, behold, thou art my son" (Moses 1:3–4). This divine identity far exceeds in importance any other feature, title, or status by which we might come to define ourselves. Indeed, being a child of God is our first and most important identity. As such we have a perfect Father in Heaven who can teach us the true nature and meaning of life, both temporal and spiritual.

THE SOURCE OF OUR NEW LIFE

When it comes to finding the help we need spiritually, to what source should we look? The answer is abundantly clear in the following words from the prophet Nephi:

> As the Lord God liveth, there is none other name given under heaven save it be this Jesus Christ, of which I have spoken, whereby man can be saved. . . . For we labor diligently to write,

> to persuade our children, and also our brethren, to believe in Christ, and to be reconciled to God; for we know that it is by grace that we are saved, after all we can do . . . and we are made alive in Christ because of our faith; yet we keep the law because of the commandments.
>
> And we talk of Christ, we rejoice in Christ, we preach of Christ, we prophesy of Christ . . .
>
> Wherefore, we speak concerning the law that our children . . . may look forward unto that life which is in Christ, and know for what end the law was given. And after the law is fulfilled in Christ. . . And now behold, I say unto you that the right way is to believe in Christ, and deny him not; and Christ is the Holy One of Israel. (2 Nephi 25:20–29)

Several key doctrinal principles in these verses can be at the forefront of our minds and deeply embedded in our hearts. We are divinely commanded to be obedient to the commandments of God. This is no small or easy task. In this case, Nephi is referring to obedience to the law of Moses. Such obedience was obviously important. However, even keeping the commandments laid down in the law of Moses was not sufficient to save the people in the days of Moses. In and of itself the law was not living, and it could not save even one man from sin and death.

However, there is something that can save us from sin and death. Or rather, there is *someone* who can. Jesus Christ, the literal living Son of the literal living Father, is the true source of salvation. He is the one person who lived on this earth that has life in Himself. He is free from the consequences of personally committing sin that entices, traps, and entangles the rest of us. He is also free from the chains of physical death that bind all the rest of us. To look to Him as the one and only source of salvation is to look forward, upward, and onward to a holier, happier, and better life. It is to look with faith in Him. It is to believe that He has power to save us and the desire to save us. We are made "alive in Christ" through our faith in Him. There is no other way to be made alive in the deep spiritual sense. There is no newness of spiritual life except through Him. There is no lasting spiritual life except that which comes through

His goodness and grace. Through the lens of faith in the true and Living Christ everything else looks better.

Consequently, obedience to divine law is necessary but not sufficient. There must also be a Savior, a Redeemer, a Deliverer. That Messiah is Jesus Christ. There is simply no other way, name, person, means, or plan by which humanity can be saved (see Mosiah 3:17). Hence this is the key doctrine that Nephi taught to his children in the firm hope that they would grasp the significance of this message. This explains why Nephi talked about Christ, preached about Him, and prophesied of Him with so much clarity and relentless determination. It is also why every other true prophet that ever lived on this earth has done likewise. Notice also that Nephi said he rejoiced in Christ. To rejoice implies energy, passion, excitement, enthusiasm, and exuberance. Rejoicing is not casual or indifferent. It is happy and powerful. It reminds me of what children do at Christmas time when they receive the gifts they deeply want. To rejoice in Christ is to be grateful to Him and thankful to Him. It is to know Him, love Him, and bless His name.

HOW IS THIS NEW LIFE POSSIBLE?

How does Jesus Christ bring about this new life where we go from being asleep or even dead to being alive in Him? The answer is given in the revealed word. Amulek teaches us, "For according to the great plan of the Eternal God there must be an atonement made, or else all mankind must unavoidably perish; yea, all are hardened; yea, all are fallen and are lost, and must perish except it be through the atonement which it is expedient should be made" (Alma 34:8–9). What does this mean? Unless Jesus Christ comes into the mortal world to take our sins away, every person in the human family will be subject to an inevitable perishing. I understand the word *perishing* to mean both spiritual and physical death—with no opportunity for reprieve from either condition. In other words, every single one of us will have hard hearts, fall from grace, and be endlessly lost unless the Atonement of Jesus Christ is successfully accomplished. There simply would be no escape from this inexorable destiny without the Atonement. Without Christ we would be subject to all the consequences of our personal sins that we could never repent of. Every mistake, error, misstep, and misdeed would become compounded in our lives and we would have no way out. Nor could we ever be healed from the pain inflicted upon us through the sins of others. We could never have a mighty change of heart. There would be no such thing as repentance. We would descend further and further into the abyss of unrighteousness with no opportunity for redemption. Further, there could be no resurrection.

In fact, it is even much worse than this. The prophet Jacob explains why: "Save it should be an infinite atonement . . . our spirits must become subject to that angel who fell from before the presence of the Eternal God, and became the devil, to rise no more. And our spirits must have become like unto him, and we become devils, angels to a devil, to be shut out from the presence of our God, and to remain with the father of lies, in misery, like unto himself" (2 Nephi 9:7–9).

CONCLUSION

If there had been no infinite Atonement of Jesus Christ, then not only would there be no repentance or resurrection, but we would also inevitably have fallen under the eternal unrighteous dominion of the devil. He would be our master and we would be his slaves. Further, we would have become like he already is—carnal, sensual, devilish. We would have been miserable forever with no chance of ever being reclaimed from this evil nightmare. We would have become the ultimate sinners in our natures and would lie, conspire, and so on. This outcome by any conceivable standard is diabolically terrible. Thus, it is in this context that we must see the marvelous goodness of Christ. He saves us not only *from* terrible suffering and evil. He also saves us *for* great good and wonderful blessings. It is the marked contrast that makes the sharp distinction between these two outcomes so poignant. Instead of everlasting evil we are rewarded with "never-ending happiness" (Mosiah 2:41) if we accept the new life that can only come to us through the Redeemer.

2

ALIVE IN CHRIST

What does it mean to become alive in Christ, and how does it occur? The Book of Mormon gives us a clear explanation of what is involved: "And the Lord said unto me: Marvel not that all mankind, yea, men and women, all nations, kindreds, tongues and people, must be born again; yea, born of God, changed from their carnal and fallen state, to a state of righteousness, being redeemed of God, becoming his sons and daughters" (Mosiah 27:25).

We ought not to be surprised that spiritual rebirth is necessary. This is to essentially say that every person born into mortality must be born again, spiritually speaking. All means all. This includes people of all races, creeds, countries, and nations. This includes all—women and men, black and white, rich and poor, famous and unknown, strong and weak, genius and ordinary, well-educated and unschooled. This covers everyone past, present, and future whether in Uganda, China, Iceland, or Mexico. This mighty change is to be one of disposition, tendency, and condition. It is to be deep, not superficial; lasting, not temporary; significant, not trivial; and fundamental, not optional. It is to be a substantial change of mind and heart. This cannot happen through will, riches, education, or worldly power. It is not a question of intellect or worldly networks or holding positions of power. It is instead a matter of knowing the source of that power to change. It is to know the source of our salvation. It is to come to know—deeply, experientially, gratefully, and eternally—that true and living God who alone has power to give us a different type and degree of life. It is to become a son or daughter of Jesus Christ through spiritual rebirth.

To become alive in Christ is to be spiritually born again into the saved family of God. It is to be made into a new creature, to be renewed in righteousness, changed in the inward man or woman, altered in our thinking, shifted in our behaviors, and moved to different actions. It is essentially to become a better type of person with higher and holier attitudes, perspectives, desires, thoughts, feelings, dispositions, tendencies, and lives. It is to put off the natural man, to let the man of sin die, to conquer the natural man, to rise above worldly aspirations. Each of us has a new life to be discovered. This newness of life is a spiritual awakening. It is a rebirth to a different kind of living—a loftier, better, and happier way of being. This can only happen through Jesus Christ. He is the light, life, truth, and hope of the world. If we let Him, He will uproot all the weeds of disbelief inside of us and plant the flowers of faith in their place. This change of life can be everlasting.

The Lord Jesus Christ is the bread of life and the fountain of living waters. I love the following scriptural passage taught to both the Nephites and the Jews at Jerusalem: "Ask, and it shall be given unto you; seek, and ye shall find; knock, and it shall be opened unto you. . . . If ye then, being evil, know how to give good gifts unto your children, how much more shall your Father who is in heaven give good things to them that ask him?" (3 Nephi 14:7–11). I know that in my own life, when I have asked things of the Lord, He has given me more than I asked for. When I sought Him, I found Him. When I knocked, the door to unexpected possibilities was opened, as were the windows of heaven. Instead of giving me a stone, not only has He given me bread, but He has also given me an array of delicious breads—as well as milk and honey. Instead of giving me a serpent, or even just a fish, He has given me a diversity of fish, which was enough not only to feed me, but also my family and others in my sphere of influence. His food can feed the whole world. His water can satisfy the thirst of all the world. Just as the prophet Lehi found the fruit of the tree of life to be white, desirable, delicious, sweet, joy-inducing and happiness-promoting (see 1 Nephi 8:10–12), I have found the feast of the restored gospel to be nourishing, mouth-watering, delicious, soul satisfying, and life giving. It is healthy, helpful, hopeful, healing, hearty, and great for the heart, mind, spirit, and body.

Yes, Christ has the power to give us an abundant life of rich blessings. We thus obtain a new vision for our lives, a new way of seeing, an improved way of acting, a better way of judging, an enlightened way of discerning, and a happier way of living. He wants to live in us. He can supply us with an unceasing flow of light, life, truth, knowledge, power, and beauty if we will let Him do so. The life the Savior gives is one of hope, healing, strength, comfort, encouragement, and peace. The beautiful gift of life He gives us is a precious treasure to be valued, enjoyed, and experienced with richness. His invitation to us is to find new purpose, meaning, significance, fulfillment, and joy in the transcendent bounty only He can offer. God is truly the giver of every good gift. His power to transform our lives is remarkable. His ability to give us a newness of life is potent. He is the great sculptor of souls, the great worker of wonders and the great Father of our Faith. The blessings that come into our lives by learning of God and drawing close to Him are both numerous and rich.

I will now discuss some specific ways in which a new life comes to us through the Savior.

ALIVE IN THE SENSE OF BEING BORN INTO MORTALITY THROUGH THE CREATIVE POWER AND GOODNESS OF CHRIST

This earth is the garden of the Lord. Each of us is like a flower in that garden. The Lord knows how to help each flower bloom beautifully. We can be more wondrous than we conceive of through God's mighty help. The sights, sounds, and fragrances of God's garden are wonderful to behold. God is the most wonderful designer and creative artist of all. The beauty of His creations is all around us. His greatest creation is His children. To be born into this mortal, fallen world might be accurately and productively understood as being a blessing stemming from Christ Himself. As the creator of this earth He made mortal life a possibility in the first place. Without His act of creation there could be no Fall and hence no procreation and human birth. This doctrine is taught clearly in the Book of Mormon. I would not have been born without my mortal parents, and they would not have been born without theirs. In a similar vein, Adam and Eve could not have come upon this earth in the first place save the earth had been created. Mortality is not possible without the creative power and act of God. While we are still breathing, we have a work to do on this earth. Our work is to serve God and bless others.

ALIVE IN THE SENSE OF BEING A CHILD COVERED BY CHRIST'S ATONEMENT

Consider these instructive verses from the book of Mormon:

> And even if it were possible that little children could sin they could not be saved; but I say unto you they are blessed; for behold, as in Adam, or by nature, they fall, even so the blood of Christ atoneth for their sins.
>
> And moreover, I say unto you, that there shall be no other name given nor any other way nor means whereby salvation can come unto the children of men, only in and through the name of Christ, the Lord Omnipotent.
>
> For behold he judgeth, and his judgment is just; and the infant perisheth not that dieth in his infancy; but men drink damnation to their own souls except they humble themselves and become as little children, and believe that salvation was, and is, and is to come, in and through the atoning blood of Christ, the Lord Omnipotent. . . .
>
> And moreover, I say unto you, that the time shall come when the knowledge of a Savior shall spread throughout every nation, kindred, tongue, and people. (Mosiah 3:16–21)

That is to say that little children are not saved purely by some reference to their own innate goodness. Rather, they are covered by the Atonement of the Son of God. He shields, protects, and blankets them through His marvelous goodness. Those without law (meaning without accountability due to limiting factors) are likewise covered by His mighty powers of salvation. All accountable persons need a Savior. There simply are no exceptions to this. In fact, these verses are abundantly clear in that we are being taught that the day will come when all persons will come to know that Christ is the Savior. This obviously includes men and women of all creeds, nationalities, backgrounds, time periods, financial status, and philosophical beliefs. In other words, there is no person of any time or place that is exempt from the need to come to know the true Messiah. This knowledge will become so widespread that no individual will be left with doubt as to who the source of their salvation must be. In 2 Nephi we are taught:

> He doeth not anything save it be for the benefit of the world; for he loveth the world, even that he layeth down his own life that he may draw all men unto him. Wherefore, he commandeth none that they shall not partake of his salvation. . . .
>
> But he saith: Come unto me all ye ends of the earth, buy milk and honey, without money and without price. . . .
>
> He hath commanded his people that they should persuade all men to repentance.
>
> Behold, hath the Lord commanded any that they should not partake of his goodness? Behold I say unto you, Nay; but all men are privileged the one like unto the other, and none are forbidden. (2 Nephi 26:24–28).

So it is that every individual is potentially capable of salvation. Each person can triumph over sin and iniquity with divine help. Every individual is to be invited and indeed persuaded to come unto Christ through faith and repentance. This is clearly predicated on the fact that each person can choose to follow God if they will. This ability to follow the Lord does not depend on wealth, fame, status, background, or education. It depends on spiritual humility and receptivity to the truth.

ALIVE IN THE SENSE OF BEING BORN AGAIN THROUGH SPIRITUAL REBIRTH

The scriptures teach with purity and plainness that Christ is the one who bears the cost of our selfishness, fear, pride, laziness, anger, and greed. "He is despised and rejected of men; a man of sorrows, and acquainted with grief. . . . Surely he has borne our griefs, and carried our sorrows; yet we did esteem him stricken, smitten of God, and afflicted. But he was wounded for our transgressions, he was bruised for our iniquities; the chastisement of our peace was upon him; and with his stripes we are healed" (Mosiah 14:3–7).

The great promise of the prophets is that peace and healing will come to those who accept Jesus Christ as the Only Begotten Son of God and the Messiah—with a covenant and promise to have faith in Him, follow Him, covenant with Him, abide with Him, and witness of Him. He is the suffering servant whose voluntary and intense crucible of affliction allows us to repent, be resurrected and find a newness of life. The prophet Alma taught:

> And he shall go forth, suffering pains and afflictions and temptations of every kind; and this that the word might be fulfilled which saith he will take upon him the pains and the sicknesses of his people. And he will take upon him death, that he may loose the bands of death which bind his people; and he will take upon him their infirmities, that his bowels may be filled with mercy, according to the flesh, that he may know according to the flesh how to succor his people according to their infirmities.
>
> Now the Spirit knoweth all things; nevertheless the Son of God suffereth according to the flesh that he might take upon him the sins of his people, that he might blot out their transgressions according to the power of his deliverance; and now behold, this is the testimony which is in me. (Alma 7:11–13)

In other words, the scope and scale of Christ's suffering is sufficient to cover all accountable persons. He actively took upon Himself the tremendous burden of every conceivable hardship so that He would have power to aid us through every possible difficulty and to rescue us from the stain of sin and the finality of physical death. This succoring of the Savior involves spiritual and emotional support in times of dire need. It ought to be noted that we cannot rightly declare that the Savior does not understand what it is like to have cancer or depression or hopelessness. We cannot correctly think He has no understanding of betrayal, humiliation, disappointment, or breached expectations. There is no situation He does not understand, no trial He has not faced, no burden He has not carried, no heartache He is oblivious to. His redemptive apprehension is full, total, and complete.

He was the King of Israel, yet He experienced the ultimate denigration, the lowliest position, the most awful brutality, and the most galling treatment. The Holy Spirit bears record of both the spoken and written word of God. Jesus of Nazareth did triumphantly atone for the sins, pains, and sicknesses of the world. He lived for us and died for us. All of this was done to help us achieve eternal glory. As we remember and follow Him, we are greatly, deeply, and everlastingly blessed.

Consider this striking declaration from Elder Bruce R. McConkie: "I feel, and the Spirit seems to accord, that the most important doctrine I can declare, and the most powerful testimony I can bear, is of the atoning sacrifice of the Lord Jesus Christ. His atonement is the most transcendent event that ever has or ever will occur from Creation's dawn through all the ages of a never-ending eternity. It is the supreme act of goodness and grace that only a god could perform. Through it, all of the terms and conditions of the Father's eternal plan of salvation became operative."[1] This is a mighty testimony of eternal truth from a true apostle, prophet, seer, and revelator. He is teaching us the critical importance of the Atonement as the central core event and the most vital reality of our lives. As we sense the spiritual power of these words, we are edified, inspired, and transformed. This witness will bolster, bless, and beautify our lives. We will be deeply and eternally thankful for the immortal Son of God and His amazing power to redeem us.

---

1   Bruce R. McConkie, "The Purifying Power of Gethsemane," April 1985 general conference, churchofjesuschrist.org/study/general-conference/1985/04/the-purifying-power-of-gethsemane?lang=eng.

In contradistinction to atheistic views that say there is no God, how important it is to know not simply that God exists, but also what kind of being He is. God does far more than exist. He lives! He loves, He creates, He governs, He guides, He teaches, He redeems, and He blesses. God is great. He is supreme, endless, eternal, omnipotent, omniscient, and almighty. These are matters of undeniable certainty and import. And we are His children, created in the image and likeness of Him. We are endowed with amazing abilities. We can become far greater than what we were and what we already are. We are destined to become transcendent. If we believe and obey His word, then we will rise to heights that will astound us. I am a believing witness of these words. Jesus Christ is the Father of our spiritual rebirth through baptism of water and baptism of fire. He is a loving Father who wants us to become more like Him. He is a being of truth, light, glory, law, and love who wants us to know Him. He is a sharer of secrets who eagerly reveals His knowledge to us. We have a pure potential for greatness as children of Christ. We can learn, grow, develop, and progress. We can ask, seek, inquire, pray, look, see, behold, view, watch and observe. We can understand, perceive, know, discern, and comprehend His ways and mysteries.

To be a mortal father is to be richly blessed. Our children are our deep treasures. We are to love them dearly, teach them wisely, and bless them generously. Fatherhood is about responsibility. It is about being an example in word and deed. It requires self-sacrifice and hard work. It demands discipline and devotion. It evokes tender regard and joyful love. It is fun, educational, inspirational, life-changing, rewarding, and bounteous. Fathers are to be heroes that their children look up to, examples that their children appreciate, and men that will encourage them to reach for the deepest and most powerful divinity they are capable of. God is the ultimate Father, the best example of what glorious manhood means. Great fathers are great men of good character. Be the sort of father that your children can always respect and look up to. In like manner, we should think of Jesus Christ as our Father by means of spiritual rebirth. He will go great distances to bless and save us. This is a soul transformation, a change in identity. This is a coming forth in a newness of life. This gives us a new nature. This is not simply ideal sounding rhetoric—it is sure and certain reality.

What is the meaning of this new life? The meaning is joy. Happiness is our purpose. And how do we discover this amazing joy? There is only one way. It involves filling our lives with growth and service. Those two things will bless our lives in marvelous ways—personal growth and service to others. We can grow as a person, develop our skills and abilities, increase our knowledge, and expand our talents. We can become something more than we already are. We can learn a new skill, read a useful book, take up a new hobby. We can be grateful and thankful. We can serve in small and large ways. We can reach out to others, help others, share our knowledge with others, share our time with others, love others, and pray for others. This will help us be more content, healthier, and full of hope. Joy will increase in our lives and happiness will abound. Does this mean we will never have sorrow, loneliness, loss, disappointment, or pain? No, of course not. We will still have plenty of those things. But even these can help us to grow as persons and help us to love others more deeply. Joy is the purpose of life. And it will come to us naturally and eternally if we pursue the path that leads to it—the path of growth and service. This is the legacy and birthright we receive as born-again sons and daughters of Christ through genuine spiritual transformation.

God can perform a mighty change of heart within every willing soul. This mighty change is essential, fundamental, basic, necessary, elemental, vital, crucial, and critical. God's goodness is made manifest in His ability to transform the inner man or woman. A shift in internal perspective is a miracle within, giving us a new heart with new feelings and a new mind with new thoughts. This involves a mighty change of life, a thorough reformation of character, a fundamental alteration in nature, and an essential revision in our state of being. This transcendent transformation lifts us to a higher place, a different plane, a loftier location, and a new level of living. We are thus blessed to transcend the profane, petty, temporary, mean, trivial, and irrelevant. This allows us to inhabit the beautiful, lasting, truthful, benevolent, generous, enlightened, insightful, miraculous, and wonderful. This is what spiritual transformation is all about—total, complete, entire, full, encompassing, engaging, endowing, overflowing, immersing, and life affirming. This newness of life is like the change from deep sleep to alert awakening. From the dreary to the enthusiastic, from the dead to the alive, from the boring to the excited, from the apathetic to the passionate, from the cynical to the hopeful, from the despairing to the believing, from the blind to the seeing, from the indolent to the energetic and from the frustrated to the successful.

ALIVE IN THE SENSE OF REPLACING WEAKNESS WITH STRENGTH

As we come to sense this new life in Christ our limitations are overcome through the development of new qualities and proclivities. Our fears are replaced with courage. "For God hath not given us the spirit of fear; but of power, and of love, and of a sound mind" (2 Timothy 1:7). Our fear dissipates when we sense the truth of these words. God wants us to be strong in faith and firm in testimony. He seeks for us to know of His love, wants us to draw upon His power, and hopes that we will be confident in our balanced understanding of His truths. His doctrines make both spiritual and intellectual sense. We can be gently courageous in knowing the great power of God. "Brethren, shall we not go on in so great a cause? Go forward and not backward. Courage, brethren; and on, on to the victory! Let your hearts rejoice, and be exceedingly glad. Let the earth break forth into singing. Let the dead speak forth anthems of eternal praise to the King Immanuel" (Doctrine and Covenants 128:22). What an inspirational call to action from the Prophet Joseph Smith. If not this, then what? If not us, then whom? If not now, then when?

Similarly, our doubts can be replaced with faith. "God is merciful unto all who believe on his name; therefore he desireth, in the first place, that ye should believe, yea, even on his word" (Alma 32:22). To believe in God is to believe His goodness, greatness, and generosity. To trust in God is to trust His plans, promises, powers, and perfection. To remember God is to remember His word, wonders, and works. To love God is to love His person, peace, patience, and purity. His word is His eternal bond. "Doubt not, but be believing" (Mormon 9:27). When we are told to fear not, doubt not, and shrink not, we can remember that there is good reason to be confident about the source of our assurance. Why? Because the Lord lives, loves us, and knows us. There has never been a better time than now to believe. There has never been a stronger need to have faith than now. There has never been a greater urgency to have assurance than now. Believe in God. Have faith in Christ. Believe in hope, love, truth, beauty, comfort, and peace. Trust in courage, compassion, kindness, and joy. Life is good, God is good, and the best is yet to come.

Consider this marvelous statement of vision, imagination, and hopeful optimism: "We need men who can dream of things that never were and ask, Why not? . . . We do not worry about HOW AND WHEN AND WHY. We say WHY NOT."[2] We can envision a new righteousness. We can change the world by changing our personal world. We can increase our expectation, raise our sights, and deepen our commitment to making good things happen. As we focus on God, we will find the powerful solution to any challenge. The solution will always involve the true and living God.

"And it came to pass that I, Nephi, said unto my father: I will go and do the things which the Lord hath commanded" (1 Nephi 3:7). This is a profound statement of deep faith, a message of pure resolve, an expression of serious intent, and a determination to act with persistence. God has already prepared the way for us to achieve every good thing, every commendable task, every worthwhile achievement, every purposeful action of truth, beauty, love, hope, and peace. We can be willing to believe and show that firm commitment by acting with courage and endurance. We are here in mortality to learn about failure but not sent to fail. We are here to succeed. We can go and do. Each one of us can rise in righteousness, become alive in Christ, and go the spiritual distance with Him.

In like manner bondage can be overturned with freedom. Debt of any kind is a form of bondage. The adversary wants us

---

2   Spencer W. Kimball, Regional Representatives Seminar, October 1974.

to always remain in debt because it is a form of slavery that prevents us from reaching our divine potential. The living prophets have warned us about the dangers of debt. They have taught us about the law of the harvest in that we reap what we sow. We are agents with a temporal stewardship. We are free to do good. We are therefore accountable to God for what we do with our temporal resources. We are wise to live within our means and spend less than we earn. Our leaders have encouraged us to pay tithing no matter what, to pay fast offerings, to have food storage, to prepare for possible difficulties, and to save for emergencies. This is prudential and wise doctrine. It is not incidental or insignificant. It is part of the plan of salvation in which we believe. In the Doctrine and Covenants we read, "For it is expedient that I, the Lord, should make every man accountable, as a steward over earthly blessings. . . . The poor shall be exalted, in that the rich are made low. For the earth is full, and there is enough and to spare; yea, I prepared all things, and have given unto the children of men to be agents unto themselves" (Doctrine and Covenants 104:13–17).

It is our responsibility to strive to get out of debt. We can practice sound principles of financial management. If necessary, we can change our priorities and attitudes to reconcile them with the inspired counsel of our prophets, seers, and revelators. We are asked to be self-reliant, which means we rely on our own resources first. We do all we can to help ourselves. "Behold it is my will that you shall pay all your debts" (Doctrine and Covenants 104:78). God will help us to be freed from the burden of excessive debt if we put our trust in Him. He is our good shepherd and can teach us what to do to escape danger and harm. This will take time and effort, but it is possible. As we counsel together in our families, we will find unity over financial matters. We will then use wisdom and frugality in our purchasing decisions. Sometimes we may need the help of our priesthood leaders and others. We should ask them for help. They are willing and eager to assist us. If we show obedience to this inspired counsel, we will reap the blessings of heaven, including temporal blessings. We will be rewarded with an improved sense of well-being, improved family relationships, more resources, and draw closer to God. We will also be better positioned to serve and strengthen others.

"He has promised you that if ye would keep his commandments ye should prosper in the land" (Mosiah 2:22). Our scarcity can be turned to abundance. The scriptures are replete with God's promise that He will turn famines to feasts, drought to living waters, desolation to fruitfulness, scorched land to green pastures, and death to life. The lack of His help is always described in terms of scarcity, while His help is always designated in terms of overflowing abundance. With divine help evil can be eradicated from our lives and good incorporated into our lives. As we turn devotedly to the Lord, the traps of temptation become less enticing to us. We turn to goodness instead. Today is a good time to do what is good, be what is good, love what is good, and share what is good. There is a constant need for principles of goodness in our lives and in our world. God is the master of goodness. He is good to the core and can teach and train us in His ways.

Our hate can die, and our love can live. President Howard W. Hunter said:

> This year, mend a quarrel. Seek out a forgotten friend. Dismiss suspicion and replace it with trust. Write a letter. Give a soft answer. Encourage youth. Manifest your loyalty in word and deed. Keep a promise. Forgo a grudge. Forgive an enemy. Apologize. Try to understand. Examine your demands on others. Think first of someone else. Be kind. Be gentle. Laugh a little more. Express your gratitude. Welcome a stranger. Gladden the heart of a child. Take pleasure in the beauty and wonder of the earth. Speak your love and then speak it again.[3]

This is a powerful statement from a gentle giant and deeply loving man. How many wonderful things are accomplished when we show our love to others through encouraging words and quiet acts of service? Love is potent. Whether for the young, middle-aged,

---

3   Howard W. Hunter, First Presidency Christmas Devotional, December 1994.

or elderly, love is necessary. Whether in times of tragedy or jubilation, love is precious. Whether we are strong or weak, we need love. Love is powerful. Whether giving it or receiving it, love is tremendously important. It will never be outdated, irrelevant, or useless. How beautiful true love is. Everything worthwhile looks better through the lens of love.

Our holding of grudges can give way to a quest for forgiveness. "But behold I say unto you, love your enemies, bless them that curse you, do good to them that hate you, and pray for them who despitefully use you and persecute you" (3 Nephi 12:43–45). This is one of those tough doctrines that most of us find challenging. God believes in us. He has confidence that we can do hard things with His help. He trusts us to do the right thing. The right thing is to treat people with loving kindness and courageous civility—even if they do not return the treatment. So, forgive your enemies. Forgive your friends. Forgive your parents. Forgive your children. Forgive your colleagues. Forgive them all, and most especially forgive yourself. Love, bless, serve, do good, pray, and help others. There is no substitute for true Christianity. To yield to forgiveness is to find a victory of monumental proportions. Similarly, desires for contention can yield to a longing for unity. "Behold, this is not my doctrine, to stir up the hearts of men with anger, one against another; but this is my doctrine, that such things should be done away" (3 Nephi 11:29–30). The doctrine of Christ says that contention and anger should be banished from our lives, homes, and nations. Angry words are a destructive weapon. Harsh words wound the soul. Hatred destroys peace, love, and brotherhood. Aggressive conflict derails relationships. So instead let us be kind, uplifting, generous, loving, gentle, calm, forgiving, merciful, compassionate, thoughtful, caring, and benevolent.

ALIVE IN THE SENSE OF AWARENESS, CONSCIOUSNESS, ALERTNESS, BEING AWAKE TO NEW OPPORTUNITIES, AND SEEING WITH NEW EYES

This involves new perspective and improved understanding. This is how we become discerning and wise. We become alert, awake, and perceptive to a spiritual view of the world. We gain access to wonderful knowledge, amazing insights, and uncovered mysteries. We obtain high mountain revelations that transform our vision of everything. "But behold, if ye will awake and arouse your faculties, even to an experiment upon my words, and exercise a particle of faith, yea, even if ye can no more than desire to believe, let this desire work in you" (Alma 32:27).

So, the Lord wants us to wake up, to stir from slumber, to become conscious, to gain a sharp alertness to the precious realization that life is for living and gospel life is not dull. Rather, it is exciting, interesting, and amazing. God wants us to be alive to potential, awake to possibilities, aware of opportunities, conscientious of what is going on inside us and around us in the life of faith. To arouse our faculties is to shock them out of stupor, to bring our abilities to life, to discern our spiritual talents, and to live with deep purpose. The "desire to believe" in God's word is no small thing. It is good to want the word of God to be true, to believe it is true, to hope it is true, to sincerely trust and earnestly wish for it to be true. And it is good to want to have a believing heart and a mind willing to take a leap of faith. A believing disposition is a powerful thing.

"And the Lord spake unto Enoch, and said unto him: Anoint thine eyes with clay, and wash them, and thou shalt see. And he did so. And he beheld the spirits that God had created; and he beheld also things which were not visible to the natural eye; and from thenceforth came the saying abroad in the land: A seer hath the Lord raised up unto his people" (Moses 6:35–36).

We are led by a prophet. Prophets see the spiritual truth for what it is—undiluted, pure, unsullied, diamond truth. They see through the mortal mists of darkness that cloud the perspective of others. They see beyond the superficial, the temporary, and the false. God be thanked that living prophets, seers, and revelators lead and guide us in these latter days. Along with the prophets, we too can learn to see with new perspective. As we come unto Christ we inevitably come to new ideas, perceptions, viewpoints, and understandings that greatly enrich our lives. We can learn to see spiritual realities for what they are. These truths will be far beyond those perceived by physical sight alone, and far deeper than merely academic opinions, intellectual insights, or intelligent conceptions. They are more profound than logic and rationality alone could ever be.

ALIVE IN CHRIST AS IN GAINING NEW PURPOSE, MEANING, AND VISION FOR OUR LIVES.

This includes the precious endowment of a healthy sense of our divine worth. To see our own lives from God's vantage point is radically important. The Son of God can give us a new vista of who we were are and who we are to become. To sense how God perceives us can jolt us from disabling negative self-perceptions. If we only discern our lives in terms of transitory and temporal desires and aspirations, we greatly limit our sense of self. This is not to suggest we ought to have an inflated sense of self-importance. Rather, when we approach having the mind of Christ, we come to sense ourselves as being deeply precious to God. This makes us humble, not arrogant. It allows us to be grateful, not angry. We can see meaning in our lives in a whole new way. We see divine design in our life. We are special, valuable, important, and loved. This means that our life is of tremendous value and significance. It also means we should believe in ourselves, our capacity for growth, and our ability to influence others for good.

ALIVE IN THE SENSE OF VIVACIOUS, ENERGETIC, AND EXCITED

This means becoming more active, excited, vibrant, vivacious, enthusiastic, exuberant, ebullient, animated, full of life, spirited, zestful. Through the Son of God, we partake of the more abundant life. I understand that to mean abundance in every sense of the word. This means a plenitude of opportunity, experience, growth, development, progress, and realization. It means land, food, water, sunlight. It means energy, excitement, ebullience, and rejoicing. It means passion and purpose.

ALIVE IN THE SENSE OF HEALING OF THE BODY AND MIND FROM SICKNESS.

Can the Son of God rebuke illness and disease? In the Book of Mormon, we have many excellent examples of the power of Jesus Christ to heal the wounded soul. One example is that of Zeezrom, who had initially opposed the work of the Lord but then through the preaching of Alma became converted. The account is very revealing:

> And also Zeezrom lay sick at Sidom, with a burning fever, which was caused by the great tribulations of his mind on account of his wickedness. . . . And this great sin, and his many other sins, did harrow up his mind until it did become exceedingly sore, having no deliverance; therefore he began to be scorched with a burning heat. . . . And then Alma cried unto the Lord, saying: O Lord our God, have mercy on this man, and heal him according to his faith which is in Christ.
>
> And when Alma had said these words, Zeezrom leaped upon his feet, and began to walk; and this was done to the great astonishment of all the people. (Alma 15:3–12)

What a marvelous story this is. Here we have a great illustration of what is involved in this process of accessing the power of the Savior to heal both body and spirit. Notice that Zeezrom was originally an enemy to the Lord's work. However, he had a change of heart. He wanted to be rescued from his physical and spiritual affliction. Notice that Alma said that such deliverance was only possible through faith in the power of Christ unto salvation. The healing of the mortal body and the forgiveness of sin offered by the Savior to us in this life is simply a reflection of the much more powerful and profound salvation involved in resurrection and granting of eternal life. Notice also that the Lord and His mortal servants held no grudge against Zeezrom for his prior actions. Rather they rejoiced in his change of heart and were eager to assist him. Zeezrom had the requisite faith in Christ to be healed and was blessed immediately with healing. He was then baptized and started to preach about Christ's redemption. The people were literally astounded at this healing.

ALIVE IN CHRIST AS IN SAVED FROM PHYSICAL DEATH

Christ can give us physical life in the face of death. "And again, it shall come to pass that he that hath faith in me to be healed, and is not appointed unto death, shall be healed" (Doctrine and Covenants 42:48–51). This is comfortingly true. For those whose time has not yet come to pass on, there is life still to be lived. There are lessons to be learned, works to be done, joys to be had, and destinies to be achieved. Regardless of circumstances facing us, our strong belief in the Messiah is a powerful antidote to the poisons of doubt, discouragement, despair, and even death. These deadly dangers are overcome by the revitalizing, renewing, restoring, rejuvenating powers of faith in the Living Christ, the Only Begotten Son of God in the flesh. To be bolstered in our belief is to see, hear, leap, and be healed.

ALIVE IN THE SENSE OF HEALING OF THE SPIRIT THROUGH FORGIVENESS OF SIN

This is about having our sins remitted. This means not only having badness removed but goodness cultivated within us: "And behold, he shall be born of Mary . . . even the Son of God. And he shall go forth, suffering pains and afflictions and temptations of every kind; and this that the word might be fulfilled which saith he will take upon him the pains and the sicknesses of his people" (Alma 7:10–11).

The Son of God not only gives us peace, but He also takes upon Himself our pains, afflictions, sicknesses, weaknesses, suffering, sorrow, sins, and even death. This means He knows precisely what it is to suffer a toothache, a headache, or a heart attack. He knows what it means to be in a car crash, to have back pain, and to be paralyzed. He understands what it involves to lose a job, to be passed over for a desired opportunity, to be abandoned, ignored, forgotten, and neglected. He knows what it means to be faced with the enticement to lie, cheat, steal and commit other sins. In fact, it means that He knows what it is like for us personally to have these kinds of experiences. He understands from the inside what I feel like when

I sin or am sick or am dejected. He roots out all the bad from our lives and replaces it with goodness, joy, and rejoicing. As we journey through the fiery furnace of affliction, He is with us to strengthen, uphold, and bless us. This is our cause for celebration at every season and indeed always.

"Therefore may God grant unto you, my brethren, that ye may begin to exercise your faith unto repentance. . . . Yea, cry unto him for mercy; for he is mighty to save" (Alma 34:17–18). Jesus Christ will redeem us from sin if we repent. He is eager to help, willing to assist, and capable of saving us. He is not disinterested, asleep, or neglectful. He is not distant, powerless, or bored. He is ready and empowered to lift us up to where He already is. This gives me powerful cause to rejoice and remember Him. We can activate His help by exercising confidence in Him, even when we have little or no confidence in ourselves.

ALIVE IN CHRIST AS IN GAINING NEW STRENGTH, POWER, AND ABILITY.

When we come unto Christ, we often receive divine endowments of strength and power. These can be physical, mental, emotional, social, and spiritual. They can empower us to do things we could not do alone, to travel distances we could never travel alone, to face challenges we could not face alone, to surmount obstacles that would otherwise overcome us, and to achieve things that would normally be impossible. "But I am like as yourselves, subject to all manner of infirmities in body and mind; yet I . . . have been kept and preserved by his matchless power, to serve you with all the might, mind and strength which the Lord hath granted unto me" (Mosiah 2:11). The scriptures teach that we can thus become vigorous in the work of the Lord, even in our old age. We can likewise find new insights, uncover new mysteries, learn new truths, discover new doctrines, endure new challenges, and avoid new dangers with divine help.

> And all saints who remember to keep and do these sayings, walking in obedience to the commandments, shall receive health in their navel and marrow to their bones;

And shall find wisdom and great treasures of knowledge, even hidden treasures;

And shall run and not be weary, and shall walk and not faint.

And I, the Lord, give unto them a promise, that the destroying angel shall pass by them, as the children of Israel, and not slay them. Amen. (Doctrine and Covenants 89:18–21)

ALIVE IN CHRIST IN THE SENSE OF HAVING OUR RELATIONSHIPS ALTERED

We become sensitive to the attitudes and moods of others. Our love for others deepens, and in turn their love for us deepens. To come unto Christ is to strengthen bonds of affection, increase ties of caring, deepen links of love, and support brotherhood and sisterhood. It is to increase compassion, develop empathy, enlarge connections, and promote togetherness. "And they did wax strong in love towards Mosiah; yea, they did esteem him more than any other man . . . therefore they did esteem him, yea, exceedingly, beyond measure" (Mosiah 29:40). "Art thou a brother or brethren? . . . In remembrance of the everlasting covenant . . . I receive you to fellowship, in a determination that is fixed, immovable, and unchangeable, to be your friend and brother through the grace of God in the bonds of love" (Doctrine and Covenants 88:133). Relationships become much more solid, stable, lasting, and deep through Christ. We become more interested in helping, serving, blessing, and loving others around us as we are more aware of the Savior. We are then less self-centered and far more sealings-centered and service-oriented. We look outwards more to encourage, praise and comfort those in our circle of concern.

ALIVE IN THE SENSE OF GLORIOUS RESURRECTION

Christ is not dead. He is very much alive. He is real, physical, tangible, and glorious: "We saw the Lord standing upon the breastwork of the pulpit, before us; and under his feet was a paved work of pure gold. . . . His eyes were as a flame of fire; the hair of his head was white like the pure snow; his countenance shone above the brightness of the sun; and his voice was as the sound of the rushing of great waters, even the voice of Jehovah, saying: I am the first and the last; I am he who liveth" (Doctrine and Covenants 110:2–4).

We worship the glorious Living Christ. He is a resurrected personage. He has eyes, hair, hands, feet, and a countenance. He can be seen and heard. He can be loved and listened to. He can be known, touched, and hugged. How wonderful to know and celebrate this powerful truth. Even after the terrible ordeal of the Atonement the Lord was about His Father's business. He visited the spirit world and preached His word to the righteous who were eagerly awaiting Him (see Doctrine and Covenants 138:18–24). He brought the joyful message of redemption to them and they rejoiced exceedingly. This message transcends the boundaries of death. It is vital to know that the resurrection of Christ impacts each of us. We will be likewise resurrected. We will come forth from the grave as physical beings. We will see and be seen, know and be known, love and be loved. We will speak, learn, grow, and rejoice. This is a mighty gift from the atoning one. Our hope in Him is now and forever. This resurrection will bring a literal newness of life to each of us.

ALIVE IN THE SENSE OF OBTAINING ETERNAL LIFE

"For behold, this is my work and my glory—to bring to pass the immortality and eternal life of man" (Moses 1:39). This is a statement of resolve, purpose, and power from the greatest being in the universe. God's purposes and plans for each of us are glorious. He wants us to live forever—not simply in the memory of others, not simply with good deeds done, not simply in some sort of allegorical way. He wants is to live literally as conscious, thinking, feeling beings with eternal longevity. He wants us to live in a perfected body forever. He wants us to live with Him and to live like Him forever. These are no small doctrines, no trivial plans, no indicators of unimportance. Whatever we think we can accomplish, the truth is that we can do more, be more, and achieve more than what we think we can. God has a higher vision for us, a grander purpose, a more elevated plan. He knows us better and loves us more than we do. To live forever is a reality. However, His plan for us is not simply to live forever—it is to live forever in love, joy, peace, happiness, and glory. This also can be our reality as we follow the plan He has for us. God does not make mistakes. He made us with a purpose in mind. He made us for joy, for love, for growth, for happiness, for beauty. He made us to be a blessing to the lives of others. He counts us as His greatest treasures. Our joy will be an everlasting one when we enter God's Kingdom (see 2 Nephi 9:18). This will be a place of peace, plenty, power, and purity. This will be a tranquil time and a state of solace. This will be a palace of perfection. We will never have to leave that holy and blessed abode.

How important it is to remember that God is the Lord of Life. He comprehends the nature of true living in a way that we can only appreciate partially. He possesses living love, abiding joy, constant hope, lasting peace, never-ending faith, and eternal life. The word of God is likewise living as it stems from a living source—powerfully impacting as in moving, lifting, changing, restoring, renewing, forceful, mighty, and transforming. The word of God must be "in" us. The living word aligns with our beating heart, our thinking brain, our functioning organs, our seeing eyes, our flowing blood, our moving arms, our walking legs and so on. The eternal spirit animates the physical body. The word of God is to be as essential, as fundamental, as vital, as crucial, to our living lives as all these other realities are to be. This is part of what it means to have an eye single to God's great glory.

CONCLUSION

There neither is, nor can there be, a higher or better type, kind, and degree of life than that made possible through Christ.

3

MESSIANIC MESSENGERS

When I was ten years old, I attended a missionary cottage meeting with my mother at the home of a fellow church member. The room was full of people. The missionaries showed a video of the First Vision of the Prophet Joseph Smith. While I already had a testimony at that time, I was nevertheless strongly touched and remarkably moved by the Spirit. I knew that Joseph Smith was a seer and that he saw what he said he saw. I knew that he was called of God just as the ancient prophets had been. I knew it with certainty. I am glad to say that this conviction has remained with me throughout my entire life. I feel blessed that I received that spiritual witness that has proved important to me in facing many tests of faith. Why did the Lord give me this sublime witness and peaceful reassurance? I was not rich, famous, educated, or of high standing in the world or Church. I was obscure, young, weak, and hesitant.

I suppose this is exactly the point. Like most people, Joseph Smith was not a man of worldly credentials or high standing. God was teaching me—although I did not perceive it at the time—that worldly achievements are not the litmus test for God's rewards. While there is nothing inherently wrong with worldly success, it is essential to note that we must humble ourselves to hear His counsel.

God desires to share with all His children His truths as soon as they are ready to receive them. He was further teaching me of the worth of my soul. Even though I was of no moment in terms of my worldly standing, from God's vantage point I was His child, someone of importance to Him. I feel deeply blessed by that witness and by comprehending the meaning and significance that underscores it. God called Joseph Smith in these times as a clear and direct witness to all the world that He is interested in us and our lives. God wants us to know that we matter to Him and that He knows we know it. There can be no effective evading of this reality.

THE CALL OF A MODERN PROPHET

It is vital to note that the Messiah is not a lone witness of His identity and purposes. To evidence this sublime truth, He calls Messianic messengers—prophets and apostles—to take upon themselves His name with full purpose of heart and to declare pure and powerful witness of Him throughout the world. As far as the dispensation of the fulness of times is concerned, the Lord called Joseph Smith as His chief prophet, seer, and revelator to lead the work of salvation. Joseph thereby became the first witness of the Living Christ in modern times. To find salvation in this day and age, we must accept the teachings and testimony of Joseph Smith as the anointed servant and mouthpiece of the Lord to this generation. This is not optional, but necessary. To accept Joseph is to accept the Master that sent Him. To be instructed by a prophet of God is to hear divine truth. A true prophet will always declare that salvation is found in coming unto Christ and in no other way or means.

In the revelations we learn about the process by which the Lord calls prophets and apostles. It is interesting to note that this process itself brings these brethren to a newness of life. In other words, this is part of this divine journey of becoming alive in Christ. If we take the prime example of the Prophet Joseph Smith, we can see this process in marvelous plainness. Clearly, young Joseph was unsure about the salvation of his own soul and which church to join. He states that "so great were the confusion and strife among the different denominations, that it was impossible for a person young as I was, and so unacquainted with men and things, to come to any certain conclusion who was right and who was wrong" (JS—History 1:8).

I think this clearly evidences that he was in a state of dark distress about what to do. From the revealed account we know that he determined to pray about the matter. While in the process of prayer we know that he was confronted by the adversary, who wanted to prevent his prayer and destroy him. Joseph called upon God and was delivered from his enemy. Joseph then received an answer to his prayer and much more. I believe he felt a great sense of relief, comfort, and reassurance from this divine encounter. To him personally this must have felt like a deeply precious experience. It is also abundantly clear that he went forth from the Sacred Grove with a sense of clarity, purpose, and resolution that he had not previously enjoyed. This significance of this event—and the impact it had on him—should not be overlooked. This experience, and many others that followed, gave Joseph the knowledge, strength, and dedication he would need to successfully do a mighty work for the Lord.

As we carefully examine the process by which Joseph Smith became a mighty Prophet of God, we can detect some vitally important elements:

- **He saw a divine light.** This light chased away the darkness and allowed him to see with clarity.
- **He heard a divine voice.** He heard both the Father and the Son. He was called by name—how reassuring that must have been. The voices bore witness of eternal truth and spoke directly to his concerns and needs.
- **He stood in a holy council.** This was a place of meeting where divine destiny was manifest. This was a sacred gathering, a holy convocation, a foreordained convergence between heaven and earth. In this special setting Joseph received a revelation based on new understanding about the reality of God.
- **He saw divine personages.** Joseph saw both the Father and the Son in this visitation. This was a profoundly important experience for him to have. He thereby became a witness—

one who knows by direct first-hand experience. This was no fiction or fantasy. He said, "When the light rested upon me I saw two Personages, whose brightness and glory defy all description, standing above me in the air. One of them spake unto me, calling me by name and said, pointing to the other—*This is My Beloved Son. Hear Him!*" (JS—History 1:17). It is noteworthy that the glorious brightness of the two individuals was beyond description. That makes perfect sense to me. How else does one properly give credit to such a remarkable encounter? God is a being of light, power, and majesty. It rings true that He would be surrounded by a light beyond human experience. I also find it telling that the Father bore direct and clear witness of His Only Begotten Son. What more powerful testimony could possibly be borne?

- **He had a vision.** The word *vision* is important. It suggests the power to see something remarkable. This was no ordinary experience. It was eye-opening, soul-stretching, and life-enhancing. By any standard this is a tremendous spiritual perceiving.

- **He was taken out of the world for a time and set apart from worldly concerns.** The Lord often uses high mountains, tabernacles, or temples as the setting for sacred encounters of this nature. He also uses groves. In this case He used a small grove of trees. The significance of this is not hard to see. Trees are deeply embedded in the gospel as symbolic of many vitally important truths such as knowledge, life, love, power, family, the Atonement of Christ, and so on. Everywhere from the Garden of Eden to the vision of the tree of life and the allegory of the olive tree we see trees and forests as occupying a central place in God's plans and purposes. The fact that the First Vision occurred in a grove of trees indicates its special nature of being set apart from the world. This time was not to be a time of distraction or amusement—it was for the serious business of saving souls. Nor was the experience to be contaminated by impure influences or unholy diversions. This was a sacred setting for a sanctified purpose.

- **He was given a book of prophecy to read.** Joseph received the Book of Mormon and translated it by the gift and power of God. There is no question that this was an eye-opening experience for him as he learned truths he did not previously know. No doubt the revelations of the Book of Mormon were instructional, surprising, edifying, and inspiring to the young Joseph.

- **He obtained revealed knowledge of the plans and purposes of the Almighty.** Joseph was there for a majestic reason. He was not only to receive an answer to his earnest prayer but also to learn that God was now intervening in the affairs of men according to a timetable and plan. This was no chance, luck, or random event. This was designed and destined for a grand purpose to save the world. Joseph learned that God had a work for him to do and this was to be approached sincerely and devotedly.

- **He received a divine commission of authority/keys as prophet, seer, and revelator.** There is no question that Joseph was divinely called to do a marvelous work and a wonder. Joseph would later receive the priesthood and its keys that would empower him to direct, control, govern, and preside over the work of salvation on both sides of the veil. It is interesting to note that Joseph received knowledge, gifts, powers, laws, ordinances, covenants, and commandments. He would not only be a prophet called to represent God to the world, but he would see things hidden from mortal view and make these known in abundance. It is virtually impossible to overestimate how important his work and how impressive his accomplishments would be.

- **He was endowed with persuasive power for the ministry of saving souls.** Joseph was interested not only in his own salvation but also that of his family and friends, his enemies, and indeed all people of all time. His work would extend—through preaching and ordinances/covenants—to many millions of people on both sides of the veil. Joseph was known for his capacity to teach the gospel with authority and power. His understanding was revelation based. His was a great gift to persuade others to faith unto repentance. This talent would prove to be essential in building up and strengthening the kingdom of God on the earth.

- **He was washed, anointed, and given a new name and new garments.** In accordance with the divine pattern, Joseph was called out of the life he had been in to embrace a new life, a new identity, a new purpose oriented through his divine call. Just as Abram became Abraham, Jacob became Israel and Saul became Paul, so Joseph became the choice seer.
- **He had his spiritual eyes opened.** There were things Joseph simply could not know prior to his divine encounters. He was schooled, trained, taught, and prepared by having new information, a new perspective, a new grasp, and a new comprehension of spiritual reality. As with many prophets before him, his awareness was fundamentally opened to truths, principles, and powers he could not possibly have discerned prior to his spiritual awakening.
- **He was given sacred instruction, information, and special blessings.** A review of the scriptures brought to light through Joseph and the doctrines taught in the temple indicates with sublime clarity that he learned great and precious principles that have the power to change the world when believed and acted upon.
- **He made sacred covenants through ordinances.** Joseph did not preach doctrines that he did not live. He was required to partake of the laws, ordinances, and covenants of the restored gospel before teaching them to others. He was required to show commitment, dedication, devotion, and persistence in the face of his divine call. These precious promises were not to be discarded for any purpose.
- **He exercised agency, faith, and good works.** Joseph was called to be a doer of the word, not a hearer only. He was

not called to teach intellectual truths and abstract concepts devoid of practical purpose. He had to show forth belief, action, diligence, work, effort, and consistency. His religion was not a belief system only—it was a call to live according to spiritual principles in daily life.

- **He taught and testified of the Only Begotten Son of God.** There are those who suppose that Joseph taught his own doctrine, promoted his own fame, sought his own riches, and advanced his own cause. This is simply not the case. Joseph was called as an instrument to do a divine work. He was called to teach that Jesus Christ is the Only Begotten Son of the Father in the flesh. He did so in purity, plainness, and power. He did so continually, relentlessly, and unyieldingly. He was not interested in building his own kingdom and promoting his own glory. He taught truth even when it was hard. He did not seek for popularity but for principle. He did not want to be worshipped but rather wanted to be true and faithful to the divine charge he had received.
- **He preached faith, repentance, covenants, and ordinances.** The things that Joseph taught are available for all to hear and see. He preached the doctrines that were given to him by revelation. He preached the absolute need for faith in the Lord Jesus Christ, for a change of heart, for entering into sacred agreements with God, and for partaking of special ordinances. He taught loyalty to God no matter the cost. These truths are core, consistent, and evident. He did not preach worldliness, laziness, fear, hatred, lust, or pride. He taught truth, honor, integrity, courage, wisdom, love, obedience, generosity, humility, and service.
- **He traveled to a land of promise.** Like the Israelites in the old world and Lehi in the Book of Mormon, Joseph encouraged his people to settle in places where they could endeavor to live the principles of their religion.
- **He gathered a people.** Like Melchizedek and Enoch before him, he gathered his people in centers of strength together. It is no easy task to unify people under principles

of righteousness. While there were complex difficulties with this project, Joseph nevertheless did a remarkable job.

- **He built a temple—a house to the Lord.** Joseph and the Saints built temples in Kirtland and Nauvoo. This is a remarkable accomplishment when understood in the light of the poverty and persecution of the Saints. Given the sacred nature of temples and their central role in the plan of salvation, I regard this as strong evidence of the divine call of Joseph Smith. There is no exaltation in the celestial kingdom without the doctrines, covenants, and ordinances of the temple.

- **He established a city of holiness—Zion.** Although Joseph did not entirely succeed in getting his people to live the law of consecration in full, there is no question that this is what he was endeavoring to do. In my view, he did remarkably well in teaching and training his people to build Zion. It is important to note that many wonderful Saints were true and faithful to Joseph and his divine vision for Zion. So, in a sense, a form of Zion was established. When we look at the amazing work done by the pioneers and their descendants in building the global Church we now have I think that we have succeeded far more than we have failed.

- **He faced severe opposition with faith and resolve.** By any measure, the opposition Joseph faced was tremendous. It was regular, deep, and persistent. However, he faced it with a determination and courage that amazes me. He had real faith—not the kind that is transitory and dependent on things being good all the time but rather a faith that persists through difficulty and challenge. He was no fair-weather disciple. He proved his absolute devotion again and again. He was a man of true character.

- **He persisted through difficulty and endured to the end no matter the cost.** Joseph was loyal and faithful to the end. The price he paid was unquestionably high. We honor him by being true to the legacy of light and love he left for us.

- **He was taken up to heaven.** While Joseph was not translated like Enoch or taken up like Alma, it is accurate to say that he died firm in the faith. He received the reward of a faithful prophet. He was taken home to that God who gave him life. He went immediately to the paradise of God to await the day of a glorious resurrection. There can be no greater gift than that held in reserve for the Prophet Joseph and those who are like him.

The importance of the calling and ministry of Joseph Smith goes far beyond his own salvation. It also strongly impacts us. As we carefully review the calling of the Prophet, we will discern that the Lord acts similarly—although perhaps in less dramatic ways—toward each of us. As we consider our own lives, we will see that the same essential pattern applies to all the Lord's people. This is how the Lord brings us to a newness of abundant life.

It is important to note that Joseph was not expecting these things to happen. He simply expected to find spiritual forgiveness and learn which church was true when he prayed in the Sacred Grove. I am convinced that he was surprised at his encounter. We know that he was surprised that Moroni visited him four times in a twenty-four-hour period (see JS—History 1:46) and when he received the Aaronic Priesthood from an angel (see Joseph Smith—History, note 6). It is my belief that he was similarly surprised at the content of many of the revelations he received and the experiences he had. Why is this important? The reason is that in a most fundamental sense, the restored gospel was radical (in a good way). The knowledge he obtained was revolutionary, considering many widespread views held at that time. It was new in thought, strange in action, distinctive in meaning, original in implication, and in many ways shocking in significance, even to people of deep religious faith. This is intentional and in a certain sense it should not surprise us.

The work of God is a marvelous work and a wonder (see Doctrine and Covenants 4:1). It is a work of miracles, wonders, gifts, glories, powers, amazements, signs, manifestations, and newness. It is intended to be counter-cultural, fresh, sensational, and shocking.

And why not? Many of life's moving moments are sublime, transcendent, unexpected, touching, and powerful. They radically reach us and transform us. They do not fit neatly into tradition, routine, or commonly accepted ways of thinking. I wrote in an earlier chapter about how the Savior's mortal ministry was intentionally different to what virtually everyone expected. So, it makes complete sense to me that the restoration of His gospel would be, in like manner, essentially disruptive to the normal or standard pattern of thinking of many people, even pious ones. So it is that talk of visits of angels, new scripture, divine authority, dreams, visions, revelations, unfolding of doctrine, sacred ordinances, and binding covenants is supposed to test our faith. We need to be prepared to be caught off guard and astonished at God's workings in this world.

In many ways, such is the case with more poignancy today. We now live in a time of great technological advances, pronounced scientific understanding, comprehensive philosophical discourse, enlarged educational opportunities, and phenomenal knowledge availability. I think these are amazing and welcome developments to be cherished. However, we have also become sophisticated intellectually as we suppose. We live in a world where talk of angels and miracles seems absurd to many people, unbelievable, incredible, irrational, ridiculous, and outdated. Many regard this modern age as being advanced, developed, mature, educated, learned, wise, and as having outgrown the superstitious underpinnings of religious thought and belief that characterized much of the history of the world. We see that some think that the idea of God is not sustainable in this intellectually advanced climate. However, when we rightly consider a harmonized spiritual and intellectual view, this conclusion is a mighty mistake.

The gospel message has always had a new and everlasting element to it. While it is eternal, it is also new, lively, fresh, stark, and intellectually and spiritual challenging. It confronts us to face inconvenient truths such as deep meaningfulness, personal responsibility, individual accountability, our own limitations, notions of divine justice, the problem of evil, and the possibility of righteousness. The restored gospel is a message that must be faced head on. Dodging it, denying it, ignoring it, laughing at it, pretending it is not there, finding it hard to accept—these are approaches that will not yield true satisfaction. It takes courage, faith, bravery, conviction, determination, resilience, humility, patience, and endurance to accept the restored gospel in our minds and hearts and to seek to align our lives with it. Confronting the stubborn natural man within us, being asked to endure pain and injustice with resolve, having to face breached expectations, having to submit our desires and demands to a Supreme Being who seeks to direct our lives for a good we do not always perceive as readily apparent—these are mighty tests of mortality. So, life will test us to the absolute core. We cannot escape the test, trial, trouble, and tribulation that inevitably confronts each one of us in deciding whether God is real or not. The only question that really requires answering is the following. How we answer that single question has ramifications in time and in eternity for us and those we love.

> "And we have beheld that the great question which is in your minds is whether the word be in the Son of God, or whether there shall be no Christ.
>
> And ye also beheld that my brother has proved unto you, in many instances, that the word is in Christ unto salvation. . . .
>
> And now, behold, I will testify unto you of myself that these things are true. Behold, I say unto you, that I do know that Christ shall come among the children of men. . . .
>
> For it is expedient that an atonement should be made; for according to the great plan of the Eternal God there must be an atonement made, or else all mankind must unavoidably perish; yea, all are hardened; yea, all are fallen and are lost, and must perish except it be through the atonement which it is expedient should be made. (Alma 34:2–10)

Thus, the great question that all women and men of all ages, nations, creeds, backgrounds, and stations must eventually answer is whether or not Jesus is the Christ, the living Son of God. It is my conviction that our answer to that question overrides everything else in importance. Our devotion to accepting that He is the Christ will have everlasting implications for us. If we accept that core truth—

and all the consequences that follow from it, regardless of the difficulty inherent in doing so—then we will be blessed beyond measure in time and eternity. To accept the Messianic message of the true prophets—though such a decision will be hard, unpopular at times, inconvenient, costly, demanding, challenging—is to find a newness of life with a scale, scope, grandeur, power, beauty, and meaning far in excess of any possible alternative that might be offered to us in terms of worldly desires, fame or power.

THE PROPHETIC MESSAGE IN OUR DAY

The living prophet becomes the covenant spokesman that represents Jesus Christ to the entire world. The words of the living prophet are the messages that the Savior Himself wants us to hear, believe, live, and share. I note some key invitations from the President of the Church.

Stay on the Covenant Path

> With our thoughts and feelings so focused on the Savior of the world, what, then, do we need to do to receive these gifts offered to us so willingly by Jesus Christ? What is the key to loving as He loves, forgiving as He forgives, repenting to become more like Him and ultimately living with Him and our Heavenly Father? The key is to make and keep sacred covenants. We choose to live and progress on the Lord's covenant path and to stay on it. It is not a complicated way. It is the way to true joy in this life and eternal life beyond.[1]

This way is the path of promise. It is the strait and narrow path of obedience and discipleship. The Savior is the perfect man, full of integrity. His word is His bond. To believe in Him is to pursue the path He pursued. True discipleship cannot be disconnected from the discipline of striving to live a godly life. This covenant path is indeed the road of Christ. These covenants bind us to God, link us to our families, connect us to peace, weld us to faith, unite us to

---

1   Russell M. Nelson, First Presidency Christmas Devotional, December 2018.

hope, and seal us to charity. How critically important it is for us to be true and faithful to these sacred everlasting covenants. Our word can thus be our firm bond.

Increase Our Individual Capacity to Receive Revelation

> And it came to pass after I, Nephi, having heard all the words of my father, concerning the things which he saw in a vision, and also the things which he spake by the power of the Holy Ghost, which power he received by faith on the Son of God—and the Son of God was the Messiah who should come—I, Nephi, was desirous also that I might see, and hear, and know of these things, by the power of the Holy Ghost, which is the gift of God unto all those who diligently seek him. (1 Nephi 10:17)

Lehi received the vision of the tree of life through the power of faith on the Son of God—who was the Messiah who should come. We need to specifically believe in Jesus Christ as the literal Son of God. This is to be the core of our faith. This is how we obtain the power to see visions, dream dreams, resist temptation, overcome evil, persuade others to repentance, establish Zion, and eventually inherit eternal life.

> And now, my sons, remember, remember that it is upon the rock of our Redeemer, who is Christ, the Son of God, that ye must build your foundation; that when the devil shall send forth his mighty winds, yea, his shafts in the whirlwind, yea, when all his hail and his mighty storm shall beat upon you, it shall have no power over you to drag you down to the gulf of misery and endless wo, because of the rock upon which ye are built, which is a sure foundation, a foundation whereon if men build they cannot fall. (Helaman 5:12)

We are to build our foundation of faith upon Christ as the literal living and loving Son of God. Each of us will face the storms, winds, rains, and floods of opposition. The only way to be secure in our faith is to build on the right foundation and remain there. This foundation simply cannot crumble. We are to stand on the holy ground of divine revelation—having received a personal witness of the rock of our religion, the rock of our redeemer, the stone of Israel. He is the cornerstone of our faith.

Minister as the Savior Does

This means being on the Lord's errand and going forth in His name to bless individuals as He would. It means to prayerfully perceive the spiritual and temporal needs of those we serve and to meet those needs lovingly, and diligently.

Come, Follow Me Curriculum

Note that the focus is to declare the doctrine of the Father and the Son. It is to teach the Divine Sonship and doctrine of Christ. We are to learn of Him, love Him, serve Him, and emulate Him. We are to come unto Him ourselves and invite and persuade others to do likewise.

Use the Full and Correct Name of the Church

> I promise you that if we will do our best to restore the correct name of the Lord's Church, He whose Church this is will pour down His power and blessings upon the heads of the Latter-day Saints, the likes of which we have never seen. We will have the knowledge and power of God to help us take the blessings of the restored gospel of Jesus Christ to every nation, kindred, tongue, and people and to prepare the world for the Second Coming of the Lord.[2]

This is a marvelous revelation-based statement. There certainly is a prophet in Israel. For me, there was a distinct spirit of inspiration, prophetic power, and reassuring certainty that accompanied President Nelson's message. We are richly blessed as we go forward with the courage to sustain the Lord's anointed servants and work diligently to bring to pass God's powerful promises and purposes.

---

2   Russell M. Nelson, "The Correct Name of the Church," October 2018 general conference, churchofjesuschrist.org/study/general-conference/2018/10/the-correct-name-of-the-church?lang=eng.

Sometimes individuals separate the person of Christ from His Church as if we can accept one but not the other. This arises from an incorrect understanding. The salvation that the Savior offers is a "package deal." This means that we are to accept all the truths of salvation. To pick and choose which aspects we want to believe in and which we want to discount puts the entire deal at risk. We believe all that God reveals. This is especially important when certain doctrines, policies, and practices may be difficult for us personally. In such circumstances, we need to have faith not simply in the Lord alone but in all the facets of His work, which inherently includes His Church, His priesthood, His doctrines, His laws, His ordinances, His covenants, and indeed all His plans and purposes.

As I reflect on the instruction from President Russell M. Nelson to align ourselves more consciously as members of The Church of Jesus Christ of Latter-day Saints, I am reminded of the scriptural concept: "Now ye may suppose that this is foolishness in me; but behold I say unto you, that by small and simple things are great things brought to pass; and small means in many instances doth confound the wise. And the Lord God doth work by means to bring about his great and eternal purposes; and by very small means the Lord doth confound the wise and bringeth about the salvation of many souls" (Alma 37:6–7). To remind us of the name of the Church is small in one sense. In another sense it is deeply and profoundly significant (see Mosiah chapter 5). We need to always remember and never forget who created and directs this Church. It is the living Lord Jesus Christ Himself. He knows the name by which He is called and knows the name by which His Church and His disciples are to be called. This is not the Church of men, which can be remolded and reshaped according to popular opinion. It is of divine origin and has a divine mandate. In my view, this revelatory reminder will serve to further clarify in a unique way what the Church truly represents to all the world—both to those inside it and those looking at it from the outside. God be thanked that we have a prophet, seer, and revelator with the spiritual insight, courage, and determination to receive divine instructions and bring them to fruition.

Home-centered, Church-supported, Christ-centered Families

The home is to be a place of faith in, testimony of, and devotion to the Lord Jesus Christ. As parents bear testimony to their children of the Divine Sonship of Christ and children gain that personal revelation for themselves, we will continue to establish a church of revelation-based homes and families. Essentially this means we will have more Christ-centered homes.

The Work of Salvation Extends to Both the Living and Dead

This is scripturally mandated. Eternal life can be given to those who are dead on conditions of their repentance and the performance of vicarious ordinances done on their behalf. It is hard to conceive of a doctrine that reveals the clear justice and mercy of God any more convincingly than redemption for the believing and obedient dead: "And so it was made known among the dead, both small and great, the unrighteous as well as the faithful, that redemption had been wrought through the sacrifice of the Son of God upon the cross" (Doctrine and Covenants 138:35).

Make the Sabbath a Delight

"And I, God, blessed the seventh day, and sanctified it" (Moses 3:3). It is no accident or coincidence that the Sabbath day is designated as being blessed and sanctified by God. This is intended to mean that it is set apart as special, dedicated as distinctive, and consecrated to be holy. Sunday is my favorite day of the week. It is a day of rest, reflection, revelation, and resolution. It is a special day—set apart from every other day. It is the day of the sacred sacrament. It is a day for doing God's work, which is to bless and serve others. On this day we are renewed in righteousness. It is apparent that each of us, as we participate in each of these revelatory pronouncements, will become closer to the divine standard and closer to heavenly joy in our own lives.

CONCLUSION

When I was twelve years old, Elder Neal A. Maxwell of the Quorum of the Twelve Apostles was to speak at a fireside in Dublin,

Ireland. I had a head cold and cough, but my mother encouraged me to go with her. I am deeply grateful that she did. We sat up front. I was not expecting what followed. I was astounded that when Elder Maxwell spoke, my cough subsided (it returned afterwards!). I was overwhelmed by the Spirit. I was spellbound by his message. I knew he was a true living Apostle who represented the Savior Jesus Christ. I remember the feeling of sensing a new reality, figuratively speaking. I was inspired to acquire the Christlike qualities Elder Maxwell spoke of, and demonstrated. This was a preliminary change in mind and heart from the Savior. It was a spiritual convergence between heaven and earth giving me an appreciation of new life in Christ. It would be followed by many events binding my soul to God eternally. I believe Saints across the world have had similar experiences. I later wrote a letter to him about how the revelation touched me personally. He wrote back and said that the Lord had been good to me in sharing His generous spiritual experiences. He was wisely deflecting praise away from himself.

The point of all of this is to suggest that God sends living witnesses to share powerful testimony of Him. Their words, example, and power of influence radiate the fact that God lives, loves, and seeks to bless us. It does not make sense to speak of accepting God while at the same time refusing to accept and hear the servants He sends in His stead. On the contrary, to accept the Lord's servants with enthusiasm is to likewise accept Him.

4

HIS HOLY NAME

Drawing close to Father in Heaven leads to emulating His character, following His example, partaking of His goodness, sharing in His knowledge, loving His soul, hearing His voice, doing His deeds, learning His plans, understanding His purposes, valuing His ways, and preparing to receive His glorious joy. This is something the Savior did perfectly well, and it is something we need to learn to do. One of the core essential ways that we draw close to our Father in Heaven is through understanding, respecting, and relying on the holy, special, and sacred name of His Beloved Son.

> And Adam and Eve, his wife, called upon the name of the Lord. . . .
>
> Wherefore, thou shalt do all that thou doest in the name of the Son, and thou shalt repent and call upon God in the name of the Son forevermore. . . .
>
> And in that day Adam blessed God and was filled, and began to prophesy concerning all the families of the earth, saying: Blessed be the name of God. . . .
>
> And Adam and Eve blessed the name of God, and they made all things known unto their sons and their daughters. (Moses 5:4, 8–12)

So, our first parents called on the name of God in prayer. They were soon instructed by an angel to conduct their worship in the name of the Son of God. They were told to repent and pray to the Father in the name of the Son going forward. We are told that Adam blessed the name of God. What does this mean? How can someone bless the name of God? I am reminded of what the Savior said when he prayed: "Our Father who art in Heaven, hallowed by thy name." That is simply to say, thy name is holy, sacred, sublime, special; may it be retained in holiness. May it be spoken with care, uttered with reverence, used only in authority, and not blasphemed or spoken in vain or in anger or profanity. So, a hallowed name is one that is respected, revered, and spoken with care. The name of God is most sacred. Therefore, I understand Adam to be honoring the name of God, showing deep gratitude and sacred sanctity regarding the use of the name of God, because it signifies His nature, character, authority, and stature as the Supreme Being. Adam praised and thanked God for His plan of salvation. Indeed, we are told that both Adam and Eve showed this tender and special recognition toward the divine name. Obviously, relying on the name of God in this way shows that they had a correct understanding of God's goodness and of the sublime redeeming action that the Father would bring to the world through the Son. Salvation is in the name of Christ; it always has been and always will be.

> Verily, thus saith the Lord: It shall come to pass that every soul who forsaketh his sins and cometh unto me, and calleth on my name, and obeyeth my voice, and keepeth my commandments, shall see my face and know that I am. . . .
>
> Therefore, in the beginning the Word was, for he was the Word, even the messenger of salvation. . . .
>
> And I, John, bear record that I beheld his glory, as the glory of the Only Begotten of the Father. . . .
>
> I give unto you these sayings that you may understand and know how to worship, and know what you worship, that you may come unto the Father in my name, and in due time receive of his fulness. . . . The glory of God is intelligence, or, in other words, light and truth. (Doctrine and Covenants 93:1, 8, 11, 19, 36)

We are thus informed that each person who calls on the name of God in prayer in the spirit of humble obedience can come to see the person who bears that sacred name. Christ is the living word of God, the word made flesh, the word now made immortal and celestial. He is the messenger of salvation, which is to say, He brings the Father's message of salvation to the world. He is the glorious Only Begotten Son in the flesh. We are taught this so we can comprehend that to come to the Father, we must proceed in the name of the Savior. There cannot be any other way, in time or eternity, for us to gain the salvation the Father plans for. If we grow in light and truth, in the manner shown to us by the Son of God, then eventually we will obtain the fulness of the Father. This means we will become intelligent, glorious, full of light and truth ourselves. This gives us a clear indication of why we must know the name in which salvation is promised and secured.

THE SPECIAL NATURE OF CHRIST'S HOLY NAME

Jesus Christ's holy name was given to Him by His dear Father. He loves, respects, and honors it. His name is distinctive, unique, special, and significant. His is the only name under heaven whereby we may be saved. His name indicates His authority, power, Atonement, mission, ministry, and character. This noble and distinguished designation is laden with precious meaning. There is only one person in all eternity who correctly and properly carries this title: "For unto us a child is born, unto us a son is given; and the government shall be upon his shoulder; and his name shall be called, Wonderful, Counselor, The Mighty God, The Everlasting Father, The Prince of Peace" (2 Nephi 19:6).

It is interesting to note the names that shall be given to this special child, this gift to the world. He will be known as Wonderful. I think that suggests the greatness of His character. It also conveys the image that He would work wonders and miracles, things that would surprise, astonish, and amaze people—even the people of God. He would show forth power to do acts not normally done.

He would be known as Counselor. He would be wise in judgment and profound in insight. His teachings would penetrate to the crucial heart of questions of significance. He would discern truth, perceive the ways of wisdom, and recognize falsehood in all its forms. He would be trustworthy, reliable, conscientious, and capable of giving sound advice to anyone and everyone. His knowledge would reach to heaven, and He would know what to say, do, and be in every circumstance. His guidance of others would be without selfish ambition. His directions would be solid and sure.

He would be called the Mighty God. Not weak, incapable, redundant, powerless, or useless. He would be strong and faithful, able, resilient, eager, and dependable. He would need this special endowment of strength to face His foes, surmount difficulties of all kinds, move consistently forward against constant opposition, and accomplish the most challenging test of His life in the performance of the infinite and eternal Atonement.

He would be named the Everlasting Father. What other child is known as the Everlasting Father? How can a child be a father? I think this scripture comprehends the eternal nature of Christ's redemptive power. Even before He was born into mortality, the prophets understood that He would be the father by spiritual rebirth of those who would be born again through His ordinances and powers. He would be the Father in this sense of all the faithful. He would give them a newness of life.

He would be termed the Prince of Peace. He would discern clearly between truth and error. He would preach comfort and consolation. He would bring assurances of conquering evil and wickedness. He would use the sword of truth and righteousness to cut through deception, trickery, error, and lies. He would bring peace to the troubled, comfort to the conflicted, harmony to the divided, confidence to the confused, and love to the forsaken. However, He would recognize and enable not only peace within but also between persons. Despite being hated and persecuted He would return good for evil. He would be royalty of the highest, noblest kind. He would walk and talk with dignity and honor. His attributes would be those of unimpeachable integrity. He would be a master of goodness, an example of how to think, speak, act, and live for the greatest benefit to oneself and others. He would surmount sin, defy death, and defeat the devil. He would preside over a whole new type of world.

He is appropriately and reverentially designated as follows:

- A premortal God by the name of Jehovah. He is the Great I AM. This perfectly illustrates His ongoing life, permanence, and marvelous power.
- The Creator. His was the power to bring this world into being. This was a life-giving and life-sustaining act of goodness.
- The Christ in mortality. This essentially means the same as Messiah, the Anointed One. The Savior was anointed to proclaim liberty to the captives and to bind up the broken-hearted. He is the rescuer, deliver, and redeemer of our souls—both body and spirit. There is no other way to salvation, no other name for salvation, and no other Messiah. There is no salvation of any kind or degree except that which is made available through His atoning sacrifice.
- Wonderful. He is amazing, astounding, impressive, majestic, and magnificent by any degree or standard we wish to consider.
- Counselor. He is the perfect teacher, guide, comforter, consoler, listener, and enabler.
- The Only Begotten of the Father in the flesh. He inherited unique abilities from His Father that allowed Him to perform in a way that is marvelous. His Divine Sonship gave Him power to do things that no other person could.
- The Son of God. He is like His Father in His goodness, appearance, and proclivities.
- The Son of Man of Holiness. He is good to the core, perfectly pure, generously gentle, victoriously virtuous, constantly courageous, relentlessly hard-working, and deeply loving.
- Emmanuel. He is indeed God with us. To see Him is to see the ways and wonders of the Almighty. He brought heavenly ways to the earth so we could sense and feel what heaven is like through his deeds, teachings, and personality.

- The Mighty God. He is powerful beyond comparison, able to deliver us, strong when we are weak. He is both tough and tender. The most difficult task is possible for Him.
- The Holy One of Israel. He is chosen, selected, commissioned, authorized, empowered, and acknowledged as the only Lord and Savior that has ever or will ever atone.
- The Lamb of God. He is a worthy sacrifice, a perfect offering, a pure vessel, and an acceptable expiator. He is the lamb without blemish from the foundation of the world. Think of that. No pride, selfishness, ignorance, laziness, hatred, or contamination stained his pure soul. He was a whole person—kind, courageous, virtuous, loving, honorable, hard-working, gentle, strong, believing, and faithful.
- The Savior. He saves us from sin, death, foolishness, regret, remorse, guilt, sadness, pain, and avoidable suffering. He protects and heals the willing soul.
- The Redeemer. He sets us free from bondage, perishing, conquest, and defeat. He redeems us from sin and death to which we are so easily exposed and enslaved.
- The Deliverer. He rescues the slaves, releases the captives, unchains the bound. He takes us away from our bondage and brings relief to our weary and sick souls.
- The Mediator. He pays our debt and ransoms us from sin on conditions of repentance.
- The Advocate. He pleads our cause before the Father with conviction, sincerity, and passion. His ability to argue our case is unmatched.
- The Prince of Peace. He is the supplier of every good thing and the bestower of every good gift.
- The Lord of Lords. He is our leader, master, help, and strength.
- The King of Kings. He is royalty of the highest order, worthy of worship, granter of mercies, maker of rules, and master of power.
- The Everlasting Father. He is the spiritual Father of the righteous, the one who gives life to His seed, the enduring source of our salvation.

- The Good Shepherd. He lays down His perfect innocent life for His people. He is good above all and generous beyond our expectation. He thinks on us, is concerned for us, and watches over us.
- The Lord. He is our Master, our unfailing guide, and our constant director. He will teach and train us if we are humble and penitent.
- The Lord of Hosts. He governs many, leads many, blesses many, helps many, knows many, and is acknowledged, known, and loved by many. This is not the fame of the notorious or the fortune of a moment. He can be admired by all, loved by all, remembered by all, and trusted by all.

HIS NAME IN HOLY SCRIPTURE

The scriptures proclaim with clarity that His name is the only name under heaven whereby salvation can be found. The Book of Mormon speaks clearly and frequently on the importance of the name of Jesus Christ. It is the only name through which salvation in the kingdom of God can be found: "There is no other head whereby ye can be made free. There is no other name given whereby salvation cometh; therefore, I would that ye should take upon you the name of Christ" (Mosiah 5:8). This sacred scripture teaches us that faith in the Lamb of God leads to spirit-filled ordinances and covenants. This is how the Holy Ghost changes our hearts from desiring carnality to righteousness—the process of being born again to receive a newness of life. This can only happen because the name of Christ indicates His authority, power, nature, character, mission, and Atonement. In other words, obtaining this new life in Christ requires us to have faith in his holy name unto the performance of ordinances and covenants and enduring compliance with them subsequently.

"Now I say unto you that ye must repent, and be born again; for the Spirit saith if ye are not born again ye cannot inherit the kingdom of heaven; therefore come and be baptized unto repentance, that ye may be washed from your sins, that ye may have faith on the Lamb of God, who taketh away the sins of the world, who is mighty to save and to cleanse from all unrighteousness" (Alma 7:14). This process of being born again is not trivial or superficial. It is mighty, magnificent, and meaningful. We are to have a mighty change of nature through faith in His name. This is reliance on His redemptive power. This is a transformation in our soul of phenomenal proportions. Thus, we can be saved only through faith in the name of the Son of God:

> And now I ask of you on what conditions are they saved? . . .
>
> Behold, I can tell you—did not my father Alma believe in the words which were delivered by the mouth of Abinadi? . . .
>
> And according to his faith there was a mighty change wrought in his heart. . . .
>
> And now behold, I ask of you, my brethren of the church, have ye spiritually been born of God? Have ye received his image in your countenances? Have ye experienced this mighty change in your hearts?
>
> Do ye exercise faith in the redemption of him who created you?" (Alma 5:10–15).

Similarly, the Doctrine and Covenants leaves us with no doubt about the source of our power. We are told that we must take upon ourselves the name of Christ through ordinances and covenants and endure to the end in following that lifestyle. How important it is to know that we must be called after His name, bear His name, and become part of His divine family. His name is to be our name. This is the doctrine of salvation in the family. As Christ is the rightful heir of God, then we too become rightful inheritors as joint heirs with Christ, but only through the complete acceptance of His name through rights, rituals, promises, and powers:

> Behold, Jesus Christ is the name which is given of the Father, and there is none other name given whereby man can be saved;
>
> Wherefore, all men must take upon them the name which is given of the Father, for in that name shall they be called at the last day;
>
> Wherefore, if they know not the name by which they are called, they cannot have place in the kingdom of my Father. (Doctrine and Covenants 18:21–25)

The Pearl of Great Price also plainly teaches that reliance on the name of the Only Begotten is the only way we can find everlasting salvation. This reliance is shown in listening, believing, trusting, obeying, repenting, being baptized, receiving the Holy Ghost, and enduring on the covenant path. This is the key that unlocks the door to all heavenly blessings. There neither is, nor can there be, a different way than this to find eternal happiness: "And he also said unto him: If thou wilt turn unto me, and hearken unto my voice, and believe, and repent of all thy transgressions, and be baptized, even in water, in the name of mine Only Begotten Son, who is full of grace and truth, which is Jesus Christ, the only name which shall be given under heaven, whereby salvation shall come unto the children of men, ye shall receive the gift of the Holy Ghost" (Moses 6:52).

The New Testament is likewise a testimony to this doctrine of believing in the name of the Son of God as being the sure way to achieve a newness of life promised by God: "But these are written, that ye might believe that Jesus is the Christ, the Son of God; and that believing ye might have life through his name" (John 20:31).

What about the Old Testament? Does this bear witness of the name of Christ? Well, let us consider the vital interchange between Jacob and a messenger from God:

> And Jacob was left alone; and there wrestled a man with him until the breaking of the day. . . .
>
> And he said, Let me go, for the day breaketh. And he said, I will not let thee go, except thou bless me.
>
> And he said unto him, What *is* thy name? And he said, Jacob.
>
> And he said, Thy name shall be called no more Jacob, but Israel: for as a prince hast thou power with God and with men, and hast prevailed.
>
> And Jacob asked him, and said, Tell me, I pray thee, thy name. And he said, Wherefore is it that thou dost ask after my name? And he blessed him there.
>
> And Jacob called the name of the place Peniel: for I have seen God face to face, and my life is preserved. (Genesis 32:24–30)

This is a most instructive account. The event shows us that Jacob was visited by a divine messenger. Jacob struggled to obtain a blessing from this heavenly being. We do not know exactly what this entailed, but certainly it was a time of spiritual searching, stretching, and effort. Jacob refused to yield to weakness. He wanted a divine blessing and would not permit himself to give up before he got it. The messenger was impressed by this man's devotion. Significantly, he asked him what his name was. Jacob told him. However, then the visitor changed his name to Israel in token of the fact that he had persevered and gained divine approbation. Then, Israel asked the messenger what his name was. The messenger asked Israel why he was asking about his name. I understand that to mean that it ought to have been evident to Israel who this messenger was. He did not need to be told his name as he already knew. The messenger then proceeded to give him a blessing.

After that blessing Israel called the name of that area Peniel, indicating that he had there seen God face to face. In other words, he had a divine encounter with God. So, what was the name of the heavenly being? It was the name of God. Jehovah is the name of God. Jehovah who later became Jesus Christ. He was the God of the Old Testament after the Fall. Interestingly, Israel said after this that his life was preserved. This suggests that his life had been in danger. However, he was preserved, protected, defended, saved. He was searching for, wrestling with, getting to know, and recalling the identity of God. It was God that blessed him. It was God that preserved his life. It was God that would give him a posterity like the sands of the seashore. It was God that would exalt his life. It is my conviction that this story teaches us of the name of God bringing salvation to those who bind themselves in close covenant with God. This was an incident that showed Jacob, renamed Israel, that salvation comes in knowing the name of God and taking that name upon ourselves. There are many other accounts in the Old Testament that are likewise similar, although their meaning and significance is veiled until our eyes are opened through the truths revealed so plainly in modern scripture.

HIS HOLY NAME AND THE PROPHETIC COMMISSION

What of prophets and apostles? In whose name do they teach, testify, and baptize? The scriptures of latter days give us the answer. Called and ordained apostles are commissioned in the name of the Lord. They declare His gospel, live as His disciples, take upon themselves the name of Christ with intentional devotion, preach to all the world, and baptize in the name of the Savior: "Yea, even twelve; and the Twelve shall be my disciples, and they shall take upon them my name; and the Twelve are they who shall desire to take upon them my name with full purpose of heart. And if they desire to take upon them my name with full purpose of heart, they are called to go into all the world to preach my gospel unto every creature" (Doctrine and Covenants 18:26–29).

So it is that these apostles do not go forth in their own name. They do not preach their own doctrines, present their own agendas, or labor to promote their own interests. Rather, they are sent in His holy name, preach His doctrine, perform His ordinances, regulate His church, gather His elect, build His temples, and give their lives and energies to His cause. They are empowered by and protected by His sacred name. They teach with His power and love with His divine love. So, this is what it means to take upon themselves His name with full purpose of heart—with pure intent, with consistent consecration, with deliberate determination, and with lasting longevity. Their great energy and enthusiasm come from having the right name written on their hearts, lodged in their minds and at the forefront of their focus.

HIS HOLY NAME AND FULL-TIME MISSIONARIES

In like manner, our full-time missionaries who serve throughout the world are living the commandments, interviewed by their priesthood leaders, recommended to serve, called by a prophet, endowed with power in the holy temple, set apart by their stake presidents, given a badge to remind them of the two names that should always be written in their hearts—their own name and the name of their Lord—trained in the ministry, and go forth to love, teach, serve, and bless others. Thus, they are full-time servants of the

Savior, acting in His name, preaching His words, performing His ordinances, promoting His work, encouraging others to come to His covenants, and rejoicing in His ability to save. It is only through the power of His name that missionaries can endure opposition, work extremely hard, sacrifice time and interests, find the elect, and build God's kingdom on the earth: "And ye are called to bring to pass the gathering of mine elect; for mine elect hear my voice and harden not their hearts" (Doctrine and Covenants 29:7).

ACTING MIRACULOUSLY IN HIS HOLY NAME AND PRIESTHOOD

Can miracles be performed in the name of Christ? Consider this powerful passage:

> Behold, are not the things that God hath wrought marvelous in our eyes? Yea, and who can comprehend the marvelous works of God?
>
> And who shall say that Jesus Christ did not do many mighty miracles? And there were many mighty miracles wrought by the hands of the apostles. . . .
>
> And he ceaseth not to be God, and is a God of miracles. . . .
>
> Behold, I say unto you that whoso believeth in Christ, doubting nothing, whatsoever he shall ask the Father in the name of Christ it shall be granted him; and this promise is unto all, even unto the ends of the earth. (Mormon 9:16–21)

Thus it is that God has always been, is, and will always be a worker of miracles. All that He does is a miracle. Creation, healing, redemption, salvation, and exaltation are all miracles. The Lord Jesus Christ healed the sick, gave sight to the blind, cleansed the lepers, walked on water, and raised the dead. These are not metaphors. They are plain and precious truths. Although we live in a day and age when many see the notion of miracles as preposterous, we can know that God is not defined by the speculations of humans. He has power to create worlds, people them, control the elements, and overcome sin and death.

It is critical to note that miracles must be done in the right name, by the right power. It is the name of God that provides for miracles.

It is the name of Christ that saves. The Savior's apostles performed many miracles. All of these were done in the name of Christ by His recognized messengers. Miracles of the body and spirit are not trivial things. They are special and sacred, and are done in a spirit of humility. Miracles are real, and they continue today among those who have faith in the name of the Son of God. All people who develop true faith in Christ can know miracles. Those holding priesthood offices can perform miracles according to the will of the Lord. Those who receive delegated priesthood authority—such as sisters in the kingdom—experience many miracles, small and large. Even those presently not yet holding the priesthood or its power can still experience miracles—such as the miracle of conversion—although this still requires a preacher with priesthood to be speaking God's words. However, the key component for all participants is faith in the Son of God. We must believe in the name of Christ to experience miracles in the posture of faith.

HIS NAME IN HOLY PLACES

It is interesting to me that each of our dedicated Church buildings display the name of Christ and His Church on the facade. This is a clear indication of who founded the Church and who governs and directs it: "For thus shall my church be called in the last days, even The Church of Jesus Christ of Latter-day Saints" (Doctrine and Covenants 115:4). The name of the Church is given by divine revelation. It bears His holy name. When we enter the Church building, it is good to remember the name of the owner and show the deference and respect to His holy name that should guide our lives. As the Church is made holy by His sacred name, so are our lives.

Likewise, and in a more significant way, our dedicated temples contain the same name at the entrance to the temple grounds. On the facade of the temple we see the words "HOLINESS TO THE LORD. THE HOUSE OF THE LORD." So it is that each temple belongs to the Savior. These are His properties, and His name protects them, sanctifies them, and makes them places of power. "And it shall be upon Aaron to minister: and his sound shall be heard when he goeth in unto the holy *place* before the LORD, and when he cometh out, that he die not. And thou shalt make a plate *of* pure gold, and grave upon it, *like* the engravings of a signet, HOLINESS TO THE LORD" (Exodus 28:35–36).

To be endowed and sealed in the temple of the Lord is to take upon us the name of Christ in holiness, with a sacred resolve to be holy as He is. The temple is where we come to understand in deeper measure the scale, scope, and importance of His name in the plan of salvation. The temple is a place of living water and renewing bread, where we find a new source of spiritual life. As it is the Lord's house, His Spirit is there, His power is there, His blessings are there, and He may visit there.

In like manner, our homes, which ought to be places of righteousness, are holy places where we remember the Lord, love the Lord, pray in the name of the Lord, give and receive priesthood blessings in the name of the Lord, study the words of the Lord, and rejoice in the great goodness of the Lord. His name should be in our own homes and hearts. Can we have full divine love at home without the name of the Lord being part of our homes? Significantly, when the Nephites at the temple Bountiful could not understand all the doctrines the Lord was trying to teach them, He specifically said they should return to their homes to ponder and pray in His name for understanding, and then He would visit them again: "Therefore, go ye unto your homes, and ponder upon the things which I have said, and ask of the Father, in my name, that ye may understand, and prepare your minds for the morrow, and I come unto you again" (3 Nephi 17:3). No doubt there is a message for all of us here. Our homes should be places of pondering, prayer, and revelation. The name of the Lord should be invoked for special purposes there.

TAKING UPON OURSELVES HIS HOLY NAME THROUGH SACRED ORDINANCES AND COVENANTS

When I think of the ordinances of the restored gospel, it is apparent that we perform each of these in the name of the Lord:

- Baptism is a similitude of Christ's death, burial, and resurrection. Baptism is performed in the name of all three members of the Godhead. We witness our willingness to take

upon ourselves the holy name of Christ by the baptismal covenant. The old sinful person dies, is buried, and comes forth in a newness of life—one of spiritual righteousness.
- The sacrament is a renewal of the baptismal covenant. It is performed in the name of Jesus Christ. It allows the humble and repentant to be renewed in righteousness through the name of the Only Begotten.
- The priesthood. Whether we are talking about receiving or using the priesthood, it must be done in the name of Jesus Christ. The priesthood is the authority and power of God and is used to bring life and salvation to God's children. All priesthood pronouncements have efficacy in and through the Atonement of the Lord. The priesthood gives us the opportunity to experience a newness of life that would otherwise be impossible.
- The temple endowment. The endowment is a sublime gift of knowledge and power. It is through the name and Atonement of the Son of God that the ordinance has power, vitality, meaning, and significance. It represents our ascent to heavenly glory. We are endowed with power through His holy name and learn how to become more as He is. In other words, this is a necessary channel for us to receive the full divine type of life.
- The temple sealing. The sealing ordinance is performed in the name of God. In other words, it is dependent on His nature, authority, power, plans, and purposes to have effect. It is how we are bound to God and our families in time and eternity. The kind and degree of life envisaged by this is both wonderful and everlasting.

Indeed, all ordinances, in order to have saving power in time and eternity, must be done in the type and name of the Only Begotten Son of God. The ritual is symbolic of the deep. The meaning of all that we do in these ordinances and covenants is the immersion of our souls in the knowledge and power of God. We are to be sealed to God through the actions of our heart, mind, body, and spirit.

HAVING FAITH IN THE NAME OF CHRIST

There are several elements to the process of how this new life occurs. We are to develop faith in the name of Christ, to make and keep sacred covenants through participation in ordinances, and to develop the characteristics and attributes of Christ in our own lives. In considering the importance of the name of Jesus Christ it is of no small moment that the Book of Mormon teaches, "And he shall be called Jesus Christ, the Son of God, the Father of heaven and earth, the Creator of all things from the beginning; and his mother shall be called Mary. And lo, he cometh unto his own, that salvation might come unto the children of men even through faith on his name" (Mosiah 3:8–9). That is to say that His name is one of eternal significance, import, and power. His name is holy, special, sacred, and distinctive. His name identifies Him as the one and only Messiah that ever has had, ever does have, and ever will have the power of salvation. His many names have meaning. To truly know His name is to know the singular source of our salvation. The holy scriptures are united in teaching that salvation can come through only one name: "And now, my son, I have told you this that ye may learn wisdom, that ye may learn of me that there is no other way or means whereby man can be saved, only in and through Christ. Behold, he is the life and the light of the world. Behold, he is the word of truth and righteousness" (Alma 38:9).

What does it mean to say that we are saved through faith in His name? His name indicates His divine nature, calling, life, mission, example, teachings, Atonement, resurrection, and power. To have faith in His name is to trust in Him, believe in Him, learn of Him, accept Him, follow Him, serve Him, sacrifice for Him, live like Him, and endure to the end by abiding with Him. Faith in His name is a process, not a once off event only. As we come to know Him in a deep and meaningful way, there is a significant transformation in our souls. Our faith in Him is tried and tested. As we learn to conduct our lives in alignment with His Holy truths, then our faith in His name inevitably increases. Over time that faith becomes unshaken and unshakable, and we find the newness of life He promised to those who abide in Him.

Salvation is simply the natural outgrowth of pursuing faith in His name consistently and sincerely.

Faith is wonderful. Faith can alter thoughts, heal hearts, bolster resolve, engender courage, transform souls, bless relationships, and fortify each of us. Now is the time for faith, the season for belief, and the opportunity for conviction. This is the day for delight, the moment for miracles, and the chance for change. Faith can and will transform the world. To believe in God is to trust in His towering promises. Through faith in the Living Christ all of life is made better. Whatever we do in life, it is essential that we do not permanently abandon our living faith in the true and living God. We are well advised to keep faith, retain faith, increase faith, develop faith, and always act in faith.

PRAYER IN HIS NAME

"Therefore ye must always pray unto the Father in my name; And whatsoever ye shall ask the Father in my name, which is right, believing that ye shall receive, behold it shall be given unto you. Pray in your families unto the Father, always in my name, that your wives and your children may be blessed" (3 Nephi 18:19–21).

We are to pray according to the divine mandate. Prayer needs to be directed to the Father and offered always in the name of the Only Begotten Son. This is a divine directive. This is a spiritual imperative. Our prayerful pleadings need to be humbly submissive. We are to rely on God's goodness and trust in His promises. If we pray for the right thing—those things which in the heavenly economy are expedient—and we believe that we shall be blessed according to the promises, then our prayers will be answered in the affirmative. This is a process we learn over time as our prayers are refined and polished from being self-seeking to pure. Obviously, we are not only to pray with our lips but with our minds, hearts, bodies, and spirits. Our prayers are to be sincere and intentional so that we live in accordance with our stated desires. How vital it is to know that we are commanded to always pray in the name of the Savior. This is the way, means, and channel appointed for true prayer. The blessings that attend such proper prayer are multifaceted and great.

MIRACLES THROUGH HIS NAME

"For I am God, and mine arm is not shortened; and I will show miracles, signs, and wonders, unto all those who believe on my name" (Doctrine and Covenants 35:8). We are thus promised that to believe on His name is to see the arm of God in our lives. It is to witness miracles, to see signs, and to experience wonders. It is to discern the workings of God in our world. God is not absent, slumbering, bored, distant, indifferent, or incapable. He is alive and well; strong and powerful; good and great; generous and gracious. He is a God of the routine and the majestic; of the individual person and the whole world; of the smallest kind deed and the greatest works of heroism. God lives, loves, lifts, and leads. Blessed be His eternal name.

Always Remember His Name

"I say unto you, I would that ye should remember to retain the name written always in your hearts, that ye are not found on the left hand of God, but that ye hear and know the voice by which ye shall be called, and also, the name by which he shall call you" (Mosiah 5:12).

When it comes to the name of the Only Begotten Son of God, Jesus Christ, there is great and lasting importance in a name. His name is to be upon us and written deeply into our hearts—at the very central core of all that we believe, do, and are. This is far beyond procedure and superficiality. We are to have His name printed, embedded, indelibly woven into our hearts. This is to be deep, meaningful, and ongoing. We are to be His witnesses, His disciples, His followers, His servants, His children, His sheep, and His friends. His name is one we should always remember and never forget. We are to honor His name, love His name, and glorify His name—now and eternally. We need to know that at the last day He will call us in the name He has given us—His name. We need to recognize His voice calling us, pleading with us, guiding us, directing us, and assisting us.

CONCLUSION

We do not find hope in this world. We cannot find real and lasting hope in worldly treasures, secular riches, transitory fame, fleeting pleasures, status-based accolades, or popular opinions. While these may provide the illusion of deep-rooted foundations, they are inevitably shallow and short-lived. Rather, we find real and deep hope in Christ. We find peace in Him, love in Him, goodness in Him, faith in Him, and joy in Him. We seek for Him, come to know Him, draw close to Him, and serve Him. He eagerly seeks for us to learn of Him. Through Him we find abundant life. There simply is no other way to find true happiness and lasting peace. He is the only true hope that the world has ever had. Jesus Christ is truly the living Son of God. The King of Kings is not merely *a* way, He is *the* way. The Lord of Lords is not just *a* truth, He is *the* Truth. The Priest of Priests is not simply *a* life, He is *the* Life. The Redeemer of Israel is not only *a* light, He is *the* Light. He is the good and Great I Am, the majestic Messiah, and the strong Savior of our souls.

5

ABOUNDING THROUGH COVENANTS

The entire restored gospel revolves around the notion of connection—connection with God, connection with Christ, connection with the Holy Ghost, connection with ancestors and descendants, Church leaders, characters and stories of the scriptures, other members of the Church, and indeed all people. Therefore, we talk of things like brotherhood, sisterhood, meeting together and ministering, and so on. These are all concepts involving our connection with others. It is also why the great work of the gospel concerns itself with words and powers such as united, sealed, bound, welded, joined, linked, and forged. While the gospel offers salvation to us on an individual and personal basis, it does not end there but locates this important individual salvation within the overall context of family exaltation. God seeks to save us all, and He does this by means of covenant religion. This is the process by which we are literally tied back to—or restored to—God Himself in the first instance and our families in the second instance. In other words, true religion will always be about connection. To fulfill this plan of connection God has invited us to participate personally in holy ordinances and thereby to make and keep the associated sacred covenants.

THE NATURE OF SACRED ORDINANCES

An ordinance is a holy act we are commanded to perform by divine revelation. It is a physical act with spiritual meaning that is performed under the authority of the keys of the priesthood and is performed in a special place designated for a sacred purpose. We often refer to the mode or manner of baptism as being by immersion. This suggests that the physical ordinance itself is a symbolic manifestation of the deep spiritual purpose of the act. Immersion is total, complete, entire, whole—this obviously indicates that our immersion in water is intended to represent a full commitment rather than a partial, half-hearted one. We know that baptism is symbolic of the death, burial, and resurrection of Christ. It is symbolic of the dying of the old man of sin, His burial in the grave, and His resurrection to a newness of life. In this way the old person of worldliness dies, and the new person is born to a new life of righteousness. In all of this it is apparent that the death of the old man of sin is intended to be permanent and the new man of holiness is also intended to be a change to a state that will last forever.

All this is contingent on the atoning sacrifice of the Son of God. Without His triumph over sin and death any baptism we might engage in—and indeed any other holy ordinances—would essentially be dead works devoid of any life-giving powers of renewal or regeneration. We are not saved by the ordinance of baptism itself. While we need to enter the waters of baptism, we must also have the baptism of the spirit—which is a complete cleansing of our souls by spiritual fire brought to us through the power of the Holy Ghost. Of course, this spiritual cleansing is entirely dependent not only on our personal submission to God but, importantly, on the redemptive act of the Son of God in Gethsemane and on Calvary. In fact, the wording of the following revelation on baptism teaches this principle clearly: *"And again, by way of commandment to the church concerning the manner of baptism*—All those who humble themselves before God, and desire to be baptized, and come forth with broken hearts and contrite spirits, and witness before the Church that they have truly repented of all their sins, and are willing to take upon them the name of Jesus Christ, having a determination to serve him to the end . . . shall be received by baptism" (Doctrine and Covenants 20:37; emphasis added).

In this verse the manner of baptism does not focus on physical immersion. Instead it specifies that the manner of baptism includes the baptismal candidate as being in the posture of humility, willingness, submission, contrition, repentance, acceptance of the Savior, having a desire to endure and being sincere. In other words, immersion is not simply a physical act of complete covering with water but is concerned with the inner workings of the spirit. It is our internal devotion to God and our understanding that Christ is the key in this divine renewing that counts most. Clearly, our body is to be immersed and our spirit is to be completely submissive. This is the manner of true baptism. This is not to suggest that physical immersion is not required as it is needed. The immersion asked of us is both physical and spiritual—and must be centered on the Son of God to be acceptable to God and to fulfill the designated divine purpose. The Savior invites us as individuals and families to take upon ourselves His name by covenant and promise. Those who are true and faithful thereby receive a newness of life.

THE NATURE OF COVENANTS MADE WITH GOD

The ordinances always involve covenants. A covenant is a personal sacred and binding promise, performed in the presence of witnesses and having blessings attached to it for obedience and penalties for disobedience. Covenants are important and precious. It is wise to approach them seriously and genuinely. As we grow and mature in understanding, we will keep our covenants with more comprehension.

TWO BAPTISMS

I love the doctrine of two baptisms. We are to have a baptism of water and a baptism of fire. Both are necessary. Consider this verse: "Wherefore, my beloved brethren, I know that if ye shall follow the Son, with full purpose of heart, acting no hypocrisy and no deception before God, but with real intent, repenting of your sins, witnessing unto the Father that ye are willing to take upon you the name of Christ, by baptism—yea, by following your Lord and your Savior down into the water, according to his word, behold, then shall ye receive the Holy Ghost; yea, then cometh the baptism of fire and of the Holy Ghost; and then can ye speak with the tongue of angels, and shout praises unto the Holy One of Israel" (2 Nephi 31:13). That is to say that following Christ sincerely, purely, honestly, and intentionally requires genuine repentance and showing our willingness to accept a new name as evidenced in the manner of baptism by water. This water baptism is symbolic of the death, burial, and resurrection of the Lord. Our water baptism is therefore following the baptismal example of the Lord. Then we need to receive the Holy Ghost by confirmation. The Holy Ghost cleanses us by fire. He removes sin and sinful tendencies from us. The Holy Ghost will allow us to speak with revelatory power like the angels do and to glorify the Savior through witnessing words.

It is interesting that these two baptisms are elemental—as both water and fire are elemental. They cleanse, purify, and sanctify us. Baptism by water cleans us on the outside, and baptism by fire cleans us on the inside. We are washed clean totally, completely, and intensely. We are quickened in the inner man, changed to a new state, transformed for a life of righteousness, made worthy to hear, see, and speak wonderful things. Both baptisms are necessary and wonderful. A newness of life comes to us through these two baptisms.

SACRAMENTAL NEWNESS

Consider the sacred sacramental ordinance and its associated covenant. The sacrament is the central act of the week for every striving Latter-day Saint. We ought to carefully ponder on the dignified solemnity associated with administering the sacramental emblems. We should conscientiously consider the sacred nature of the sacrament. It is important to consciously think and reflect on the deep meanings of the atoning sacrifice of our Lord as we experience each element of this organized ordinance:

- The holy hymn that always teaches doctrine of divine deliverance through Christ.

- The precious prayer that asks our Heavenly Father to bless the emblems to our sanctification.
- The peaceful passing that reflects honor, respect, and sobriety among young, active, vivacious men.
- The broken bread that reminds us that only because Christ was broken can we be made whole.
- The wholesome water that reminds us that the pure blood shed was not poured out in vain.
- The sacred sublimity that envelops us with spiritual peace, promptings, and ponderings.
- The cherished covenants which bind us to God with everlasting remembrance.

As we hear the words spoken, see the priests kneeling, say amen to the prayer, touch the bread, and drink the water, we use all of our temporal and spiritual senses to be entirely encompassed in the special atmosphere. The cleansing power of Jesus Christ washes through us and we are renewed in righteousness.

There is profound importance in this weekly act of remembering our Redeemer. For example:

- I remember the **body** of the Lord as the temple of divinity.
- I remember His **Spirit**, which is attuned constantly to that which is righteous, true, and beautiful.
- I remember His **heart**, from which deep goodness proceeds.
- I remember His **eyes**, which see the need of each soul.
- I remember His **hands**, which bless and heal the sick.
- I remember His **feet**, which walked far and wide to serve the people and thus do the Father's will.
- I remember His **blood**, which was pure and was shed to save our sick souls.
- I remember His **ears**, which hear the deep pleading of many needy persons.

To always remember Him obviously involves much more than occasional reminiscence. The sacramental hymn "We'll Sing All Hail to Jesus' Name" says, "Ye do remember Him" (Hymn no. 182). We do not forsake or abandon Him. We ought not to ignore or neglect Him. We must not despise or trivialize Him. We remember, think about, reflect on, dwell on, focus on, and cleave to Him. We wait on, run to, long for, praise, and abide with Him. We love Him, need Him, believe in Him, rejoice in Him, and prove loyal to Him. In my fear I am grateful for His courage. In my loneliness I am grateful for His companionship. In my weakness I am grateful for His strength. In my slumbering stumbling I am grateful for His waking overcoming. I remember the glorious goodness of God. We can be grateful for our great God. We are blessed by His beautiful bounty.

DEVOTION TO COVENANTS

It is not intended that we enter covenants casually or that we keep them apathetically. Our integrity and dedication to covenants are no small things. It does matter if we keep our word, especially when it comes to sacred promises with eternal implications. Obviously, this is not easy, as our commitment and resolve are often tested, particularly in areas where we may feel we are weak. However, it is not impossible to become devoted, especially with God as our ally.

> And we are willing to enter into a covenant with our God to do his will, and to be obedient to his commandments in all things that he shall command us, all the remainder of our days. . .
>
> And now, these are the words which king Benjamin desired of them; and therefore he said unto them: Ye have spoken the words that I desired; and the covenant which ye have made is a righteous covenant.
>
> And now, because of the covenant which ye have made ye shall be called the children of Christ, his sons, and his daughters; for behold, this day he hath spiritually begotten you; for ye say that your hearts are changed through faith on his name; therefore, ye are born of him and have become his sons and his daughters.
>
> And under this head ye are made free, and there is no other head whereby ye can be made free. There is no other name given whereby salvation cometh; therefore, I would that ye should take

upon you the name of Christ, all you that have entered into the covenant with God that ye should be obedient unto the end of your lives.

. . . I say unto you, I would that ye should remember to retain the name written always in your hearts . . .

For how knoweth a man the master whom he has not served, and who is a stranger unto him, and is far from the thoughts and intents of his heart?

. . . Therefore, I would that ye should be steadfast and immovable, always abounding in good works, that Christ, the Lord God Omnipotent, may seal you his, that you may be brought to heaven, that ye may have everlasting salvation and eternal life. (Mosiah 5:5–15)

It is therefore right for us to make and keep sacred covenants in the name of Christ. True religion will always promote the making and keeping of promises, oaths, obligations, duties, and responsibilities. Of course, through this process we are made new. The power of the Savior flows to us through faithful adherence to righteous covenants. This power will allow us to face every difficulty, surmount every obstacle, obtain every blessing, and lay hold upon eternal reward. Christ saves us through His atoning power. However, this power comes to us through entering and showing devotion to sacred ordinances and covenants. The full blessings of the Atonement of the Savior cannot come to us outside the covenants He has designated for us to accept and live. It is critical to note that covenants allow us to serve, remember, think about, and know the Lord. This devotion of the heart binds us to God with sincerity and loyalty, and He is thus bound to us.

THE COVENANT PATH

We are to walk the path of promise, the road of righteousness, the journey of joy. While this might seem restrictive or difficult, it is really for our benefit and blessing. It is a trek that can be made. It is not impossible. It is a way of devotion, diligence, duty, and determination. These are sacred matters of the soul—"O then, my beloved brethren, come unto the Lord, the Holy One. Remember that his paths are righteous. Behold, the way for man is narrow, but it lieth in a straight course before him, and the keeper of the gate is the Holy One of Israel; and he employeth no servant there; and there is none other way save it be by the gate" (2 Nephi 9:41). This is simply to say that God is a being of truth and righteousness. His plans and purposes are likewise true and good. His path is one of faith and faithfulness. While the path of promise is narrow—meaning it provides for requirements and demands which are strict and onerous—it is also straight, which means it is not full of trickery and treachery. The path of the Lord is sure. God does not play games with us. He makes promises and He keeps promises. It is plain and precious. He is trustworthy and reliable. He does not change His truths arbitrarily. He is constant and kind. He sticks to His standards. He requires us to learn His ways and live His laws if we want His rewards. In this sense, He levels with us and expects us to do likewise. He holds Himself responsible to ensure that salvation comes to those who follow the way prescribed, not a way of their own devising. To me, this reality gives assurance and comfort. Indeed, to travel the covenant path is to ascend toward a destiny of glorious grandeur. The bounteous joy that rests upon us as we traverse this narrow way knows no parallel. It is simply the road of righteousness, the trek of triumph, and the journey of jubilation. It is the path of the Holy Messiah, and He encourages us, blesses us, instructs us, comforts us, and journeys with us along the way. There is no one that can take us away from that path, except ultimately ourselves.

THE BLESSINGS OF COVENANTS

God wants us to draw closer to Him, become more like Him, and eventually enter His presence. We draw closer to God by making covenants to obey the commandments and by keeping those covenants. Through obedience we will find the abundant life of joy, righteousness, peace, and happiness and draw closer to God and our heavenly home. The prophet Alma asked, "And now behold, I ask of you, my brethren of the church, have ye spiritually been born of God? Have ye received his image in your countenances?"

(Alma 5:14). This is a wonderful reminder that we need to radiate the image of God in our countenances to the world, not radiate the image of the world in our countenances to God. We are to have His image in our face—that of humility, truth, faith, hope, love, mercy, courage, and virtue, not the image of the natural man or woman whose image is in the likeness of a worldly idol—that of selfishness, lust, jealousy, pride, anger and rebellion.

The sacrament prayer on the bread reads, "O God, the Eternal Father, we ask thee in the name of thy Son, Jesus Christ, to bless and sanctify this bread to the souls of all those who partake of it, that they may eat in remembrance of the body of thy Son, and witness unto thee, O God, the Eternal Father, that they are willing to take upon them the name of thy Son, and always remember him and keep his commandments which he has given them; that they may always have his Spirit to be with them. Amen" (Doctrine and Covenants 20:77). Through His marvelous goodness and superb generosity, Christ allows us to take upon ourselves His holy name. He kindly bestows upon us a portion of His power. He humbly shares His great knowledge with us. He mercifully calls us His friends. He invites us to partake of His divine nature. He eagerly promises to give us peace in this life and a glorious resurrection and eternal lives in the world to come. We are to be born again, transformed, changed, altered deeply, daily, and everlastingly through His marvelous divine help. This is how we obtain the mind of Christ and become partakers of the divine nature. This transformative process of becoming alive in Christ is a blessing beyond compare.

President Nelson said, "Your commitment to follow the Savior by making covenants with Him and then keeping those covenants will open the door to every spiritual blessing and privilege available to women, men, and children everywhere."[1] Covenants are sacred spiritual promises between us and our Father in Heaven to keep His precious commandments. These promises are keys to special power, protection, and peace. We will receive great and wonderful blessings

---

1 Russell M. Nelson, Special Broadcast to the Church, January 16, 2018.

as we voluntarily choose to live on the covenant path of obedience now and always. Covenants with God are powerful. They enable growth, consolation, transformation, and joy. They bind us with the divine, link us with loved ones, and unite us with eternal principles.

> And this greater priesthood administereth the gospel and holdeth the key of the mysteries of the kingdom, even the key of the knowledge of God.
>
> Therefore, in the ordinances thereof, the power of godliness is manifest. . . .
>
> For without this no man can see the face of God, even the Father, and live.
>
> Now this Moses plainly taught to the children of Israel in the wilderness, and sought diligently to sanctify his people that they might behold the face of God;
>
> But they hardened their hearts and could not endure his presence; therefore, the Lord in his wrath, for his anger was kindled against them, swore that they should not enter into his rest while in the wilderness, which rest is the fulness of his glory. (Doctrine and Covenants 84:17–24)

This marvelous revelation teaches us that the ordinances and covenants of the priesthood are necessary for us so that we might learn the true nature of God, be prepared to see Him in person, have power to stand in the divine presence, and gain the kind and type of life that comes with entering into the restful glory of the Lord. If we want respite and refuge from the world and safety and security that goes beyond worldly powers and possessions, we need to be covenant disciples of the Lord. By doing this we gain access to peace, rest, love, and hope of a godly, eternal nature. There can be no greater promises and privileges than these in either time or eternity.

COVENANT CONNECTION

The core of the restored gospel is connection—connection to God, connection to family, connection to friends, connection to our true divine nature. The covenants of the gospel provide a powerful and permanent connection to all the things that we truly aspire to. When I live the gospel, I am connected—not distant, alone, isolated, fragmented, separate, distinct, fractured, and lonely. I am linked, sealed, joined, united, bound, gathered, and welded. This is the great work of God's religion—to tie us back to Him and His beloved family. We are to be gathered in one. This is truly a family matter. Sincerity is required for us to connect with heaven. We can link into God's purposes and accomplish His work on earth and in the world to come. In this connection we find hope, meaning, resolve, purpose, and power. As we clearly link each gospel principle and practice to God and His Son, we find the binding saving power. If we want to be connected in strength to those who are important to us, we need to invest heavily in covenants with God.

THE PROTECTION OF COVENANTS

Covenants protect us from our own short-sightedness, weakness, distraction, and from the cunning of the adversary. They also protect us from the sophistries of the worldly wise. As we reflect on our covenant promises, we can gain the wisdom to focus on the important, live with integrity and persist through difficulty.

Family Covenants

We are to come unto Him ourselves and invite and persuade others to do likewise. We are to learn of Him, love Him, serve Him, and emulate Him. We are to teach the Divine Sonship of Christ to others. In addition, our families are to be centered on Christ. The home is to be a place of faith in, testimony of, and devotion to the Lord Jesus Christ. As parents bear testimony to their children of the Divine Sonship of Christ and children gain that personal revelation for themselves, we will continue to establish and build a church of revelation-based, Christ-centered homes and families. Indeed, salvation comes to those who believe on His name. A family rooted in Christ is a family with new life in it. This means new potential for growth, new opportunities for unity, and new experiences for joy. We know that just as individuals grow close to God through covenants, so do families. Family covenants are likewise blessed with spiritual power, protection, and permanence.

"Pray in your families unto the Father, always in my name, that your wives and your children may be blessed" (3 Nephi 18:21). This is a moving charge to each husband and father to gather his wife and children together and then to pray to God, in the name of our Savior, that his family will be heaven blessed and that this very practice will be a blessing to his wife and children. We need family prayer as a buttress and unifying device. Wives and children need to see their husband and father on his knees in humble prayer. This will strengthen homes and families. And if there is no man in the home, then women and children should pray together. This practice will change individuals, families, and the world for the better. This divine injunction comes with divine reward.

CONCLUSION

In the holy name of Jesus Christ, we pray fervently, are baptized, perform sacred ordinances, make cherished covenants, are endowed with precious power, and are sealed up unto eternal life. His name is one of power, of might, of strength, of ability, of capacity, and of sacredness.

6

SAINTHOOD THROUGH CHRIST'S ATONEMENT

We obtain sanctified sainthood through the Atonement of the Lord Jesus Christ: "For the natural man is an enemy to God, and has been from the fall of Adam, and will be, forever and ever, unless he yields to the enticings of the Holy Spirit, and putteth off the natural man and becometh a saint through the atonement of Christ the Lord, and becometh as a child, submissive, meek, humble, patient, full of love, willing to submit to all things which the Lord seeth fit to inflict upon him, even as a child doth submit to his father" (Mosiah 3:19).

So it is that sainthood would not have been possible for any of the children of God subject to the Fall of Adam if there had been no Atonement of Christ. This saintliness is essentially the capacity for humble submission to God's will. It is patience, kindness, long-suffering, courage, gentleness, meekness, and pure love. To become a saint is to become the best possible version of ourselves, the self that we were always capable of, the kind of person we would have been all along if we had never defected from the ways of God either in small or large amounts. Sainthood is our divine destiny, and our righteous Redeemer has made it possible for us.

THE ATONEMENT OF THE LORD

I marvel at the infinite Atonement. In a sense, this is the process of at-one-ment. He comes to know us, and we learn about Him. We come to understand the following about each other: name, needs, desires, and hopes; pains, sorrows, temptations, afflictions, weaknesses; strengths, joys, successes, triumphs, and ministry. To truly grasp the Atonement of the Lord one must compare it with what could have happened. The Savior could have lived a life of ease, comfort, and rest. He could have lived forever. Instead, He chose the thorny path. He volunteered for trials and tribulation. He surrendered to suffering. He submitted to a painful death. He did this to heal, bless, lift, and save the weary soul who willingly comes to Him for help. A deep, thorough, and lifelong study of the Atonement yields precious dividends. We need to learn the doctrine involved to the full extent we are capable of. Consider the following:

This was a mighty struggle.

"And lo, he shall suffer temptations, and pain of body, hunger, thirst, and fatigue, even more than man can suffer, except it be unto death; for behold, blood cometh from every pore, so great shall be his anguish for the wickedness and the abominations of his people" (Mosiah 3:7). This reflects the fact that the Savior suffered phenomenally. He faced profound contradiction and intense opposition. He knew physical pain, hunger, thirst, and exhaustion beyond what human beings can bear. His suffering was so sore that he sweat blood, not simply water. This was on account of our evil intents and doings.

> He is despised and rejected of men. . . .
> Surely he has borne our griefs, and carried our sorrows. . . .
> But he was wounded for our transgressions, he was bruised for our iniquities; the chastisement of our peace was upon him; and with his stripes we are healed.
> All we, like sheep, have gone astray; we have turned every one to his own way; and the Lord hath laid on him the iniquities of us all. (Mosiah 14:3–6)

This atoning experience was deeply difficult for the Savior. He suffered for sins He had not committed; He felt guilt even though He had done no wrong; He felt pain even though He had inflicted none on others. It was a suffering of body, heart, mind, and spirit—a holistic and complete suffering. He knew deep sadness, intense betrayal, serious loneliness, overt rejection, and tragedy. This was the ultimate punishment for someone who really was innocent of all crimes, who was bereft of any badness. We viewed Him as someone whom God had abandoned. We turned away in fear while He bravely bore punishments rightfully ours. The affliction He endured was caused by our pride, selfishness, stubbornness, envy, jealousy, lust, fear, anger, and rebellion. While we so often have walked the path of self-indulgence, He walked only in the covenant path. In bitter irony he then paid the price for our wandering so that we could return to peace and safety.

It is experienced through all the senses.

In my opinion, the Atonement was total. That is to say that the Savior had no part of His system that was untouched by His ordeal. It was before Him in living color. He was immersed in difficulty and surrounded by darkness. For example, if we were to have a traumatic holistic experience in which we saw terrible things, felt deep emotional hurt, touched hot objects, heard ugly words, and ate poisoned food, then we would be in a very limited sense experiencing the range of challenge He went through in the sense of it being all encompassing, although He did so all at once and to a degree far beyond what we can envision or relate to.

It is revealed to a degree through the Holy Ghost.

Obviously, no human can comprehend fully the scale and scope of the Atonement of the Lord. However, I feel that through the power of the Holy Ghost we can sometimes gain some small appreciation of what Christ may have endured. When we are encompassed about by many difficulties and feel swallowed up in darkness and despair, or when others we love are caught in the vice of tragic suffering, the Holy Ghost can open our minds and heart to a sense of the Atonement. We get a spiritual glimpse into the nightmare of the soul that He faced. This is beyond words. It is not really something we can articulate. We sense it, feel it, and apprehend it intuitively. In this sense our dark night of the soul can give us some appreciation for the spiritual price that has been paid for us so that we may be redeemed from the prison of sin and the despair of death.

It is transformative in its nature and impact.

When we come to comprehend the Atonement and benefit from its blessings, we are always changed by the experience. We cannot remain as we were. We are moved, altered, transformed, and made different in positive and helpful ways. The Atonement of the Lord is the ultimate self-improvement opportunity. It will inevitably improve our viewpoint of everything.

Its power comes through sincere investment in ordinances and covenants.

These ordinances and covenants are the channel through which God's transformative power enters into our souls—both spirit and body. We are educated by them, focused by them, moved by them, reoriented by them, made aware through them, and empowered by them. They show us the true source of our power—God. As we carefully, consciously, and devotedly participate in these outward rituals and ceremonies, it is intended that our hearts and minds will be changed. We are to be holistically involved and partake of the power of these rites. They are to mean something precious to us, to point us to God, and to remain as powerful motivators and reminders of the sacred promises we have made in holy places to follow Christ in thought, intent, word and deed. Ordinances focus us on Christ, His power, plans, and purposes. His power comes to those who honor and obey ordinances and who prove loyal to covenants.

SAINTHOOD THROUGH CHRIST'S ATONEMENT

We can use it to resist temptation, heal from sin and strengthen resolve. This is marvelous enabling power.

The Atonement does not just cleanse us from past sins. It also helps us to resist sin, to transcend the desire for sin, and to perform works of righteousness consistently and even when it is difficult to do so. We are enabled and empowered to lift the burdens of others, to look forward with faith, to do hard things, and to remain cheerful in our quest for divinity. Like the electrical device that needs to be recharged to continue to function, we need the enabling power of the Atonement of Christ to help us to continue onwards, upwards and forwards in the journey of lasting discipleship.

Requires a Divine Sonship—"And he shall be called Jesus Christ, the Son of God" (Mosiah 3:8)

To comprehend why Christ had to be the Son of God, it is needful to consider the Father. He is the Supreme Being. He is embodied, perfected, and glorified. He possesses great and genuine goodness. His love is both lasting and lifting. His might is marvelous and majestic. His peace is perfect and profound. We need to consistently take hold upon this thought—that God the Father is good, gentle, generous, and great. Indeed, brightly beams our Father's mercy (see Hymn no. 335). As the Father is powerful, so is the Son. His Divine Sonship refers to His relationship to His Father. Jesus Christ had abilities, power, and capacities that no other mortal has ever had. He had power to live a sinless life. He also had power to cleanse others from sin. He had power to suffer far beyond what we can. He had power to die and then rise again. These attributes enabled Christ to perform the infinite and eternal Atonement.

Possible due to divine character of the Lord

The Savior was not given to following the dictates of the natural man in the way we sometimes are. Although He was tempted, He rose above that seductive carnality with which all are faced. He was a holy man who gave way always to righteousness. He was a true saint, always doing truly pure things. He surrendered to His Father by doing the right thing consistently. His character was one of sublime goodness. Indeed, without the attributes of Christ the Atonement could not have been accomplished. What were His personal attributes?

- Believing, knowledgeable, obedient, good, great, virtuous, honest, full of integrity, discerning, wise.
- Consistent, conscientious, determined, devoted, diligent, deliberate, dutiful, faithful, loyal, persistent, hardworking.
- Compassionate, kind, gentle, loving, long-suffering, charitable, merciful, patient, considerate, sensitive, thoughtful, forgiving, generous, benevolent, hopeful, joyful.
- Courageous, brave, powerful, strong.

Why are these characteristics which were embedded in His being so important for Him to possess to be the Savior and Redeemer? He would not give up on goodness when opposed. He would not relinquish His righteousness in the face of discouragement and despair. He would only offer His innocence so that we could benefit from it. Indeed, He does the following:

- Goes the distance with us, however long that takes.
- Takes the long view and knows that greatness takes patience.
- Persists through difficulty knowing that it is to be overcome and not yielded to.
- Believes in us, even if we do not believe in ourselves.
- Wants us to succeed and is willing to invest heavily in that proposal.
- Is willing and able to help us, not in a derogatory or selfish way, but with genuine care.
- Is good to the core, not superficially or apparently so.
- Sees the individual and our needs, the real needs of our souls.
- Is both tough and tender, having gentle compassion and mighty strength. This is a powerful and necessary combination in a Master servant.
- Is relentless, resolved, and determined rather than casual, full of apathy, or careless.

- Is flawless and perfect, rather than dragged down by his own demons.

I stand all amazed at His generous greatness, suffering sacrifice, devotion to loving duty, commitment to covenants, and mighty majesty. We need to remember Him, reflect upon Him, and rejoice in Him. To remember Him always is to spiritually connect to Him.

LINKING THE ATONEMENT OF CHRIST WITH THE RESTORATION

Through modern-day revelation we understand that the blessings of the Atonement of the Savior are interwoven with all other parts of the plan of salvation. We need to explicitly link the Atonement with the restoration of prophets, doctrine, priesthood, commandments, ordinances, and covenants. The Restoration gives us access to the powers of the Atonement of Christ. Consequently, we cannot focus on it exclusively and neglect or reject other aspects of the plan. Truth is non-divisible. The Atonement of our Redeemer is a part of the great mosaic of revealed religion. As I studied the issue of how the jigsaw pieces of the gospel fit together, I was especially interested in how the latter-day restoration combines all gospel elements into one great whole. While the Atonement of our Messiah is the means of salvation, it is evident that the gospel kingdom is one of law, order, structure, and authority. Hence, we need the priesthood and its doctrines, ordinances, and covenants to gain access to the redemption of Christ. The Church is not separate and distinct from the Lord. Thus, priesthood authority and doctrine are essentially connected with the saving powers of Christ's Atonement. In other words, the Prince of Peace is essentially connected with priesthood power. We are not saved individually and independently, but as part of the gospel family in God's government kingdom.

The revealed scriptures indicate how this is so as shown in the following table.

LINKING	PRIESTHOOD AUTHORITY WITH	THE PRINCE OF PEACE
Scripture	Doctrine	Lesson
	LAW & ORDER	
D&C 88	Law of kingdoms	To abide in God's law is to receive glory
Alma 13	Patriarchal order of the Melchizedek Priesthood	Faithful priesthood holders are types of prophets/Christ
	PRIESTHOOD AND ITS KEYS	
D&C 121	Dispensational priesthood	The priesthood is an everlasting principle
D&C 13	Restoration of the Aaronic Priesthood	Name of "Messiah"
D&C 84	Priesthood authority and power	How to enter the rest of the Lord
D&C 110	Priesthood keys restored in Kirtland Temple	Keys give efficacy and power to priesthood work
D&C 128	Restoration of keys and baptism for the dead	The work of salvation applies on both sides of the veil
D&C 138	Vision of redemption of the dead	Christ holds the keys of the Resurrection
	ORDINANCES & COVENANTS	
D&C 20	Duties of the priesthood	Importance of ordinances/ covenants under proper authority
D&C 132	New and everlasting covenant	The ancient order is restored

	ORGANIZATIONS & KINGDOMS	
D&C 107	Church organization in latter days	The Lord's house is a kingdom of order
Moses 7	Enoch establishes a city of Zion	Heavenly principles lived on this earth through preaching
D&C 29	Second Coming of the Lord	Fulfillment of ancient prophecy
D&C 45	Second Coming of the Lord	Day of righteous power
	ETERNAL FAMILIES	
D&C 131	Qualifications for exaltation	Marriage is a sanctifying sacrament
Moses 6	Lineage of the fathers	Be a strong link in the righteous family chain
Abraham 1	Rights of the fathers	Our desires determine our divine instruction
Abraham 2	Priesthood blessings upon the seed	Eternal families are the highest order of divine blessings

HUMILITY

For us to truly come to Christ we need to develop a humble dependence on the Lord. Humility is a prerequisite to being taught of the Lord:

> Wherefore, I the Lord, knowing the calamity which should come upon the inhabitants of the earth, called upon my servant Joseph Smith, Jun., and spake unto him from heaven, and gave him commandments; . . .
>
> The weak things of the world shall come forth and break down the mighty and strong ones, that man should not counsel his fellow man, neither trust in the arm of flesh. . . .
>
> And inasmuch as they erred it might be made known;
>
> And inasmuch as they sought wisdom they might be instructed;

> And inasmuch as they sinned they might be chastened, that they might repent;
>
> And inasmuch as they were humble they might be made strong, and blessed from on high, and receive knowledge from time to time. (Doctrine and Covenants 1:17–28)

Only those who are humble and penitent before God can be made strong in spirit, receive heavenly blessings of power, and obtain revelation to guide their path on a consistent basis. We are taught that if we are humble before God—meaning meek enough to seek His guidance and follow His direction—then we will be divinely led and receive answers to our important questions and solutions to our pressing problems. We are instructed that when we do not have wisdom that we must humble ourselves and pray for help. Then our spiritual eyes will be open to see things we have never seen and hear things we have never heard (see Doctrine and Covenants 136:32). We are informed that those who become sufficiently humble will see the Lord with their spiritual eyes (see Doctrine and Covenants 67:10). Humility is an essential component in our spiritual journey to learn the things of God. To bow before God intellectually and attitudinally is to open the door to coming to know new things, to learning new ways, and to partaking in new experiences. Humility prepares us for a new life in Christ and allows us to retain that new life over time.

FAITH IN CHRIST

The Savior often said to others, "Thy faith hath made thee whole." I think this means their faith in Christ made them fixed, renewed, healed, complete, and transformed. Faith is powerful. It is strengthening, enabling, enduring, meaningful, resolve-promoting, and all-encompassing. How has faith in the Living Christ done this in my life and the lives of other people that I know? Well, there are the matters of overcoming hardship, enduring persecution, transcending betrayal, surmounting weakness, growing beyond abuse, and facing illness with hope—not always in the direct and immediate sense of being delivered from these things but rather in the sense of learning, growing, developing, and resolving in the midst of challenges of all kinds and degrees. To be saturated with faith in Christ is to be immersed in purpose, covered with courage, filled with rejoicing, and swallowed up with peace. Indeed, through Christ we can face our fears, frighten our fears, and forsake our fears. We do this by coming unto Him, and He will enable us to find our faith, fortify our faith, feel our faith, and fuel our faith. Faith in Christ will unify us, give us internal harmony, bring us peace, and eventually provide for our perfection. This will be integrity, completeness, being finished, made new, and being at one with God.

HOPE IN CHRIST

Hope is a prevalent, vital, an ongoing feature of the restored gospel. It is an anchor to the soul. This does not mean that it holds us down or keeps us back. Rather, it is a source of stability, surety, protection, and safeguarding. Without such an anchor, we would drift off without purpose or direction. We would be exposed to dangerous places. Of course, our hope needs to be placed in the Savior. Why? So He can do what He promises. He can deliver the reward. He can guide us through treacherous seas, assist us through uncharted territory, and lead us through mountainous heights. Through Him, any precipice we encounter will not be our undoing, no road will lead to an aimless destination, no snake will fatally wound us, no enemy will overcome us, no distraction will derail us and no tragedy will consume us. Hope in Christ is a lively hope, a sure hope, a good hope, and a solid hope. It is short term and long term. It is deep and pervasive. It is strong and robust. It is a sure companion when we are facing the stormy seas, the deep ravine, the scary height, the unexpected foe, the freezing cold, the blistering heat, the dry desert, and the barren waste whether these come in the form of physical locations, difficult relationships, unforeseen financial challenges, poor health, breached promises, crises of faith, or identity confusions. Hope springs eternal because Christ is eternally in our corner, watching over us, mindful of us, encouraging us, aiding us, and emboldening us.

HOLINESS

I have been studying the characteristics of Christ and how He helps us to become the best version of ourselves, and I have found this journey to be spiritually illuminating and enlightening. One thing that has really caught my attention is the great holiness of the Savior and how amazing His life and ministry really was. In this regard, I have reviewed Alma 7, 13, 34, and other chapters of scripture. I am struck by the connection between the holiness of the Lord, the holiness of the prophets, and the holiness of high priests. I am impressed by the parallels between the callings of high priests, the callings of the prophets, and the calling of the Messiah. Obviously, this process of giving us divine opportunities to engage in the patterns of holiness is the means that the Father uses to transform us into the kind of people we need to become. This is how we become partakers of the divine nature and how we work in the process of salvation for others. Our names, callings, ordinances, covenants, priesthood, labors, attributes and spiritual experiences are all part of a divine pattern. This "priesthood pattern" shows us that we are much more like the Savior than we sometimes suppose—although we still have a long distance to travel in reaching the ideal standard we strive for. This also indicates how prophets are "types and shadows" of the Savior. This has been for me a faith reinforcing and testimony enhancing exercise.

As the Lord Jesus Christ was holy, so are we to be. Holiness is the sacred sanctity needed to assist in hastening the work of salvation. In the restored gospel we have the following:

- The Holy One of Israel
- The holy scriptures
- The holy priesthood
- The holy temple
- The holy kiss and embrace that heals, blesses, and strengthens

Should we find ourselves straying from the ways of God, we can seek to recover our holiness with determined strivings. It is interesting to me that holiness was very much part and parcel of the Savior's life. He is our holy King. Likewise, both prophets and all saints can and do learn to incorporate the facets of holiness into their lives. Consider how important and comprehensive this is.

SAINTHOOD THROUGH CHRIST'S ATONEMENT

Characteristics	Jesus Christ	Prophets	Men
Holy Name	Wonderful, Counselor, The Mighty God, The Everlasting Father, The Prince of Peace	Name given signifies mission and work. Melchizedek was a king of Salem and prince of peace. Joseph Smith was a choice seer.	A good name signifies a good work.
Holy Calling	Foreordained as the Anointed One	Chosen to fulfill the eternal covenants of the Lord—holy prophets, seers, revelators	Called and prepared as High Priests from Foundation of World
Holy Ordinance	All gospel ordinances including priesthood ordination	All gospel ordinances including priesthood ordination	All gospel ordinances including priesthood ordination
Holy Order	Order of The Son of God—the Only Begotten in the Flesh	Melchizedek Priesthood— the Order of Christ	Melchizedek Priesthood— the Order of Christ
Holy Works	Preaching, healing, ministering, infinite and eternal Atonement	Many mighty miracles and the working of mighty wonders	Faith, repentance, works of righteousness
Holy Attributes	Holy One, Holy Messiah	Humble, submissive, gentle, easy to be entreated, patient, long suffering, temperate, diligent, grateful, faithful, hopeful, charitable	Sanctified, garments washed white, just and holy men
Holy Ghost/ Spirit	Manifest His divine identity and mission through the power of the Holy Spirit	See, hear, and know of sacred mysteries through the power of the Holy Ghost	Accept the Spirit, led by the Spirit

CHANGE IN NATURE

While the ordinances and covenants are vitally crucial for becoming alive in Christ, it is not enough to achieve ordinances as if they were simply procedural steps to be taken. We are to be fundamentally conformed to a new state and condition of living. This requires more than a superficial change in outlook or a temporary transition to a different way of life. It demands more than passing through certain rituals and ceremonies, although such passing is essential. What the Lord seeks is a transformation in our nature. This means the laying down of the man or woman of sin and the explicit development of traits that are pleasing to God. The Book of Mormon clarifies our need:

> But men drink damnation to their own souls except they humble themselves and become as little children, and believe that salvation was, and is, and is to come, in and through the atoning blood of Christ, the Lord Omnipotent.
>
> For the natural man is an enemy to God, and has been from the fall of Adam, and will be, forever and ever, unless he yields to the enticings of the Holy Spirit, and putteth off the natural man and becometh a saint through the atonement of Christ the Lord, and becometh as a child, submissive, meek, humble, patient, full of love, willing to submit to all things which the Lord seeth fit to inflict upon him, even as a child doth submit to his father. (Mosiah 3:17–19).

We thus become willing to be taught and molded by God. We lay down the vices of arrogance, pride, conceit, haughtiness, selfishness, and hatred and take up instead the virtues of humility, sincerity, love, kindness, selflessness, and so forth. The Lord has promised us that we can develop these new attributes with His divine help if we are willing to do so. So how do we show our willingness to receive these highly desired characteristics?

Divine Transformation

To profoundly change the world, we must first be changed ourselves. If we seek to impact others, we first need to be impacted ourselves. To transform we must first be transformed. Real, potent, and lasting change must first come within ourselves—only then will we be able to alter our environment proactively and positively. God is the great change agent. He moves us, enlightens us, educates us, empowers us, uplifts us, comforts us, and blesses us. This is how we are empowered to transform that which we see around us. The power that God has in altering every facet of our lives is astonishing. Not only can He deeply and lastingly change us for the better, but He can also do the same for marriages, families, communities, nations, and the entire world.

Courage

In the cause of Christ, we need to develop courage to follow Him, even when it's difficult. In my study of the scriptures, I cannot locate a single incident where the Lord gave in to pressure from others, where He backed down due to fear, where He compromised His standards, or where He acquiesced to fear of others. He had valiant courage. This was courage under fire, not simply convenient courage that attends clear approval from others. He did the right thing regardless of what anyone, including His closest disciples, expected or demanded. We remember the time when Peter, the chief apostle, told Christ not to go to Jerusalem or He would face death. The Lord responded with the fact that the adversary was talking through Peter to deliver this message. Talk about courage to say the truth! We often hide our true thoughts and feelings from others because we worry about what they might think. The Savior did not let this kind of approach interfere with His mission. We would do well to judge what we should do by whether it conforms to the will of God or not, rather than whether it is acceptable to others. This does not mean we are intentionally offensive. However, we need to develop courage to do what the Lord would do, regardless of whether or not it is easy, popular, or recommended by others.

Concerning those who shall inherit the celestial kingdom, we are told:

And who overcome by faith. (Doctrine and Covenants 76:53)

Wherefore, all things are theirs, whether life or death, or things present, or things to come, all are theirs and they are Christ's, and Christ is God's.

And they shall overcome all things.

Wherefore, let no man glory in man, but rather let him glory in God, who shall subdue all enemies under his feet.

These shall dwell in the presence of God and his Christ forever and ever. (Doctrine and Covenants 76:59–62)

That is to say that we need to be valiant in the testimony of Christ, caring more about being loyal to Him than gaining approval of the world. Even the approval of close friends or family should not be more important to us than the approbation of the Lord we love above all things.

This requires us to show bravery when it is easier to be cowardly. We are told elsewhere in the scriptures that it requires courage to change our lives, to care for others, and to receive inspired correction; that perfect love casts out fear; that evidencing our faith before others requires personal courage; and that the Lord expects us to have the courage of our convictions. Courage to testify before others often comes at great personal risk:

- Adam and Eve were the first to voluntarily leave paradise to enter a lonely, difficult, and dangerous new world.
- Enoch the preacher was a wild man in the land, and all men were offended because of him.
- Noah built an ark in dry weather and preached repentance to a mocking crowd.
- Abraham went to Egypt knowing it was hostile territory.
- Moses faced powerful Pharaoh with righteous but unpopular demands to let the people of Israel go free.
- Christ was willing to submit to those who were weaker than Him in every way to come off conqueror for all willing to yield to Him.
- Peter was crucified upside down for consistently preaching the forbidden message of the Resurrection of Christ.

- Abinadi was burned at the stake for refusing to discount the message of repentance for king Noah and his priests.
- Joseph Smith was willing to continue to speak for God even though he was hounded, persecuted, assaulted, and eventually martyred for taking this course.

Many other examples could be cited throughout the range of scriptural history. Further, there are numerous examples of courage being evidenced since the restoration of the gospel of individuals and families doing hard things in accepting, living, preaching, and enduring faithfully in their membership in The Church of Jesus Christ of Latter-day Saints. No doubt many of these are known only to the persons who displayed them and to the God who honors and sustains them. There is no regret when we have the courage to follow the Lord, come what may. Courage in Christ gives us a new type and kind of life, not one free from tribulation, but one that is exemplary and worthy of commendation from the Lord of life.

THE IMPORTANCE OF MAKING SACRIFICES

Sacrifice is an essential element of true discipleship. Sacrifice is the willingness to relinquish what is precious to us so that we might obtain divine approval. We know that the Messiah would offer His life to fulfill the purposes of the Father's plan of salvation: "Wherefore, redemption cometh in and through the Holy Messiah; for he is full of grace and truth. Behold, he offereth himself a sacrifice for sin, to answer the ends of the law, unto all those who have a broken heart and a contrite spirit; and unto none else can the ends of the law be answered" (2 Nephi 2:6–7).

Interestingly, this verse also indicates that the sacrifice we must make is that of a broken heart and a contrite spirit. That is to say that hearts that are set on the world must be changed voluntarily to hearts set on righteousness. It is also to say that spirits that are fixed on doing their own will need to be transformed to spirits that are intent on doing the divine will. To make such a sacrifice is what each of us needs to do so that we might benefit from the Atonement of the Lord. In other words, both His willing sacrifice and our intentional sacrifice are necessary for the law of God to be effective in saving our souls.

Our sacrifice must mean something to us. It must cost us something. It must be symbolic of the sacrifice made by Christ in giving His pure life to save an otherwise dead world. So, sacrifices must be a type of Christ's free will offering and hence must be done in His name. Otherwise, they do not meet the divine standard given to Adam and Eve in the beginning:

> And he gave unto them commandments, that they should worship the Lord their God, and should offer the firstlings of their flocks, for an offering unto the Lord. And Adam was obedient unto the commandments of the Lord.
>
> And after many days an angel of the Lord appeared unto Adam, saying: Why dost thou offer sacrifices unto the Lord? And Adam said unto him: I know not, save the Lord commanded me.
>
> And then the angel spake, saying: This thing is a similitude of the sacrifice of the Only Begotten of the Father, which is full of grace and truth.
>
> Wherefore, thou shalt do all that thou doest in the name of the Son, and thou shalt repent and call upon God in the name of the Son forevermore. (Moses 5:5–8)

Our sacrifices are not to be selectively chosen by us, based on what we determine and limited by our own preferences and inclinations. To obtain divine approbation, our offerings are to be done sincerely, freely, and humbly, and they must also evidence a devotion to our sacred agreements with the Lord. The proof of our devotion is manifest in our obedience to the sacrifices the Lord asks us to make—whether those sacrifices involve time, resources, habits, or ambitions. "Verily I say unto you, all among them who know their hearts are honest, and are broken, and their spirits contrite, and are willing to observe their covenants by sacrifice—yea, every sacrifice which I, the Lord, shall command—they are accepted of me" (Doctrine and Covenants 97:8).

King Lamoni's father expressed a willingness to give up prized possessions and significant status so that he might obtain redemption through the Savior. Aaron instructed him that the great need was for him to show humility before God and to repent of his misdeeds. When the king heard this, he accepted it and prayed to God, stating that he would give up all his sins to come to know the God of heaven:

> The king said: What shall I do that I may have this eternal life of which thou hast spoken? . . . And it came to pass that when Aaron had said these words, the king did bow down before the Lord, upon his knees; yea, even he did prostrate himself upon the earth, and cried mightily, saying:
>
> O God, Aaron hath told me that there is a God; and if there is a God, and if thou art God, wilt thou make thyself known unto me, and I will give away all my sins to know thee, and that I may be raised from the dead, and be saved at the last day. (Alma 22:15–18)

It is instructive that King Lamoni's father was obedient to what he was asked to do. I also believe that if he had been asked to give up his property and power that he would have done that. Our willingness to do what is asked reveals the depth of our dedication to God. It is apparent to the honest in heart that possessions, power, and sins are simply not nearly as precious as true joy is.

THE SACRIFICE OF GOD

A careful reading of the scriptures shows that the sacrifice of the Savior was complete and total. He held nothing back, retained no element of stubbornness, and valued nothing greater than He appreciated His Father:

> And now Abinadi said unto them: I would that ye should understand that God himself shall come down among the children of men, and shall redeem his people.
>
> And because he dwelleth in flesh he shall be called the Son of God, and having subjected the flesh to the will of the Father, being the Father and the Son—
>
> The Father, because he was conceived by the power of God; and the Son, because of the flesh; thus becoming the Father and Son—
>
> And they are one God, yea, the very Eternal Father of heaven and of earth.

And thus the flesh becoming subject to the Spirit, or the Son to the Father, being one God, suffereth temptation, and yieldeth not to the temptation, but suffereth himself to be mocked, and scourged, and cast out, and disowned by his people.

And after all this, after working many mighty miracles among the children of men, he shall be led, yea, even as Isaiah said, as a sheep before the shearer is dumb, so he opened not his mouth.

Yea, even so he shall be led, crucified, and slain, the flesh becoming subject even unto death, the will of the Son being swallowed up in the will of the Father. . . .

And now I say unto you, who shall declare his generation? Behold, I say unto you, that when his soul has been made an offering for sin he shall see his seed. And now what say ye? And who shall be his seed? . . .

For these are they whose sins he has borne; these are they for whom he has died, to redeem them from their transgressions. And now, are they not his seed? . . .

The Lord hath made bare his holy arm in the eyes of all the nations; and all the ends of the earth shall see the salvation of our God. (Mosiah 15:1–12, 26–31)

The doctrine taught in this passage is powerful. The Savior's sacrifice consisted in his willingness to take upon Himself:

- The responsibility of being the Redeemer of all
- Birth into humble and difficult circumstances
- The subduing of any natural inclinations of the mortal body He acquired in favor of doing the will of God
- The duty to live by spiritual principles rather than worldly ones
- The hardship of facing all types and degrees of temptations
- Mocking
- Scourging
- Being cast out
- Being disowned by his own people
- Being led by sinful men
- Being quiet in the face of attack, insult, humiliation, and falsehood

- Being crucified
- Being slain

It is abundantly evident that this was irony in its most bitter form. The best person was treated like the worst, the most innocent was treated like the guiltiest, the most loving person was treated with the most hatred, the gentlest was treated with the most contempt. This was a sacrifice most pure and perfect. His will was swallowed up in the will of the Father with entire loyalty. There was no holding back, no bargaining, no negotiating, and no pretense. It was a submissive surrender to godliness. It is also clear from this passage that only those individuals who willfully submit to the commandments of God can be held blameless before God through the Atonement of our Lord. Our surrender to God leads to Him blessing us with the ultimate reward of salvation. Hence, the need for us to mirror the example of our Messiah in facing injustice, affliction, suffering, and unfairness with grace and resolve. Glory will follow those who offer sacrifice in the type and name of their Lord.

SACRIFICE BRINGS FORTH BLESSINGS

Sacrifice is not simply about giving things up. In fact, we always end up receiving far more than we supposedly give up. Blessings come to us from our willingness to put the Lord first and foremost in our lives. What can we achieve with divine help? What are we capable of with Godly assistance? What is the Lord's vision for us to accomplish and become? What are His plans and purposes for our lives—premortal, mortal, and postmortal? The Savior invites us to have more and be more: more righteous, faithful, courageous, pure, loving, hardworking, generous, forgiving, diligent, patient, kind, devoted, obedient, happy, successful, persistent, determined, charitable, and blessed.

He asks us to give up evil for good. "For thus saith the Lord—I, the Lord, am merciful and gracious unto those who fear me, and delight to honor those who serve me in righteousness and in truth unto the end. Great shall be their reward and eternal shall be their glory" (Doctrine and Covenants 76:5–6). He is magnanimously merciful and generously gracious to those who love, reverence, respect, and honor Him. What marvelous blessings He bestows upon us in terms of knowledge, understanding, wisdom, ability, peace, hope, love, and joy when we draw close to Him with diligent devotion. We never regret following our great God. The benefit of knowing of His loving kindness extends forever.

He turns our sadness to happiness (see 2 Nephi 5:27). Nephi and his people faced many difficulties and sorrow, but because they sacrificed to follow the Lord, they lived with happiness in their souls. Righteousness always is happiness. Joy comes from living right.

He replaces our lust with virtue (see JS—Matthew 1:10–11). As we purify our lives we will be filled with virtue, power, and divine love. That bridling of our passions will fill us with great love. We will know that God loves us, cares for us, remembers us, blesses us, and has a perfect plan for us. God is good. God is generous. He leads us with a loving hand. As we come to feel of His perfect everlasting love for us, we will likewise feel great love for Him and others. Then nothing will derail us from this path of joyful love.

He jettisons our anger and fills us with loving kindness (see 4 Nephi 1:15). God's love is perfect, everlasting, powerful, pure, majestic, and life-changing. To sense His love, to know of His goodness, to feel His compassionate mercy, and to understand His regard for us is to be transformed. To be touched by His bounteous forgiveness and generous influence is to find a newness of life. The love of God blesses us, enlightens us, heals us, uplifts us, and redeems us. Then we become vessels of love toward others. When this happens, peace, joy, hope, and joy fill our hearts and our homes.

He instructs us to abandon laziness and instead become persons of hard work:

> Now I, Nephi, did not work the timbers after the manner which was learned by men, neither did I build the ship after the manner of men; but I did build it after the manner which the Lord had shown unto me; wherefore, it was not after the manner of men.
>
> And I, Nephi, did go into the mount oft, and I did pray oft unto the Lord; wherefore the Lord showed unto me great things.

SAINTHOOD THROUGH CHRIST'S ATONEMENT

> And it came to pass that after I had finished the ship, according to the word of the Lord, my brethren beheld that it was good, and that the workmanship thereof was exceedingly fine. (1 Nephi 18:1–4)

Nephi rejected the slothfulness of the carnal man and worked hard to build the boat that would take his family to the promised land. It is instructive that the Lord showed him the manner the ship should be built after. This showing happened on a high mountain. How evident that the Lord expects us to work according to divine instructions and that this work will produce results that will draw us closer to His presence and His promised inheritance. A new life comes from doing a new kind of work—a godly work.

He pleads with us to let go of fear so that we can embrace courage: "And he went a little further, and fell on his face, and prayed, saying, O my Father, if it be possible, let this cup pass from me: nevertheless not as I will, but as thou wilt" (Matthew 26:39). The Master lived a genuinely great life that was lived in crescendo. He was no fair-weather disciple. His commitment was total, His loyalty unswerving, and His devotion to His Father absolute. When the challenges He faced grew exceedingly difficult, the true greatness of His character revealed itself. We can learn much from this. When we face weakness, difficulty, inconvenience, or pain, we can rise above our own selfish tendencies and seek to be true disciples in word and deed. To show courage under fire is to reveal what we are truly made of or what we can be made of, with divine help. Greatness can be within us, all of us.

He takes away our doubt and fills us with faith: "And there arose a great storm of wind. . . . and they awake him, and say unto him, Master, carest thou not that we perish? And he arose, and rebuked the wind, and said unto the sea, peace, be still. And the wind ceased, and there was a great calm And he said unto them, Why are ye so fearful? how is it that ye have no faith? And they feared exceedingly, and said one to another, What manner of man is this, that even the wind and the sea obey him?" (Mark 4:37–41).

What manner of man indeed! He is the light that shines in darkness. He is the bright and morning star (see Revelation 22:16).

He is our kind King, our loving Lord, and our soothing Savior. His power to heal our wounded souls never fails. He is still the master of winds, waves, mountains, and men. So, we have every reason to doubt not, fear not, worry not. He who calmed the stormy seas can likewise help us climb every mountain, surmount every obstacle, overcome every trouble, and accomplish every worthwhile aim. His power is certain. There is no need for us to continually suffer from prolonged fear or disabling doubts. We can transcend worldly concerns and be at peace. So, in truth, what we receive from God far outweighs anything He commands us to let go of for Him. We can believe in Him. We can follow Him. We can love Him. We can serve Him. He will overrule for our benefit and blessing as he is the Living Christ. His powerful promises are sure.

THE HEALER OF OUR SOULS

Can you fix a piece of glass that you broke, or that someone else broke—whether accidentally or intentionally? Can you fix a broken soul that you damaged, or that someone else damaged—whether accidentally or intentionally? Of course not. There is, however, one who can. He not only fixes broken glass but, more important, damaged and broken souls. I stand all amazed at this unique and powerful ability. I have no doubt that each of us knows deeply what it is to feel broken, alone, distraught, afraid, and powerless. There is no shortage in this world of heartbreak, danger, disappointment, conflict, sorrow, pain, confusion, distraction, and loneliness. I know by personal experience what it is to feel betrayed, abandoned, bullied, frightened, overwhelmed, and lost. This is the human condition, and there is no immunity from it. We are all broken vessels in some way or another. I know that the Son of God is the perfect friend, the master healer, the noble gentleman, the loyal helper, and the mightiest superhero we can look to, rely on, depend upon, and lean on. When we reflect on His healing capacity this can mean several different things, all of which are important and helpful. He can heal us in every way a person can possibly be healed. I love to dwell on the critical importance of His healing power.

"And Isaiah, who declared by prophecy that the Redeemer was anointed to bind up the broken-hearted, to proclaim liberty to the captives, and the opening of the prison to them that were bound" (Doctrine and Covenants 138:42). That is to say that the Messiah was specifically called and appointed to heal the hearts of the broken hearted. Who are these broken-hearted people? You and I. He was to proclaim liberty to the captives. Who are these captive people? You and I. He was to open the prison to set the prisoners free. Who are these prisoners? You and I. These promises refer not simply to those bound down by sin in vary obvious ways, but to each one of us. Even the people of the Lord have broken hearts, wearied minds, undernourished spirits, and frail bodies. Even the good people of the earth live in self-imposed prisons, or the prisons constructed for them by others, or the prisons of guilt and shame. We all need to be broken out of our bondage, to be healed of our afflictions, to have the breach in our souls repaired, to have our hearts comforted, to have our hopes renewed, to have our relationships healed. We are all in desperate, daily, and deep need of a Lord that can heal us now and eternally.

Indeed, Christ is our rescuing Redeemer. He can reclaim us from being lost, redeem us from our worst weaknesses, retrieve us from our fallen condition, reinvigorate our tired souls, refresh us with living waters, renew us with the Bread of Life, rehabilitate us from foolish errors. He can save the weary soul, help the wounded traveler, bind up the broken-hearted, console the distressed, and bring peace to the troubled. His rescue of you and I is needed if we are to rise above the past, be unloosed from the chains upon us, and go forward with a newness of life.

A HERO BEYOND COMPARE

As a child I was intensely fascinated by superheroes, especially Superman. The idea of having the power to fly, to run incredibly fast, to stop bullets, to withstand the pressures of extreme heat or cold, to have x-ray vision, and so on amazed me. No doubt we have all felt impressed by such marvelous powers. Of course, real human beings do not have such powers. However, this is not to suggest that people do not have amazing abilities in their own right—such as the ability to persist through difficult circumstances, to think wonderful thoughts, to show tremendous courage, to feel and act on deeply loving emotions, to sacrifice comforts and convenience for the good of others, to have a vision of light in a dark time—and numerous other gifts which are important and special.

As I have grown in my knowledge and understanding of the Son of God, I have come to the awareness that He truly is a superhero of the highest order. He can do amazing things, which are beyond the capacity of even the greatest humans. Not only is He a hero in the sense of being brave, loyal, true, just, and good, but He is also super in the sense of having powers and abilities that are far greater than normal human beings possess. The scriptures teach with abundant clarity that Jesus Christ is real and that His powers are far above the ordinary.

SERVICE

Having healed us, the Savior sends us forth to heal others. Service soothes, sanctifies, saves, savors, strengthens, solidifies, soldiers on, and helps us to soar. Service allows us to bless others with the Atonement of the Lord because we have first been blessed through it. We have been forgiven, cleansed, uplifted, edified, and learned to rejoice. We have felt divine love. It is therefore only right that we would deeply wish to convey that same loving aid to others. This is the context for the following verse that describes the Lord calling the righteous spirits in paradise to go forth to share the truth with the spirits in prison who have not yet found the joy of divine consolation.

> But behold, from among the righteous, he organized his forces and appointed messengers, clothed with power and authority, and commissioned them to go forth and carry the light of the gospel to them that were in darkness, even to all the spirits of men; and thus was the gospel preached to the dead.
>
> And the chosen messengers went forth to declare the acceptable day of the Lord and proclaim liberty to the captives who were bound, even unto all who would repent of their sins and receive the gospel. (Doctrine and Covenants 138:30–31)

These brethren and sisters knew their message, for they had experienced it firsthand. They had been blessed with the bounty of remission of their sins. They had known divine forgiveness. They had personal experience of the love manifest through the Atonement of the Lord. So, of course, they wanted to share that with others. They did not need to be compelled to do so. They felt the love of the Lord for them and so they understood and felt love for others. This is the redemptive basis of loving service. It is to sing the song of redeeming love (see Alma 5).

CONCLUSION

So does the Lord understand what it is to have cancer, a stroke, or heart disease? Yes. Does He know about despair, depression, discouragement? Yes. Does He comprehend disloyalty, abandonment, betrayal, and humiliation? Yes. He indeed comprehends all the physical, spiritual, emotional, social, and mental ailments that exist. However, this is not all. He descended below all things that He might comprehend all things. This comprehension is experiential. He not only understands but also rises above. He has ascended above all affliction, sin, pain, and death. He has conquered the devil, hell, and death. He is triumphant over all things. He experienced the bitter, and yet He is full of love for us and rejoices with us. Thus, He can comfort us in every way we need as he understands from the inside out. He knows our deepest struggles. There is no thought hidden from Him. He gives us strength to face every struggle, to surmount every difficulty, to rise above every affliction, to heal every illness. We are healed by gaining perspective and strength, and eventually our affliction will be healed entirely.

It is my sincere and deep testimony that He is indeed the Holy One of Israel, the redeemer of my broken soul. He has consoled me, comforted me, counseled me, uplifted me, forgiven me, cleansed me, loved me, chastised me, corrected me, blessed me, and encouraged me. How grateful I am to know these things deeply and powerfully. He indeed lives, loves, and redeems my soul from death and hell. I pray that He will be with you and I in every time of trouble and His mighty power will succor us, strengthen us, and save us.

7

THE LIGHT THAT SHINES IN DARKNESS

FROM DARKNESS TO LIGHT

As a child I was terrified of the dark. While this is not unusual, it certainly felt like I had been uniquely endowed with an especially heavy dose of fear. I was troubled about monsters hiding in the dark and just waiting to get me. When it came time to go up to bed at night, I was reluctant to do so, as the stairway was dark. My mother would simply say, "Turn on the light switch before you go up." I found this to be sound advice. When I switched on the light the darkness vanished and so did my fears. It is impossible for a monster to hide in the light. I likewise liked to have the bedroom door ajar with the light on in the hallway as I went to sleep. My reasoning was that the monsters under the bed simply had nowhere to hide if a light was coming into the room and providing visibility. I cannot adequately explain how comforting that light was to me. I have always felt that light brings assurance, comfort, consolation, safety, security, and peace.

The lesson of my childhood has not been lost on me. I am no longer afraid of the dark—either physically or spiritually. This is because I know with certainty about the power of the Light. I know enough to know that God is the Light. Jesus Christ is literally the

Light of the World. There is no mystery about this. Without Him, there would be no light of any kind or degree. There would be no sun, moon, or stars. There would be no lightning, electricity, or light bulbs. There would be no life either. If ever I am surrounded by darkness—whether it be physical darkness or the spiritual darkness that comes with confusion, uncertainty, sorrow, or pain—I remember the need for light. I remember the source of the Light, the power of the Light, the goodness of the Light, and my love for the Light. Christ is truly the Light that shines in darkness. He is the ever present, ever guiding, always consoling Light of my life. In the presence of His marvelous light, all the monsters of the dark—be they real or imagined—must shrink away in shame and defeat. We can come to know the light, live in the light, rely on the light, rejoice in the light, and abide in the light. To say that Christ shines in darkness is to say that He is actively involved in bringing light into our lives. He is apparent, clear, noticeable, present, and ready to illuminate our understanding and show us the way to Him. It is to say that He overcomes fear and dread in our lives through His shining example.

GOD IS A BEING OF LIGHT

God is a personage of light, a being of glory, a man of radiance, a person of luminosity. I associate this light with His overarching intelligence, amazing capacity, intrinsic goodness, long reaching vision, and His ability to influence all things: "He comprehendeth all things, and all things are before him, and all things are round about him; and he is above all things, and in all things, and is through all things, and is round about all things; and all things are by him, and of him, even God, forever and ever" (Doctrine and Covenants 88:41). God is the Father of us all. He is called "the Father of lights" (James 1:17). I believe this means that He is the Father Star, as Christ is the Bright and Morning Star. He is the source of all. He is the fountainhead from which all creation springs. He is the intelligent One who gives life to all others, including the Son. He is light, love, and life personified. He is the embodiment of righteous principles. He is intelligence, glory, power, and wisdom. He is the original source of all that is true, beautiful, good, and majestic. We come to know and draw close to Him as we live in the light of gospel truth. To learn of Him, we need to stand in the light, perceive the light, discern the light, pursue the light, remain in the light, and spread the light of truth.

THE WAY, TRUTH, AND LIFE

We have been instructed that Christ is the way, the truth, the life, and the light. So it is that as we come unto Christ that we are inherently seeking the truth, sensing the light, knowing the way, believing the doctrine, accepting the Messiah, and learning true wisdom. It is important to comprehend that His light allows us to see things as they really are, including God, ourselves, and other people. His light allows us to apprehend the true nature of existence, the plans of God, the purposes, meaning, and significance of reality. The light of Christ allows us to see the truth for what it is and not to be blinded, confused, and deceived. Is it any wonder that the Savior gave physical sight to the physically blind and spiritual vision to the spiritually blind? He opens the eyes of the blind—whether temporal eyes, the eye of faith, or spiritual eyes.

THE LIGHT OF GOD

By any standard, the First Vision is a most remarkable theophany, a divine experience of sublime scope, a revelatory moment of tremendous importance, and an event that has the power to change the entire world for the better. This significant and sacred visitation represents a destined convergence between the divine and the human. The vital and crucial nature of this vision is of the utmost worth to every one of us. God be thanked for the choice seer of this dispensation who was a pioneer in being chosen and prepared for this experience. One of the things we learn from this vision is that God is a being of amazing light:

"I saw a pillar of light exactly over my head, above the brightness of the sun, which descended gradually until it fell upon me. It no sooner appeared than I found myself delivered from the enemy which held me bound. When the light rested upon me I saw two Personages, whose brightness and glory defy all description" (JS—

History 1:16–17). It is interesting to me that Joseph Smith saw a pillar of light before he saw God. The brightness of this pillar was more than that of the sun. That is a profound thought. The light that accompanies God is thus glorious. It is of importance that the light rescued Joseph from his dark enemy. He noted that the brightness and glory of God the Father and God the Son was beyond description. It seems to me that this means that while the light that came before the presence of God was witnessed was greater than the radiance of the sun, the light of God Himself was even more glorious than this—as Joseph could not put that light into words. So, in this truth we see that the light of God is luminous beyond anything on earth or in the heavens. That is a powerful truth for us to remember when we are confronted by darkness in any form.

THE AUTHOR OF LIGHT

God is the creator of light. He organized it for our benefit and blessing so that we might see and know the way in which to proceed. We are told: "And God said, Let there be light: and there was light" (Genesis 1:3). What a beautiful thing is light. It is from God and bears record of His glory, goodness, generosity, and greatness. By this created light we see, we know, we understand, we discern. It guides us safely through dark places and warns us of destructive dangers. Good things are much more likely to happen in the light. Thank heavens for light.

THE LIGHT OF CHRIST

"Behold, I am Jesus Christ, the Son of God. I came unto mine own, and mine own received me not. I am the light which shineth in darkness, and the darkness comprehendeth it not" (Doctrine and Covenants 10:57–58). In truth, Christ is the being that came to this world to show us how to live. His example was evident, observable, clear, and apparent. He spoke in the light, worked in the light, and evidenced the truth in the light. His life was not conducted under the cloak of darkness, deception, or deviousness. He showed women and men how to combat error, falsehood, and iniquity. He shined in darkness. That is to say that He radiated goodness and truth in a world prone to all sorts of corruption, confusion, and consternation. The darkness did not comprehend Him, that is, it neither understood Him, nor did it overcome him. How can impurity grasp virtue? How can revenge understand forgiveness? How can hate discern love?

> Which glory is that of the church of the Firstborn, even of God, the holiest of all, through Jesus Christ his Son—
>
> He that ascended up on high, as also he descended below all things, in that he comprehended all things, that he might be in all and through all things, the light of truth;
>
> Which truth shineth. This is the light of Christ. . . .
>
> And the light which shineth, which giveth you light, is through him who enlighteneth your eyes, which is the same light that quickeneth your understandings;
>
> Which light proceedeth forth from the presence of God to fill the immensity of space. (Doctrine and Covenants 88:5–12)

The Savior is a being of truth and light. He is a being who creates powerful things such as the sun. The symbolism of such is clear. As the sun allows us to have life and light, so the Son of God permits us to have life and light. We also know that His light gives us comprehension, understanding, and knowledge. He is the law of light by which creation is governed, ordered, structured, maintained, and glorified.

> He comprehendeth all things, and all things are before him, and all things are round about him; and he is above all things, and in all things, and is through all things, and is round about all things; and all things are by him, and of him, even God, forever and ever. . . .
>
> And they give light to each other in their times and in their seasons. . . .
>
> The earth rolls upon her wings, and the sun giveth his light by day, and the moon giveth her light by night, and the stars also give their light, as they roll upon their wings in their glory, in the midst of the power of God.
>
> Unto what shall I liken these kingdoms, that ye may understand?

> Behold, all these are kingdoms, and any man who hath seen any or the least of these hath seen God moving in his majesty and power.
>
> I say unto you, he hath seen him; nevertheless, he who came unto his own was not comprehended.
>
> The light shineth in darkness, and the darkness comprehendeth it not; nevertheless, the day shall come when you shall comprehend even God, being quickened in him and by him.
>
> Then shall ye know that ye have seen me, that I am, and that I am the true light that is in you, and that you are in me; otherwise ye could not abound. (Doctrine and Covenants 88:41–50)

This is most illuminating and inspiring. It is not the intention of God that we remain ignorant of Him or oblivious to His ways. He seeks to help us grow in intelligence, ability, comprehension, and discernment. We are promised that we will come to comprehend God in due course as we learn the laws of light. Light assists knowing. The Savior wants us to understand Him better, know Him more deeply, love Him more sincerely, and emulate Him more completely. He is not out of reach. His light permeates us, actuates us, motivates us, improves us, and helps us to abound. His light gives us a new type, kind, and degree of life, and only a portion of that is readily apparent to us as we grow and develop in our capacity to comprehend His light.

THE LIGHT OF GOD'S WORD

The word of the Lord is doctrine. It is pure, unfettered, undiluted truth. It is a companion to light. They travel together. The word of God is therefore visionary, enlightening, perspective-enhancing, and clear. It is right, correct, good, and proper. If we listen to God's word we grow in truth, expand in receptivity to spiritual light, and see much more clearly. We draw closer to the Lord who radiates truth and light. "For the word of the Lord is truth, and whatsoever is truth is light, and whatsoever is light is Spirit, even the Spirit of Jesus Christ. And the Spirit giveth light to every man that cometh into the world; and the Spirit enlighteneth every man through the world, that hearkeneth to the voice of the Spirit" (Doctrine and Covenants 84:45–46).

This word and light of the Lord is so critical to our journey through mortality. Through this divine light we can discern truth from error, we can see the beauty within us and around us, we can make good choices based on eternal principles, and we can bring comfort and joy to others. As we live in the light of Christ daily and consistently, we find the abundance of a new life. This new life is not stingy, meager, or threadbare—rather it is multifaceted, multidimensional, rich, and pervasive.

The light of God's word frees us from the bondage of spiritual falsity, sin, and sadness. It wakes us up, stirs us from slumber, opens our eyes, and fills us with light. For example:

> And now behold, I say unto you, my brethren, you that belong to this church, have you sufficiently retained in remembrance the captivity of your fathers? Yea, and have you sufficiently retained in remembrance his mercy and long-suffering towards them? And moreover, have ye sufficiently retained in remembrance that he has delivered their souls from hell?
>
> Behold, he changed their hearts; yea, he awakened them out of a deep sleep, and they awoke unto God. Behold, they were in the midst of darkness; nevertheless, their souls were illuminated by the light of the everlasting word. (Alma 5:6–7)

This does not just apply to those presently outside the true fold of God. It also applies to any of us who believe in God but are nevertheless afflicted with various forms of spiritual blindness. For example, consider these verses that were given to remind covenant disciples of the darkness that attends unbelief and casualness about the Book of Mormon and modern revelation:

> And your minds in times past have been darkened because of unbelief, and because you have treated lightly the things you have received—
>
> Which vanity and unbelief have brought the whole church under condemnation.
>
> And this condemnation resteth upon the children of Zion, even all.
>
> And they shall remain under this condemnation until they repent and remember the new covenant, even the Book of Mormon and the former commandments which I have given

them, not only to say, but to do according to that which I have written. (Doctrine and Covenants 84:54–57)

Obviously, this is intended to indicate that brightness comes into our minds as we esteem highly the revealed word of God in this dispensation. Our faith in these words of truth brings spiritual vision to our lives. This capacity to see will prove vitally important as the world becomes increasingly immersed in spiritual darkness. In fact, it is gloriously evident that the more of the word of God we embrace willingly and joyfully, then the greater the light of Christ will be in our lives.

THE LIGHT OF GOD'S EVERLASTING COVENANT

We know that God is a being of light. So it is that His creations, messages, and blessings are likewise accompanied by and drenched in light. We are instructed that the new and everlasting gospel covenant is a light to the world: "And even so I have sent mine everlasting covenant into the world, to be a light to the world, and to be a standard for my people, and for the Gentiles to seek to it, and to be a messenger before my face to prepare the way before me" (Doctrine and Covenants 45:9). The covenant is therefore a way for the people of the world to see God and all things clearly, openly, and with discernment. The covenant is also a standard for the people of God. That is, it is a rule, a guide, a measure, an expectation, and a principle that we are supposed to live our lives according to. It is a way of seeing whether we are living in the right manner. The covenant is something the Gentiles need to be attracted to if they are to find salvation among the people of the Lord. Also, fundamentally, the restored gospel covenant is a messenger—or an Elias—to prepare the world for the Second Coming of the Lord. As John the Baptist very much prepared the way for the first coming of the Lord, so the covenant of these latter days is the perfect way of preparing the willing to see the Lord and to rejoice in His presence. Covenants are the means the Lord uses to test us in terms of our desire to follow Him or to follow some other way of life. Thus, the covenant is a light. It is transparent, available, open, clear, and shows us the way to live. Does the covenant of Christ give us access to a newness of life? It surely does, for it opens the way for us to have the scales of darkness removed from our eyes so that we can see things as they really are.

RECEIVING DIVINE LIGHT

Does willing obedience to divine standards allow us to obtain the light of God? Do we gain this truth from God gradually? Will we eventually receive all glorious truth and know all wonderful things if we follow the pattern of line upon line receptivity to spiritual light? The Lord's answers to these questions is a certain yes (see Doctrine and Covenants 93:28). Obedience brings bountiful blessings. These blessings include understanding, wisdom, comprehension, knowledge, discernment, assurance, confidence, and peace. God wants us to feel secure in faith, comforted by His plan, and ready to take on challenges. Keeping His commandments helps us to find joyful contentment and optimistic resolve. We are the beneficiaries when we do His will. How wise God is. Receiving light does not make it more difficult to see the truth—rather it makes it easier.

BEING FILLED WITH THE LIGHT OF GOD

God's intention is for us to eventually have bodies that are filled with light, that we are devoid of darkness, and that we will be able to comprehend all the things He wants us to know (see Doctrine and Covenants 88:67). Will this involve an increase in our capacity? Indeed. Will it also mean that we learn things that are presently unknown or mysterious to us? I believe so. It is evident that God is a being of glorious light, of stunning radiance and of transcendent splendor. His knowledge is sublime, and His majesty is triumphant. As we come to truly know Him, we are transformed so that we reach for a deeper destiny pertaining to ourselves and others. That destiny is that we are to be light bearers, light wearers, and light containers. We are to be vessels of light, love, and life.

BECOMING A LIGHT TO OTHERS

We are not simply to receive the light ourselves. Rather, we are to radiate light to others so that they might also partake in the promises of becoming filled with light too (see 3 Nephi 12:14–16). We can be a light to everyone—any people and all people. To light the world is to diminish darkness, overcome dread, and extinguish doubt. It is to shine in goodness, gentleness, and graciousness. Be the light you can be—daily, consistently, and always. We do this by being a light to one person at a time. If there are any that are lonely, frustrated, sick, tired, or afraid, we can be a source of strength to them. We accomplish this by following the Light of the World ourselves—Jesus Christ—and encouraging others to do likewise. It is the case that those who are lit from the inside themselves will also then light the world with divine love.

"For verily I say unto you that I am Alpha and Omega, the beginning and the end, the light and the life of the world" (Doctrine and Covenants 45:7). What light do we hold up for the world to see? The light of Christ. He is light—now and always. He is life—today and tomorrow. He is glorious—yesterday and forever. The darkness will bow to him, bend to him, give way to him and run from him. So, let us hold up the light of the world consistently, persistently, and gladly. He will shine our way so that we can do this.

CONCLUSION

Jesus Christ is appropriately described as the Light that shines in darkness. He is always available to us, especially when we are facing deep darkness. He is far more powerful than the adversary is—there simply is no comparison between them. I know this by my own personal experience. We are well advised to look to the light of the world. We can do this. It is a choice. "Wherefore, men are free according to the flesh; and all things are given them which are expedient unto man. And they are free to choose liberty and eternal life, through the great Mediator of all men" (2 Nephi 2:27–28). We always have a choice to follow the Lord—no matter what the darkness is that we face. If there is one thing I have come to know in this life with complete certainty, it is this: As we study the doctrine of the

Atonement of the Lord our viewpoint and our lives are changed in a fundamental way. Through the triumphant Only Begotten Son of God—who has revealed himself in glory in these latter days to His precious Prophet Joseph Smith—we come to a marvelous and wonderful new understanding and life. Let us celebrate the Light and Life of the World. He is the living Light. He is the speaking, caring, teaching, and courageous Master. He is the never-failing healer of our souls. My witness of Him is sure and certain. He is our serene Shepherd. He lives. He loves. He saves. As we come to Him completely and with everlasting determination, He will bestow power upon us to overcome all things. He is truly mighty to save. May we always remember Him.

8

THE SCHOOLMASTER

In this chapter I discuss the importance of the law of the Lord and how it is essential in facilitating our access to a new life in Christ.

THE NATURE OF A SCHOOLMASTER

If you are anything like me, you feared your school principals (schoolmasters) when you were young. These authority figures can seem larger than life, scary, and powerful. We do not want to get on their bad side, as they could make life difficult for us. We often see them as harsh disciplinarians who rule with strict control. We may sometimes assume that they love the power of dominion and exercise that control without regard to the welfare of those they preside over. While this may be a correct assessment in certain situations, I believe it is an incorrect view in others. There is another way of seeing a schoolmaster. It is that this person wants what is best for you. This leader wants to ensure that everyone under their stewardship gets opportunities and privileges to learn, grow, develop, and progress. There are schoolmasters who rule with a gentle hand and love their students. Their care is genuine. In other words, the laws upheld by such caring schoolmasters are not intended to be cruel or prohibitive. The rules are not an end in themselves but rather a means to an end. Their purpose, when crafted carefully and enacted wisely, is to ensure that the circumstances are conducive to learning and development so that the precious students can grow and develop.

However, this simply cannot happen without rules, policies, procedures, protocols, or standards. We are expected to conform to behavioral values that make the school experience viable and enhancing for everyone. If there is bullying, cheating, fighting, immorality, and so on permitted on school property, then inevitably people will be hurt and negatively impacted. In serious cases the consequences could be disastrous. The schoolmaster needs to ensure that rules are established and maintained so that order and goodwill prevail. In other words, there is simply no sense in which we can talk about effective schoolmasters without simultaneously referring to the rules and standards by which everyone in the school community must abide, if there is to be peace, an environment of safety, and an atmosphere conducive to learning. In other words, effective educational systems would simply be impossible in the absence of clearly defined codes of conduct.

THE NATURE OF LAW

In my career I have been instructed through dealing with various aspects of law, such as treaty law, human rights law, property law, tax law, employment law, and personal injury law. This has been an eye-opening experience. We sometimes see law as forbidding, limiting, or constraining. However, law is also intended to be protective, reassuring, guiding, and helpful. Law regulates, safeguards, and offers assurances so that we can know where we stand and there is fairness for all. Think of the benefits of law:

If there were no laws protecting the lives and treatment of citizens, then governments or others could kill, rob, or otherwise unfairly deal with us.

If there were no rules of the road, then chaos and death would abound.

If there were no regulations in sports, then cheating would prevail.

If there were no laws in employment, then employers or employees could perform many arbitrary injustices such as stealing without penalty.

If there were no standards expected of us at home, we would become drifters lost in a maze of confusing expectations and vulnerable to a hard world.

When we talk of the law, it is not necessarily accurate to think of it as being essentially negative or even neutral. I prefer to think of the law as being an instrument of fairness in that the same standards are expected of everyone in a particular sphere regardless of background, circumstance, or station in life. It is also an instrument of love, as it benefits those who live according to its underlying precepts.

The idea that someone in authority over us can simultaneously give us rules and love us also is not as contradictory as it might appear. When parents guide us to make wise choices, this should not be interpreted to mean that they do not care about us. Precisely the opposite is usually the case. It is because our parents love us so deeply that they are so heavily invested in giving us direction. It also explains why they are so frustrated when we ignore or rebel against their considered expectations derived from long years of experience—and often stemming from the pain they have found attached to the making of poor choices themselves in their own pasts. Of course, when we are young, we are inexperienced and sometimes proud, so we see any directives given to us as undesirable impositions on our freedom. It is usually only as we grow in experience and wisdom that we learn that having someone to guide us when needed is really a beneficial blessing rather than a wicked intrusion in our lives. Of course, this does not mean that authority figures are always wise or careful or loving when they guide us. They may often do so awkwardly and messily. As we mature, we learn to forgive them as being sincere if not always wise. And we see the pattern repeated in our own parenting. On the contrary, those who invite us to live without high standards and devoid of demanding value are not automatically to be correctly perceived as being trustworthy and caring.

THE MEANING OF DIVINE LAW

What of the law of Moses? The law of Moses essentially consisted of the ten commandments. These commandments were intended to regulate behavior between individuals in a way that God approved of. The law of Moses was not an end in itself. The observance of the rules was not to become the end all and be all of existence. The law was a means to an end. That end was the Christ and the salvation He, as the divine lawgiver, would bring to the world.

> And behold, this is the whole meaning of the law, every whit pointing to that great and last sacrifice; and that great and last sacrifice will be the Son of God, yea, infinite and eternal.
> And thus he shall bring salvation to all those who shall believe on his name; this being the intent of this last sacrifice, to bring about the bowels of mercy, which overpowereth justice, and bringeth about means unto men that they may have faith unto repentance.
> And thus mercy can satisfy the demands of justice, and encircles them in the arms of safety, while he that exercises no faith unto repentance is exposed to the whole law of the demands of justice; therefore only unto him that has faith unto repentance is brought about the great and eternal plan of redemption. (Alma 34:14–16)

Law does not stand alone. It is not devoid of purpose or meaning. The law of Moses was intended to point the children of Israel to Christ. This is because the law was necessary but not sufficient. It was required to keep the law of Moses, but it was not enough to do so. Without the Atonement of Christ, no amount of obedience to the law of Moses could save the children of Israel. So, any observance of the law—whether it was casual or exacting—was not to be confused with the transformative life-changing powers of the Atonement of the Lord. Not one of us can save our own souls based only on our own merits. However, this does not absolve us of the need for obedience. We are still expected to be obedient. The lawgiver has made that a requirement upon us. And when we fall short, we are required to repent. In truth, both obedience and repentance are possible only through Christ. They are laws given to us by the Lord.

The mistake that the Pharisees and Sadducees made was that they viewed their strict observance of the law—and numerous additional exacting standards created by men—as the great standard by which they judged their standing before God. They did not comprehend the critical and vital importance of the Atonement of Christ in making salvation possible to all. Nor was their obedience about the substance of spiritual love for God and man. Rather, it was in the form of procedural compliance with rituals and rules. Their exacting obedience to the letter of the law became the great measuring rod. And the spirit of the law became neglected and was instead transformed into a multitude of rules and regulations that were more a matter of the letter than the spirit. Obedience to the core of the Mosaic law was essential and worthwhile. Harmony between the letter and spirit of the law was possible. Thus, compliance with the heart of the divine law was vital. However, conformity with numerous man-made additions, deletions, or interpretations was not needful. Numerous rule-based obligations added without inspiration could never align with the original spiritual purposes of the law. More important, salvation requires a Savior, and therefore any salvation that is thought to occur by virtue of human effort alone is essentially impossible. The grace of Christ is needed in every time and circumstance and among every people. It is through our acceptance of divine standards through divine help that we find salvation and in no other way.

The scholars of the law are not the only ones who make this fundamental mistake in judgment. Many years ago I faced a significant challenge. I employed many efforts to find a solution. It was only after many spectacular failures that it finally dawned on me that I had not intently implored the Lord for His mighty assistance. Upon pleading with the Lord, I found the solution to my difficulty. I was surprised by His strength to help me face what had been previously a seemingly insurmountable obstacle. His power to help us far transcends even our most valiant unaided efforts. What is ironic is that this was something I should have seen far sooner. I was essentially acting like a Pharisee in relying on my own strength and wisdom to resolve a problem I faced when I should have asked the Savior for His saving strength to assist me. There is not much point in having a Savior that we do not look to for help when needed. This is obviously not to suggest that our own efforts are futile or not needed. We are expected to work out our salvation through constant effort. However, this effort needs to be carried out in the context of asking specifically for divine intervention simultaneously. We are to recognize the gracious hand of God in helping us all the days of our lives, not just when we are in dire need of help.

When we understand the law of Moses from the perspective of Jehovah who gave us the law in the first place, it will make a radical and pronounced difference to how we comprehend the law, its meaning, and purpose. In this spiritual and intellectual context, the law becomes both necessary and exciting as a basic part of experiencing a mighty change of heart. The Lord can change our hearts, and then obedience becomes much more natural. This will mean that the law is no longer the measuring rod of our lives or indeed a seemingly impossible high standard which irritates our efforts to be good. Rather, we will learn to live the law because our natures have been changed. This does not mean that our obedience to the law will always be perfect or carried out with the proper motive. However, gradually our obedience itself will become more in line with the spirit of the law and not just the letter. It will be a willing and heartfelt compliance.

THE SUPREME RULER

God controls, governs, leads, and presides over all things. He rules by law and order (see Doctrine and Covenants 88:41). Thus, the divine word records profoundly inspirational doctrine in speaking of the God and Father of us all. He is the Almighty, now and always. He is the great supreme ruler of the universe, in whom all perfection dwells. He is love in physical form or charity incarnate. He is power and purity, love and life, joy and rejoicing, might and mercy. There is no end to His wisdom, no conquering of His might, no failing of His strength, and no depletion of His love. He reigns, rules, blesses, and saves. We need to know Him, love Him, serve Him, remember Him, and become more like Him, worlds without end.

God is a being of love. He is also a man of law and order. This means that all the laws of the Lord are given in love. Can God give commandments that do not have love implicit in their design and nature? No, of course not. Will He make determinations that are not made in love? Certainly not. Will He give guidance that is in any way devoid of charity? Most definitely not. Will His judgments lack love? No. His orders always stem from love. Will God's nature, plans, and purposes be motivated by anything other than pure love and genuine concern? No.

In like manner, God's instructions evidence His great loving regard for His children. The commandment to not kill protects both the person inclined to violence and the potential victims of violent crime. The commandments to not covet and not steal safeguard both the person tempted to covet/steal and the person who may be stolen from. Every commandment has this protective element at its root. In every case, if people keep the commandments, they will save themselves from terrible guilt and save their potential victims from losing property, possessions, and their lives. To keep the commandments is to show love for ourselves and others. To break them is to hurt and maim not only ourselves but others also. God endorses, approves of, and rejoices in our keeping His commandments, as He knows this will bless us and others. The corollary of this is that He frowns upon, discourages, and is justifiably angry in righteous ways when His children plunder, murder, deceive, betray, and likewise do other heinous acts. Why? It is because He knows that such actions not only seriously harm the victims of such actions, but they also bring terrible suffering upon the instigator of such actions. I often think that the suffering of those who commit serious moral infractions ends up being way worse than the suffering experienced by those who are victimized. Both suffer needlessly. These outcomes are avoidable if we will just choose to be obedient.

Indeed, we are instructed by Alma to "bridle all your passions, that you may be filled with love" (Alma 38:12). This is most instructive. It is my experience that those who love most deeply and enduringly are those who restrain their appetites, who guard their wants, who manage their desires. In the world we are told to give vent to our desires, to live for ourselves, to enjoy our lives, to seek pleasure, to aspire after comfort, to do our own thing, and to pursue our passions. This is fatal advice. In every situation where I have seen this kind of philosophy lived out, the result has always been a lessening of love rather than a display or increase of it. The truth is that disobedience promotes a lack of love. Acting without self-restraint or control or mastery leads to all sorts of crimes and sins and is accompanied by anger, hatred, hostility, and often violence. On the other hand, reigning in our desires, appetites, and passions leads to numerous acts of loving concern, acts of goodwill, performances of unselfish service, devotions of duty, honor, and obligation. Such mastery of self is accompanied by great and deep love and blesses both the person possessing the love and the person on the receiving end of it.

Therefore, it is critical that we uncover incorrect philosophies and unmask them to see what they really are. Everything that encourages obedience to God is inspired by Him and always produces real joy and true love. The doctrines of the adversary—which are couched in terms of apparent universal love and acceptance of everyone doing whatever suits them—are in fact destructive of true love and lasting happiness. God's laws can only be ones of love. Satan's enticements can only be ones of misery, sadness, and despair. For God to truly show love for us, He must give us guidance and direction that is difficult. It stretches us beyond the spiritual flabbiness of the natural man, it contradicts our selfish tendencies, it combats our carnal proclivities, and it asks us to conform to standards, values, and behaviors that require self-discipline and genuine concern for the well-being of ourselves and others. So, law and order are not essentially to be associated with unwelcome prohibitions to our freedom. Yielding to high standards is an act of love. Giving vent to whatever desires are common to the sensual man or natural woman are the acts arising from the absence of love. On that basis, I do not share the thinking that says that allowing or encouraging people to do whatever they want and to be free from constraints and obligations is in harmony with loving them. Precisely the opposite is the case.

Of course, the law of God is not arbitrary, inconsistent, or self-serving. It is not about unreasonable demands or Him just giving orders to be obeyed, or Him exerting power and dominion to control and subject us to His whims. While men may act as tyrants, despots, and dominators, the nature of God is radically different from this. His laws are life enhancing. His laws are wise, beneficial, and useful. His laws are designed to facilitate growth in the person abiding by them. His laws regulate our behavior, improve our character, and give us clear direction on how to live after the manner of happiness. If we join a military army, we probably would not expect our commander to talk in terms of loving us, nor would we expect our generals to show us much affection, or our captains to show consideration of our feelings. However, God the Father, when He appeared to Joseph Smith, introduced His son by saying, "This is my Beloved Son, Hear Him" (JS—History 1:17).

So, the first thing our Father does is call Joseph Smith by his own name and expresses His love for the Savior. Not exactly what you would expect a harsh, unforgiving, and unloving God to do, is it? That is because He is the true God. He lives and loves us. He is not the kind of God many of us feared growing up. He is not quick to anger, eager to lord over us, and hasty to criticize and condemn us. Neither is His law only to punish us. Its purpose is to help us avoid needless suffering by living wisely, avoiding certain types of self-inflicted punishment and heartache, preventing the pain that comes from breaching our conscience and avoiding the guilt that comes from having harmed others. When we join the Lord's army we gradually come to see and experience the nature of true divine love, which is not self-indulgent and permissive. It is demanding (as in obedience), and it is compassionate (as in repentance). I am grateful to know that God's law and God's love are in harmony, being mutually reinforcing and collaborative.

THE NATURE OF RIGHTEOUS LEADERSHIP

We often hear criticisms leveled against those who are in positions of authority and influence, whether they hold status in governmental, educational, religious, or business institutions. It is common for their motives and leadership styles to be evaluated and viewed negatively. It is regularly assumed that those who hold power have only selfish ambitions. However, is it true to suggest that all leaders are like this? Is it correct to assume that authority essentially comes with corrupting values and standards? I do not believe so. Of course, holding position does not make one automatically immune to temptation, nor does it inevitably infer dubious aspirations in the office holders themselves. There is such a thing as righteous leadership. Consider the following scriptural teachings:

> Behold, there are many called, but few are chosen. And why are they not chosen? . . .
>
> That the rights of the priesthood are inseparably connected with the powers of heaven, and that the powers of heaven cannot be controlled nor handled only upon the principles of righteousness. . . .
>
> Hence many are called, but few are chosen . . .
>
> Let thy bowels also be full of charity towards all men, and to the household of faith, and let virtue garnish thy thoughts unceasingly; then shall thy confidence wax strong in the presence of God; and the doctrine of the priesthood shall distill upon thy soul as the dews from heaven.
>
> The Holy Ghost shall be thy constant companion, and thy scepter an unchanging scepter of righteousness and truth; and thy dominion shall be an everlasting dominion, and without compulsory means it shall flow unto thee forever and ever. (Doctrine and Covenants 121:34–46)

There are some essentially important truths to note from these verses. There are principles of righteousness that allow us to have access to divine power. There is such a thing as righteous dominion, which is inherently good and lasts forever. There are righteous attributes which are a beneficial blessing to those who possess them and those who are influenced by them. I note that these verses indicate that as we follow principles of righteousness that we will know an increase in our capacity to love, an enlargement of our souls, and a strengthening of our confidence before God. This is no coincidence. God's work is to enhance, expand, extend, and ennoble each of us. This is how we are added upon and thus become more like our Father in Heaven. This is precisely what is involved in becoming alive in Christ—we gain access to a new and improved type, kind, and degree of living. Leaders are blessed to become an ever-improving example of righteous leadership in the Lords way.

So, the problem is not the holding of authority itself nor is it the wielding of influence nor the exercise of power. It is the source of our authority, the way we exercise such control, and the end that we pursue in directing others that matters. God is benign, benevolent, and good in His exercise of authority. Similarly, we can become likewise as we learn the principles upon which inspired leadership is based.

THE NATURE OF RIGHTEOUS GOVERNMENT

Thankfully, there is such a thing as righteous government. The use of the priesthood is always governed by those who hold priesthood keys. Priesthood keys are the right and responsibility to direct, govern, control, and preside over the work of salvation. The keys are specific authority delegated to priesthood leaders to direct the work in a specific geographic area for a specific time. Priesthood keys ultimately belong to God. As designated by the Father, Jesus Christ holds all the keys of salvation, including the keys of resurrection. The keys of resurrection are not delegated to men on the earth at this time. The Savior has delegated to the living prophet only the exercise of all priesthood keys held by the Church on the earth. All the living ordained apostles hold all the priesthood keys, and they exercise keys to carry out their presiding and regulating roles. However, the full exercise of keys is not operational by an apostle until such time as that individual becomes the living prophet. Nevertheless, the apostles still exercise priesthood keys in performing their apostolic ministry even while also acting under the direction of the full keys exercised by the living prophet. All brethren who receive keys do so under the overall, overarching, presiding authority of the living prophet.

Good government in the kingdom of God is a lawful activity approved of by God. Indeed, the Lord instructed some of the brethren of this dispensation that faithful service in the Lord's vineyard would have the effect of ensuring the law of God was effectual, working, and holding fast. In other words, the purposes of the law would be fulfilled. The law would bring stability, surety, solidity, strength, and salvation to those who heard, accepted, lived, and taught it: "Therefore, tarry ye, and labor diligently . . . to bind up the law and seal up the testimony" (Doctrine and Covenants 88:84). To bind something is to protect it, salvage it, honor it, and hold it together. The law of God is intended to unify and rescue us from scattering, breaking up, and losing our way. Law in this sense is a helpful anchor, keeping us grounded and connected to God. The law of God is a righteous link to Him. It therefore ought to be maintained, respected, valued, defended, and safeguarded by us. To lose divine law is to lose perfect love.

THE LAW OF CHRIST AS A STANDARD OF MEASURE

The law of Christ is plain and precious. It is a rule, a guide, a standard by which all things can be judged. The gospel law of God is to be known and practiced by those who seek to follow the divine way (see Doctrine and Covenants 88:77–78). This means we righteously judge every doctrine, principle, and practice from every other source by how it compares with the revealed word in these latter days. Consider the following: "And when ye shall receive these things, I would exhort you that ye would ask God, the Eternal Father, in the name of Christ, if these things are not true; and if ye shall ask with a sincere heart, with real intent, having faith in Christ, he will manifest the truth of it unto you, by the power of the Holy Ghost. And by the power of the Holy Ghost ye may know the truth of all things" (Moroni 10:3–5). This indicates to us that we can discern the difference between right and wrong, truth and falsehood, wisdom and error by the influence of the Holy Ghost in our lives. For example, judging the accuracy of the Book of Mormon by any method not involving the Holy Ghost is not in alignment with God's standard for differentiating between scripture and uninspired writings.

> Wherefore, I the Lord, knowing the calamity which should come upon the inhabitants of the earth, called upon my servant Joseph Smith, Jun., and spake unto him from heaven, and gave him commandments; . . .
>
> The weak things of the world shall come forth and break down the mighty and strong ones, that man should not counsel his fellow man, neither trust in the arm of flesh—

But that every man might speak in the name of God the Lord, even the Savior of the world;

That faith also might increase in the earth;

That mine everlasting covenant might be established;

That the fulness of my gospel might be proclaimed by the weak and the simple unto the ends of the world, and before kings and rulers.

Behold, I am God and have spoken it; these commandments are of me, and were given unto my servants in their weakness, after the manner of their language, that they might come to understanding . . .

And inasmuch as they were humble they might be made strong, and blessed from on high, and receive knowledge from time to time.

And after having received the record of the Nephites, yea, even my servant Joseph Smith, Jun., might have power to translate through the mercy of God, by the power of God, the Book of Mormon.

And also those to whom these commandments were given, might have power to lay the foundation of this church, and to bring it forth out of obscurity and out of darkness, the only true and living church upon the face of the whole earth, with which I, the Lord, am well pleased. . . .

For I, the Lord cannot look upon sin with the least degree of allowance;

Nevertheless, he that repents and does the commandments of the Lord shall be forgiven;

And he that repents not, from him shall be taken even the light which he has received; for my Spirit shall not always strive with man, saith the Lord of Hosts.

And again, verily I say unto you, O inhabitants of the earth: I the Lord am willing to make these things known unto all flesh;

For I am no respecter of persons, and will that all men shall know that the day speedily cometh; the hour is not yet, but is nigh at hand, when peace shall be taken from the earth, and the devil shall have power over his own dominion.

And also the Lord shall have power over his saints, and shall reign in their midst, and shall come down in judgment upon Idumea, or the world.

Search these commandments, for they are true and faithful, and the prophecies and promises which are in them shall all be fulfilled.

What I the Lord have spoken, I have spoken, and I excuse not myself; and though the heavens and the earth pass away, my word shall not pass away, but shall all be fulfilled, whether by mine own voice or by the voice of my servants, it is the same.

For behold, and lo, the Lord is God, and the Spirit beareth record, and the record is true, and the truth abideth forever and ever. Amen. (Doctrine and Covenants 1:17–39)

This is a revelation of remarkable instruction. The Lord restored His gospel to the earth so that His commandments, revelation, knowledge, covenant, priesthood, understanding, wisdom, power, spirit, word, and truth would be made available to all people on both sides of the veil. His purpose is to increase our insight and expand our understanding of things divine. We can discern the voice of God in these latter days by the fact that it adds to our understanding. It increases, expands, grows, and develops all the divine attributes and capacities of our being. This is the great distinctive power of the Restoration. It adds and does not take away. It enlarges and does not diminish. This is how we know it is true. It gives us far more than we could ever have without it. The law of God does not take away from the quality, freedom, and capacity of our lives. Instead, divine law cultivates our ability to grow into the kind of fully developed spiritual beings we can become. The Lord has given His word in these days through the prophet Joseph Smith (see Doctrine and Covenants Section 5:10). To accept him as a true prophet is to accept the word of God in these times. Joseph Smith is the great revealer of the saving knowledge of Christ in this dispensation. The law of God is the law of the prophets. It is the law of witnesses. It is the law of increased intelligence, added light, expanded wisdom, advanced understanding, and developed comprehension.

The rise of the Church of Christ in these last days . . . by the will and commandments of God. . . .Which commandments were given to Joseph Smith, Jun., who was called of God, and ordained an apostle of Jesus Christ, to be the first elder of this church; . . .

After it was truly manifested unto this first elder that he had received a remission of his sins, he was entangled again in the vanities of the world;

But after repenting, and humbling himself sincerely, through faith, God ministered unto him by an holy angel, whose countenance was as lightning, and whose garments were pure and white above all other whiteness;

And gave unto him commandments which inspired him;

And gave him power from on high, by the means which were before prepared, to translate the Book of Mormon. . . . Proving to the world that the holy scriptures are true, and that God does inspire men and call them to his holy work in this age and generation, as well as in generations of old;

Thereby showing that he is the same God yesterday, today, and forever. Amen. (Doctrine and Covenants 20:1–12)

This is a marvelous revelation. This great latter-day work of restoration is definitive proof that God is at work in this world, not simply randomly, but according to plans and purposes. He is a God of law and order and instituted His latter-day Church and kingdom in a manner that would stand the test of time and eternity. It would be a miraculous work and a wonder, a source of astonishment and amazement, a work of power and purity. This work would prove categorically and clearly that the Bible is indeed true when understood in the light of revelation, and that God works through chosen servants to accomplish His work. God is good and great. This work would renew the world.

> Hear, O ye heavens, and give ear, O earth, and rejoice ye inhabitants thereof, for the Lord is God, and beside him there is no Savior.
>
> Great is his wisdom, marvelous are his ways, and the extent of his doings none can find out.
>
> His purposes fail not, neither are there any who can stay his hand.

> From eternity to eternity he is the same, and his years never fail.
>
> For thus saith the Lord—I, the Lord, am merciful and gracious unto those who fear me, and delight to honor those who serve me in righteousness and in truth unto the end.
>
> Great shall be their reward and eternal shall be their glory.
>
> And to them will I reveal all mysteries, yea, all the hidden mysteries of my kingdom from days of old, and for ages to come, will I make known unto them the good pleasure of my will concerning all things pertaining to my kingdom.
>
> Yea, even the wonders of eternity shall they know, and things to come will I show them, even the things of many generations.
>
> And their wisdom shall be great, and their understanding reach to heaven; and before them the wisdom of the wise shall perish, and the understanding of the prudent shall come to naught.
>
> For by my Spirit will I enlighten them, and by my power will I make known unto them the secrets of my will—yea, even those things which eye has not seen, nor ear heard, nor yet entered into the heart of man. (Doctrine and Covenants 76:1–10)

What an impressive revelation! We are informed that God wants us to hear and hearken to His words. He wants to share His heavenly wisdom with us. He wants to teach us of His ways. As we follow His divine law, we will learn eternal mysteries and inherit majestic rewards. Who can comprehend the full import of these promises? We can glimpse them and by the Holy Spirit we catch a measure of the vision of what is involved. The Restoration is perfect proof that God intends to keep this promise. He will pour out revelation upon us as fast as we are willing and able to receive it. The restored gospel opens our minds and hearts to truths we simply could not know otherwise. We are deeply privileged to gain an understanding that stretches us in this manner. Again, the world offers nothing comparable.

> And your minds in times past have been darkened because of unbelief, and because you have treated lightly the things you have received—
>
> Which vanity and unbelief have brought the whole church under condemnation.

> And this condemnation resteth upon the children of Zion, even all.
>
> And they shall remain under this condemnation until they repent and remember the new covenant, even the Book of Mormon and the former commandments which I have given them, not only to say, but to do according to that which I have written—
>
> That they may bring forth fruit meet for their Father's kingdom; otherwise there remaineth a scourge and judgment to be poured out upon the children of Zion.
>
> For shall the children of the kingdom pollute my holy land? Verily, I say unto you, Nay.
>
> Verily, verily, I say unto you who now hear my words, which are my voice, blessed are ye inasmuch as you receive these things;
>
> For I will forgive you of your sins with this commandment—that you remain steadfast in your minds in solemnity and the spirit of prayer, in bearing testimony to all the world of those things which are communicated unto you. (Doctrine and Covenants 84:54–61)

This is a most important revelation. We are to treat the Book of Mormon and the restored scriptures with the utmost respect and reverence. We are to remember them, rejoice in them, live their precepts, preach from them to the Church and the world, and to safeguard their doctrines and promises. As we do this, we will feel the approbation of heaven, bring forth a good harvest for the Lord, and be forgiven of our own sins. It is therefore a divine commandment that we value those scriptural treasures that have come forth specifically for our day. These doctrinal pearls have cost so much and will yield great blessings to us as we take them seriously and conscientiously.

> God shall give unto you knowledge by his Holy Spirit, yea, by the unspeakable gift of the Holy Ghost, that has not been revealed since the world was until now;
>
> Which our forefathers have awaited with anxious expectation to be revealed in the last times, which their minds were pointed to by the angels, as held in reserve for the fulness of their glory;
>
> A time to come in the which nothing shall be withheld. . . .

All thrones and dominions, principalities, and powers, shall be revealed and set forth upon all who have endured valiantly for the gospel of Jesus Christ . . .

All the times of their revolutions, all the appointed days, months, and years, and all the days of their days, months, and years, and all their glories, laws, and set times, shall be revealed in the days of the dispensation of the fulness of times—

According to that which was ordained in the midst of the Council of the Eternal God of all other gods before this world was, that should be reserved unto the finishing and the end thereof, when every man shall enter into his eternal presence and into his immortal rest.

How long can rolling waters remain impure? What power shall stay the heavens? As well might man stretch forth his puny arm to stop the Missouri river in its decreed course, or to turn it up stream, as to hinder the Almighty from pouring down knowledge from heaven upon the heads of the Latter-day Saints. (Doctrine and Covenants 121:26–33)

This is a revelation for our times. It is evidently and abundantly clear that God has designed these last days for the purpose of pouring down knowledge upon His children. He will give His church hidden knowledge that many saints and prophets from the past looked forward to being revealed in the last times. He will uncover all things to our comprehension. He will reveal all mysteries and explain His workings. We will learn His creative laws, powers, patterns, programs, procedures, policies, principles, and processes. What a marvelous message! We are being prepared to receive these transcendent, triumphant, and towering truths. For this to happen the saints will need to refine their ability to hear the voice of the Lord, study His words more deeply, and live his laws with more devotion. What a rich heritage we have that we can receive this legacy of laws from the Lord.

On the third of October, in the year nineteen hundred and eighteen, I sat in my room pondering over the scriptures;

And reflecting upon the great atoning sacrifice that was made by the Son of God, for the redemption of the world;

And the great and wonderful love made manifest by the Father and the Son in the coming of the Redeemer into the world;

That through his atonement, and by obedience to the principles of the gospel, mankind might be saved. . . .

As I pondered over these things which are written, the eyes of my understanding were opened, and the Spirit of the Lord rested upon me, and I saw the hosts of the dead, both small and great. (Doctrine and Covenants 138:1–11)

I find this to be a most illuminating revelation. Here we have an ordained prophet of the Lord and President of the Church, who was nearing the end of his mortal life, who had been a devoted student of the scriptures throughout his life and yet, he was pondering on the scriptures and was able to receive powerful revelation. He saw and heard things that he had not known or understood before. That which was closed to him previously was now open. That which was dark was now seen in the light. This was a remarkable revelation in that he saw the redemption of the dead of all ages. He exercised the gift of seership and saw things not visible to the natural eye. He saw with an eye of faith and witnessed spiritual reality by the power of the Holy Spirit. There are great lessons to be learned from this. No matter how well we know the word of the Lord, we ought to remain receptive and responsive to new truth, clearer insights, hidden messages, and powerful promptings. This is the bedrock of this church. We can seek and gain wisdom, desire and discover new things, believe, receive answers to our questions, and ask for and receive clarification to overcome our confusion. There is a type and pattern in this. We ought to be a people that search, ponder, and pray. We need to reflect and meditate on the word of the Lord. He will show us things we had not previously considered. This knowledge will uplift and edify us. It will also help others as we share it in appropriate ways. The law of the Lord is discovered through feasting on His word and delighting in His doctrines.

BIND THE LORD

I am grateful that "I, the Lord, am bound when ye do what I say; but when ye do not what I say, ye have no promise" (Doctrine and Covenants 82:10). We are told that the leading brethren were to be bound by a bond and covenant. Their stewardship was one of managing the Lord's resources in a fair way according to the Lord's law. So, this was the new commandment that was given to them, so that they would know what the Lord required of them. These commandments were directives on how they were to act, to perform their labors. This performance, according to the Lord's law, would prepare them for salvation. The law of the Lord is critically important to any discussion of how souls are to be saved. Sometimes people artificially try to separate what the law requires from what is in the interest of caring for people. I believe the Lord combines these two ideas so that they are not in competition with each other. They are cohesive. Further, we are instructed that the Lord is bound (tied, obligated, constrained) when we keep His directions and observe His commandments. In keeping His law, we have the promise of the fulfillment of His word. We will be blessed. There is no abdication of this responsibility by the Lord. On the other hand, if we do not keep His directives, then He is not obligated to bless us with the connected rewards that would otherwise have accrued to us. How important it is, therefore, that we observe to do His will, especially in the context of our covenants. When we do this, we are tied to Him in such a way that He has mandated Himself to honor. We are not simply bound to be blessed, we are bound to the Lord Himself, linked to His covenant, united with His commands, sealed to His word, connected to His law, and forged to His promises.

CONCLUSION

If we see divine law as inextricably bound up with God's goodness and grace, we will be much more likely to desire to obey it. Love and law are not mutually exclusive—rather they are two sides of the same coin. They really cannot be separated from each other. God is not endeavoring to exercise unrighteous dominion over us. Rather, the very nature of His leadership is good, beneficial, and beautiful. To move away from the requirement to know and keep divine law is to slip into spiritual apathy, fear, and hostility toward things divine. True obedience to God is always accompanied by an outpouring of genuine love for Him, for us, and for others.

9

REVELATORY RICHES

In this chapter I discuss how the overflowing revelations of the Restoration bring us to a new life in Christ.

When you have good news, it is almost certain you will want to share it with someone, especially someone you care about. In like manner, our great God is a sharer of secrets and a dispenser of knowledge. It is not His purpose to keep His knowledge to Himself. Rather, He is eager to share His understanding with us as we are prepared to receive it. He is like the earthly father and mother who delight in seeing the happiness of their children when they awake on Christmas morning to discover the presents that are specifically chosen for them. He rejoices to uncover mysteries to the understanding of His children. He wants us to be endowed with comprehensive knowledge of His plans and purposes. The treasures of the Lord are His children and His knowledge. It is no wonder that both these treasures come together in the work of the Lord. He seeks to bestow His treasures of knowledge upon us as soon as we are ready and willing to receive them. To become aware of the wise revelations of God is to be rich in time and eternity. This is also to suggest that to not have the knowledge of God revealed to you is to be in a state of spiritual poverty. God does not want any of His children to remain in this state of impoverishment. Rather, He wants each of His children to enjoy the abundance of eternal riches. To move from a state of spiritual poverty to one of spiritual abundance is obviously to find life in a new measure.

God is a being of bounteous abundance. He owns all things and has all power. He is willing and eager to share everything with us—His love, knowledge, power, opportunities, wealth, and joy. He shares His children with us. Think of it—He shares His greatest delights with us. He shares His most wonderful treasures with us—His beloved children are His precious treasures. We get to share our time, lives, and experiences with the people around us. God seeks to teach us of His ways, works, and wonders. We can learn so many useful things in this mortal probation. We can learn to love, to lift, to receive, to serve, and to bless. We can learn to heal, to share, to believe, and to grow. We can learn patience and purity; courage and bravery; mercy and magnanimity.

God wants to bless us daily, deeply, and constantly. He delights to bless us. We are blessed by obedience, guided by truth, warned by wisdom, comforted by consolations, protected by power, and renewed by revelation. We are enriched by acquiring rich treasures of revelation, gaining ever expanding knowledge, learning truths that transform us, seeing powerful perspectives that shape our attitudes and actions, engaging in covenants that protect us from distraction, and feeling a profound sense of peace that all will be well during our most dark experiences. As God uncovers His mysteries to us, we will see the previously unseen, hear the unheard, feel the unfelt, believe the unproven, learn the unlearned, know the unknown, and hope the unhoped. This will inspire us to love the unloved, bless the unblessed, heal the unhealed, save the unsaved, and do the undone.

PRECIOUS PRECEPTS OF THE HOLY GHOST

The promptings and assurances of the Holy Spirit are not trite. His teachings are vital, His communications central, and His comforts essential.

"Yea, behold, I will tell you in your mind and in your heart, by the Holy Ghost, which shall come upon you and which shall dwell in your heart. Now, behold, this is the spirit of revelation" (Doctrine and Covenants 8:2–3). This is the Lord's way of teaching us how He will manifest the truth to us. It will involve communication to both our mind and heart. In other words, it will involve personal sharing of divine truths between God and us individually. It will impact our thoughts and our feelings. It will give us new and beneficial ideas. It will also bestow upon us feelings of light, warmth, comfort, and rejoicing. Our very desires will improve as they become more spiritually grounded. The Holy Ghost wants to reach us, connect with us, share with us, and help us to see new ways of being. The personal revelation that will come to us from the Comforter will be needful, important, and crucial to our spiritual safety and development. His companionship will provide us with a core relationship in mortality. He will teach us, enlighten us, reveal things to us, console us, and warn us of danger. The things He teaches will be significant to our souls.

> And now, verily, verily, I say unto thee, put your trust in that Spirit which leadeth to do good—yea, to do justly, to walk humbly, to judge righteously; and this is my Spirit.
>
> Verily, verily, I say unto you, I will impart unto you of my Spirit, which shall enlighten your mind, which shall fill your soul with joy;
>
> And then shall ye know, or by this shall you know, all things whatsoever you desire of me, which are pertaining unto things of righteousness, in faith believing in me that you shall receive. (Doctrine and Covenants 11:12–14)

We are herein instructed to trust the invitations of the Spirit. He will not mislead us. His promptings will be for us to do what is right, to remember our dependence on God, to discern between light and darkness. His sharing with us will instruct us and bring us genuine peace and happiness. Our righteous desires must be rooted in the spirit of revelation for them to truly succeed.

"Behold, this is your work, to keep my commandments, yea, with all your might, mind and strength. Seek not to declare my word, but first seek to obtain my word, and then shall your tongue be loosed; then, if you desire, you shall have my Spirit and my word, yea, the power of God unto the convincing of men" (Doctrine and Covenants 11:20–21). The Lord has promised us that if we desire to have His Spirit with us and to know His word, then we will have divine power to do His will. This convincing power will be a powerful asset in the Lord's work. What does this convincing power do? It enables us to preach and teach the word of God in such a manner that others are touched, interested, moved, awakened, and startled. It convinces others to believe in God, trust His promises, keep His laws, endure challenges, persist in serving others, and stay the spiritual course. His convincing power is far more than intellectual or academic. Rather, it moves others to acts of righteousness.

"Deny not the spirit of revelation, nor the spirit of prophecy, for wo unto him that denieth these things" (Doctrine and Covenants 11:25). Rather than rejecting revelation and spurning spirituality, we are commanded to believe in divine inspiration and accept divine teaching. The Holy Ghost can help us to see differently, feel newly, search intently, and act obediently. The Holy Ghost is a revelator. He loves to teach good doctrine, share profound insights, and lead willing souls by means of divine guidance. The Spirit testifies of the truth and we are touched, edified, and moved. I have been strongly interested in the influence of the Holy Ghost for a long time. I note that His influence is transforming. He allows us to see with new eyes the marvelous truths of eternity. As the third member of the Godhead, His ability to communicate truth to us is pronounced and profound. His impressions are not easily forgotten or ignored. His friendship is true and helpful to us.

TREMENDOUS TEACHINGS OF THE LIVING PROPHETS AND APOSTLES

In 2015, my brother Michael and I attended a leadership meeting in Edinburgh, Scotland, with Elder Jeffrey R. Holland. When Elder Holland reached the stand, he blew a kiss to us all. This was electric preaching, a message of love without words. I am an emotional person and this got me welling up! He taught us powerfully of how our righteousness can vicariously bless others while preserving their agency simultaneously. He bore a tremendous testimony. He then blessed us. I felt as if his hands were on my head and he was giving me an individual blessing. This meant much to me, as my loved ones and I really needed that blessing at that time. He gave us a charge to bless others through the blessing he gave to us. I was so completely moved to tears I could not even sing the concluding hymn. Afterward, when I approached Elder Holland to greet him, I simply looked into his eyes and said, "Elder Holland, we love you." He looked right back at me and responded, "We love you too." I continue to be blessed, humbled, and overwhelmed by the outpouring of love and joy I felt that day. Such is the powerful impact of true Apostles upon the people of God.

BEAUTIFUL BOUNTIES OF THE BOOK OF MORMON

The Book of Mormon is a doctrinal marvelous work and a wonder. It is given to us as a pure indicator that God is serious about enriching our lives endlessly. "And if there were preaching which was sacred, or revelation which was great, or prophesying, that I should . . . touch upon them" (Jacob 1:4). These are days of fulfillment of prophecy by power. The Book of Mormon, which is written for our day, indeed contains sacred revelation of Christ, great preaching of truth, and wonderful prophecies regarding latter day marvels. It has power to heal the wounded soul. It directs us, guides us, inspires us, teaches us, comforts us, and blesses us. It establishes our faith, enriches every part of our lives, and provides an anchor to our immortal souls. If we want a deep and lasting faith that will weather every storm, then we need to build our lives on the divine truths contained in this book of books.

President Benson said, "I have a vision of homes alerted, of classes alive, and of pulpits aflame with the spirit of Book of Mormon messages."[1] In this sense, the Book of Mormon is intended to bring us new life—we are to be more alert, more attentive, more tuned in,

---

1   Ezra Taft Benson, "Flooding the Earth with the Book of Mormon, October 1988 general conference, https://www.churchofjesuschrist.org/study/general-conference/1988/10/flooding-the-earth-with-the-book-of-mormon?lang=eng.

more passionate, and more engaged about the Lord's work by dwelling on Book of Mormon moments, messages, and meanings. The Book of Mormon is God's good word. It is full of doctrinal clarity. It can transform us in powerful ways. The marvelous messages of this book of books will bring strong spiritual truth into our lives. As we study, learn, live, and teach the doctrine of Christ in the Book of Mormon, tremendous power flows into our lives to perceive truth, discern light, and lay up heavenly treasures. "Behold, great and marvelous are the works of the Lord. How unsearchable are the depths of the mysteries of him; and it is impossible that man should find out all his ways. And no man knoweth of his ways save it be revealed unto him; wherefore, brethren, despise not the revelations of God" (Jacob 4:8). We truly have a good and generous God who is eager to share His treasures of knowledge with us. He wants to reveal His mysteries. We simply need to be willing to ask Him in faith and have the courage to act on His answers.

"And now, behold, I say unto you, and I would that ye should remember, that God is merciful unto all who believe on his name; therefore he desireth, in the first place, that ye should believe, yea, even on his word" (Alma 32:22). We are invited to believe in God—to accept the reality of His goodness, greatness, and generosity. We are to trust in God—to place faith in His promises, powers, and perfection—especially when it seems hard to do. We are to remember God—to recollect and reflect on His word, wonders, and works. We are to love God—to feel deep appreciation for Him and to show loyalty to His plans and purposes. We are to know that His words reflect His greatness and grandeur. His words can be trusted and followed.

"And after this manner do they bear record: The eye hath never seen, neither hath the ear heard, before, so great and marvelous things as we saw and heard Jesus speak unto the Father; And no tongue can speak, neither can there be written by any man, neither can the hearts of men conceive so great and marvelous things as we both saw and heard Jesus speak; and no one can conceive of the joy which filled our souls at the time we heard him pray for us unto the Father" (3 Nephi 17:16–17). Even though we may have experienced wonderful things in the past such as hearing uplifting music, seeing beautiful art, reading poignant poetry, or learning wonderful truths, all of this is but a prelude to what God has in store for us. There are astonishing things yet to be discovered, amazing words waiting to be heard, precious feelings soon to be felt, astounding sights shortly to be seen, and wonderful places yet to go to. The wisdom of God far surpasses that of man. His plan is a perfect plan of progress for each one of us personally. As we come to experience the great love that He has for us we are transformed. This is the path to true happiness and deep joy. What lies ahead for us is more than we can presently conceive of.

DELIGHTFUL DIADEMS OF THE DOCTRINE AND COVENANTS

In our own day, the Lord has revealed many great and precious truths that amaze, astonish, and comfort us. "But now hold your peace; study my word which hath gone forth among the children of men, and also study my word which shall come forth among the children of men, or that which is now translating, . . . and then shall all things be added thereto" (Doctrine and Covenants 11:22). God has invited us to place our priorities on the things of eternal value. These do not consist of worldly fame, fortune, and the accolades of a fading moment. Worldly riches have transitory value, but the things of God are of infinite worth: "Seek not for riches but for wisdom; and, behold, the mysteries of God shall be unfolded unto you, and then shall you be made rich. Behold, he that hath eternal life is rich" (Doctrine and Covenants 11:7). For God to declare that those with eternal life are rich speaks volumes. That means that by the standard of measurement God uses, these blessed persons are rich in His eyes. That must give us some indication of the scope and scale of the riches involved. Given that those riches will consist of divine wisdom, knowing the mysteries of God and being with God forever, it is difficult to see how anything else could possibly be greater. "Behold . . . the riches of eternity are mine to give" (Doctrine and Covenants 67:2).

Notice that the Lord speaks herein of the riches of eternity. The riches of this life are one thing—and a great thing at that if we use them to do good—but the riches of eternity would seem to indicate something far beyond earthly riches. These riches have to do with eternal rewards and everlasting joys. These involve land, love, laughter, life, and much more. God is no stingy employer. He seeks to reward us bounteously: "For thus saith the Lord—I, the Lord, am merciful and gracious unto those who fear me, and delight to honor those who serve me in righteousness and in truth unto the end. Great shall be their reward and eternal shall be their glory" (Doctrine and Covenants 76:5–6). Indeed, He is magnanimously merciful and generously gracious to those who love, reverence, respect, and honor Him. What marvelous blessings He bestows upon us in terms of knowledge, understanding, wisdom, ability, peace, hope, love, and joy—to name but a few—when we draw close to Him with diligent devotion. We never regret following our great God. The benefit of knowing of His loving kindness extends forever.

"Treasure up in your minds continually the words of life" (Doctrine and Covenants 84:85). I find it deeply interesting that the Lord uses the phrase "words of life" to refer to treasure. We are being taught that the words of the gospel are a treasure to us. The gospel is a message about life, what it means, what it involves, and how it can be precious to us. I understand this to mean that the Lord will help us value life because He will make that life abundant—both now and forever. Our minds are to be full of the knowledge of the Lord, His views, His insights, His perspectives, and His mindset. "Draw near unto me and I will draw near unto you; seek me diligently and ye shall find me; ask, and ye shall receive; knock, and it shall be opened unto you" (Doctrine and Covenants 88:63). This is a divine invitation from the Lord of Life Himself. He beckons us to come to Him, know Him, love Him, be like Him, and be with Him. As we voluntarily choose to move closer to Him, He will teach us, train us, guide us, lead us, comfort us, and console us. He will bless us with bounties. How precious this is. We are in the driving seat in terms of our closeness to God. We have the agency necessary to learn of Him, follow Him, move close to Him, and become more like Him. It is our legacy, potential, and destiny. It is up to us. He will not compel us. However, He will invite, persuade, encourage, entice, and ask us to draw close to Him. God can be found. He is eager to listen to us, speak to us, comfort us, guide us, direct us, bless us, heal us, and help us to grow. This is his very work and glory. He lives, loves, counsels, and strengthens. This I am grateful to know with glad certainty.

"God shall give unto you knowledge by his Holy Spirit, yea, by the unspeakable gift of the Holy Ghost, that has not been revealed since the world was until now . . . a time to come in the which nothing shall be withheld, whether there be one God or many gods, they shall be manifest" (Doctrine and Covenants 121:26–33). God desires to share His secrets with us so that they are no longer mysteries but rather are "plain and precious." I delight in His revealed truths given to us through the Prophet Joseph Smith in these latter days and in the outpouring that continues institutionally and individually in the kingdom of God. I find the Doctrine and Covenants insightful, amazing, educational, inspiring, comforting, motivating, and captivating.

POWERFUL PRINCIPLES OF THE PEARL OF GREAT PRICE

Many rich truths in the Pearl of Great Price can reorient us, empower us, embolden us, and fortify us. We can be educated in the laws of the Lord, the principles of power, and the commandments that lead to covenants. "And I saw the Lord; and he stood before my face, and he talked with me, even as a man talketh one with another, face to face; and he said unto me: Look, and I will show unto thee the world for the space of many generations" (Moses 7:4). These are the powerful words of the prophet Enoch. He spoke from personal experience of a God that can be seen, heard, touched, loved, and known. The God of Glory is no mythical fantasy. Rather, He is a living reality. As we believe in Him, come to Him, and teach about Him, we will find a newness of life. What better time is there to do this than now?

Joseph Smith said, "At length I came to the conclusion that I must either remain in darkness and confusion, or else I must do as James directs, that is, ask of God. I at length came to the determination to "ask of God," concluding that if he gave wisdom to them that lacked wisdom, and would give liberally, and not upbraid, I might venture" (JS—History 1:13). When we are in confusion, we can ask God for clarity. When we are in darkness, we can ask God for light. When we are lacking wisdom, we can ask God for wisdom. We can ask God for comfort, knowledge, peace, and understanding, and He will shower down these blessings upon us in a form that will teach us, stretch us, develop us, and help us grow. We can always ask of God for guidance in important matters. He will always answer.

Concerning the First Vision, Joseph Smith said:

> I saw a pillar of light exactly over my head, above the brightness of the sun, which descended gradually until it fell upon me. It no sooner appeared than I found myself delivered from the enemy which held me bound. When the light rested upon me I saw two Personages, whose brightness and glory defy all description, standing above me in the air. One of them spake unto me, calling me by name and said, pointing to the other—This is My Beloved Son. Hear Him!" (JS—History 1:16–17)

This revelatory experience of the Prophet Joseph Smith certifies that the heavens are open in these latter days. God speaks, angels minister, authority has been given, power has been granted, scripture has been penned, miracles have abounded, prophets have been called, and the work of salvation has been declared. These are truly days of great prophecy and marvelous power. And the best is yet to come for each of us. "And whoso treasureth up my word, shall not be deceived" (JS—Matthew 1:37). To treasure the divine word is to place it in value above everything else. The word of God is safety to the soul, comfort to the heart, courage to the spirit and joy to our being. As we follow His word we will discern between truth and error. We will know joy and rejoicing. We will withstand the day of evil and temptation. We will be protected from danger and keep our promises to always honor God.

TRANSCENDENT TRUTHS OF THE OLD AND NEW TESTAMENTS

I have loved the stories and truths of the Bible since I was a child. I do not remember a time when I was unimpressed by the accounts of miracles in these books. Rather, I accepted these as divine accounts that inspired me to become better as a believer. The core truths of these testaments—or covenants—are that God is the creator and upholder of the heaven and earth. He created humankind for a purpose.

> In the beginning God created the heaven and the earth. (Genesis 1:1)
>
> And God said, Let us make man in our image, after our likeness: and let them have dominion over the fish of the sea, and over the fowl of the air, and over the cattle, and over all the earth, and over every creeping thing that creepeth upon the earth.
>
> So God created man in his *own* image, in the image of God created he him; male and female created he them.
>
> And God blessed them, and God said unto them, Be fruitful, and multiply, and replenish the earth, and subdue it: and have dominion over the fish of the sea, and over the fowl of the air, and over every living thing that moveth upon the earth. (Genesis 1:26–28)

We are created in the divine image, the likeness of the Supreme Being. How stunning is that? This truth is powerful. We are the children of God. This is a divine identity. We are guided by sacred texts to sense that we are far more than any identity that might be given to us in this world. We are more than titles, status, achievements. We are greater than our weakness, inadequacies, and deficiencies. We are sons and daughters of the divine. This powerful truth can motivate us to do hard things. We are well advised to fix this thought in our minds and hearts and know that we are children with a promise.

God makes covenants with us, and as we keep His commandments, He blesses us with both mortal and eternal blessings. He always wants to have a people of promise who honor Him and receive honor from Him. God said to Noah: "And I will establish my covenant with you; neither shall all flesh be cut off any more by the waters of a flood; neither shall there any more be a flood to destroy the earth. And God said, This *is* the token of the covenant which I make between me and you and every living creature that *is* with you, for perpetual generations:" (Genesis 9:11–13). We also learn that the Father's Only Begotten Son was born to save the covenant people of the Lord from all enemies. Eventually, this world will be refined, renewed, purified, and sanctified into a place of Godly glory. The scriptures are not intended to be lifeless words, dead ideas, or even just meaningful metaphors. Rather, the words are to leap off the page and into our hearts and minds. The words are to be brought to life by the power of the Holy Ghost—this is how they acquire the persuasive, transformative, and renewing force to change our lives.

Consider the verse that opened this dispensation: "If any of you lack wisdom, let him ask of God, that giveth to all men liberally, and upbraideth not; and it shall be given him" (James 1:5). This scripture—when activated by the power of the Holy Ghost—moved Joseph Smith to pray in faith in the sacred Grove. He was struck with a sense of the potent importance of this invitation—asking God suddenly made tremendous sense to him. He did so with pure confidence. He was deeply rewarded for doing so. Not only did he receive the answer to his prayer, but it was also what initiated this great and marvelous latter-day work of restoration which has blessed millions all over the world. As we follow this example and pray in faith we will be divinely led.

INSPIRATIONAL INSIGHTS OF THE HOLY TEMPLE

I have heard the temple described as the spiritual university of the Church. There is a tremendous insight in that designation. A university is a place of advanced learning, of higher instruction in the things of the mind. God's university is much greater. It impacts not only the mind but also the heart, spirit, and body. It touches all the senses and awakens all the faculties of our being. As the School of the Prophets existed to prepare individuals to represent God to the world, so the temple exists to prepare men and women to become royalty to God in the worlds without end that exist in the eternities.

I received my endowment in the Frankfurt Germany Temple on February 19, 1991. I wrote the following relating to this in my personal journal:

I was honestly shocked by the experience. I was transfixed and overwhelmed. I was struck by the magnanimous nature of God and what he had in store for me and all mankind. Our potential as Children of God is truly phenomenal. I was on a spiritual high the entire week. The blessings and opportunities offered in the Temple are utterly amazing, and great. The experience was life changing when I thought of what God was offering to me.

As the years have passed, I have come to understand to a much deeper degree how significant the knowledge acquired in the temple is. It is like a flowing river amid a parched desert. It is life renewing knowledge. In the holy temple we learn of the nature, plans, and purposes of the Almighty. We come to comprehend His character in a very meaningful way. We understand the Atonement of Christ with deeper personal awareness. We see behind the symbols, rites, and rituals to the meaning and significance of sacred events. The revelation there is so pointed, comprehensive, and life-affirming that we are altered in our fundamental posture to living when we receive all the ordinances and covenants of that holy place. When we are properly instructed, endowed, and sealed in the temple we gain power to live a Christlike life in a holistic, holy, and heavenly manner. We learn the patterns of thinking, acting, and becoming that are core to our ascent to eternal glory. The temple is indeed the house of God and His living, permeating, actuating, energizing, and transforming influence is felt there and suffuses through us completely.

ADDED UPON

Our Father in Heaven is purposely intent on helping us to develop, grow, increase, expand, learn, and become more than we already are. Consider the below verse from the book of Abraham:

> Now the Lord had shown unto me, Abraham, the intelligences that were organized before the world was; and among all these there were many of the noble and great ones; . . . And we will prove them herewith, to see if they will do all things whatsoever the Lord their God shall command them;

And they who keep their first estate shall be added upon; and they who keep not their first estate shall not have glory in the same kingdom with those who keep their first estate; and they who keep their second estate shall have glory added upon their heads for ever and ever. (Abraham 3:22–26)

This is powerfully instructive. I note that the spirits we are discussing are all the spirits. All the premortal spirits who kept their first estate were added upon by coming into mortality and receiving a body. If they did not do this, they could not have been added upon with the treasure of mortal experience and learning. The spirits who did not keep their first estate were only the devil and his angels, who were denied bodies and progression. Obviously, even the telestial glory is an added upon kingdom of glory compared to outer darkness. Similarly, the spirits who eventually go to the terrestrial kingdom are added upon in mortality beyond what they otherwise would have been. Of course, those who go to the celestial kingdom clearly keep their second estate through their obedience to divine commandments, and we are told they are added upon in mortality and indeed forever and ever.

So, faithfulness at each stage of existence allows us to be "added upon" so that we reach the next stage and gain the opportunities unique to it. We can grow, develop, increase, expand, evolve, and develop. We can be magnified, added upon, enlarged, enhanced. We were added upon in premortality. We are further added upon in mortality. We are then additionally added upon in the eternities. This happens in the following way:

- Intelligences are clothed upon with a spirit body. Spirit bodies are added upon with a temporal mortal body. Mortal bodies are added upon with glorified resurrected bodies (see Doctrine and Covenants 130:22).
- Premortal glory is added upon by mortal glory, which is then expanded into eternal glory (see Doctrine and Covenants 93:36 and 130:18–19. Glory is intelligence, light, and truth.)
- Spirit experience is magnified through mortal experience, which is then blessed with eternal experience (see Doctrine and Covenants 122:7).

- God's family leads to mortal families, which then become eternal families (see Doctrine and Covenants 130:2 Eternal glory through coupling between a male and female soul).

This is how the works of the Father are glorified in that His children are added upon in knowledge, wisdom, understanding, power, capacity, and might. What is also interesting is that the noble and great, who were described as good and chosen in premortality, become leaders in mortality. It is significant that they are added upon in mortality and into the eternities. So, the fact that they are noble, good, and great in premortality is not the end of their progress and development. They are enhanced through their mortal experience and improvement. Notice also that one of these spirits was like unto God in premortality. This is clearly Jehovah, who was superbly intelligent and gifted in that situation. However, He was also to be added upon in mortality with a physical body and a resurrected body in the eternities. His perfection would then be achieved, and He would receive all glory, power, and dominion in heaven and on earth. Clearly, even He was to be added upon.

We also have this great instruction in this verse: "Whatever principle of intelligence we attain unto in this life, it will rise with us in the resurrection. And if a person gains more knowledge and intelligence in this life through his diligence and obedience than another, he will have so much the advantage in the world to come" (Doctrine & Covenants 130:18–19). That is to say that our intelligence in mortality is not fixed. To attain unto a certain level means we can grow, increase, and expand in our intelligence. We can improve our spiritual gift, enlarge our spiritual talent, and gain more knowledge than we start with. Through faithful devotion we expand in capacity and ability. Doing so will give us a benefit for the life to come. How important it is therefore to desire to rise to a celestial principle of intelligence in mortality. This can be accomplished through faithfully giving heed to the word of God, to hearkening to His divine directions. This is the Liahona lesson. So, we are not static both within spiritual realms and between them. It is anticipated that we will seek to improve our goodness, develop our greatness, increase our capacity for learning, develop our nobility, further our understanding, and magnify our comprehension of God and His ways. Now is always a good time to gain an enhanced education in the ways of the Lord. God will continue to work with us to add to our glory as we are seeking, desiring, and intent on growing.

CONCLUSION

The restored gospel of Jesus Christ contains a phenomenal array of truths that are to be learned line upon line. They provide understanding, hope, consolation, and a reason to rejoice. As we are accepting and sustaining of this Restoration, we can continue to be true to the powerful distinctiveness of this restored truth. Our loyalty to the Restoration in the crucible of affliction of our refiner's fire will transform us into strong, brave souls. There is no message on the earth more empowering, soul-satisfying, or edifying than this.

So where will we go for treasures and riches of eternity if not to the restored truth? I am vividly reminded of the key importance of both institutional and personal revelation, that we are truly led by a prophet, and the crucial importance of Jesus Christ as the anointed Savior of the World. How blessed we are to have such clear and powerful leadership in these latter days. As we soak in the deep waters of revelation and immerse ourselves in the cleansing baths of revealed religion, we will sense that revelation always trumps tradition. We will know that the revelation-based rock is the only firm foundation on which to build a life of lasting faith.

> And now, my sons, remember, remember that it is upon the rock of our Redeemer, who is Christ, the Son of God, that ye must build your foundation; that when the devil shall send forth his mighty winds, yea, his shafts in the whirlwind, yea, when all his hail and his mighty storm shall beat upon you, it shall have no power over you to drag you down to the gulf of misery and endless wo, because of the rock upon which ye are built, which is a sure foundation, a foundation whereon if men build they cannot fall. (Helaman 5:12)

10

IN THE STRENGTH AND POWER OF THE LORD

The Lord expects us to use our physical strength, mental knowledge, passionate feeling, and righteous character to face challenges and surmount difficulties. However, He is both willing and able to assist us, empower us, enable us, strengthen us, and bless us. In the strength of the Lord we can find needed help, peaceful healing, restoration to health, restful harmony, and deeply embedded happiness. The Lord asks us to shoulder our burdens and move forward—even when circumstances are challenging. He wants us to rise in righteousness, which allows us to do the following:

- Carry on despite physical limitations
- Survive and surmount emotional heartbreak
- Transcend psychological setbacks
- Ascend above spiritual dangers and
- Triumph over social misunderstandings

This overcoming needs to be of a durable nature, as this victory needs to be repeated regularly, sincerely, and conscientiously. The quality to face and overcome challenges is admirable. It is impressive, remarkable, noteworthy, and wonderful. The Lord is ever available to encourage us onward, forward, and upward in this most important journey.

DIVINE STRENGTH IN TIMES OF REFINING

I have faced many trials, tests, troubles, and tribulations. On one occasion, I served as a branch president for almost ten years. This was a challenging and rewarding role. It was a genuinely bittersweet experience and an emotional roller coaster. It was extremely difficult at times. At other times I loved it, and was very enthusiastic and energetic. At times I was tired due to the constant incessantness of it all. The demands seemed never ending. My desires were tested, as were my love, knowledge, preparation, and patience. God knew what I went through during this time given that all aspects of my life were facing various challenges—my family relationships, work, Church calling, health, and personal life. In fact, it was the deepest refiner's fire of my life because I was facing eight major life challenges at one time. Ironically, even though I knew that life was a school of testing, I found myself expecting my life to be much easier than it had been. It turned out to be one trial after another but also one precious lesson after another. I continued to face many difficulties and had many wonderful opportunities. I learned so much. I would not trade that education for anything. The things I comprehended softened my heart and strengthened my resolve to stay the course, keep the faith, and travel the distance. I learned to love the Lord and the people much more personally, richly, and deeply.

The support from God was real, regular, and renewing. He was a tremendous source of strength to me. He guided me, consoled me, comforted me, inspired me, strengthened me, enlightened me, encouraged me, and empowered me. God was with me in powerful and reassuring ways. My life is a precious tapestry, a great mosaic of meaning. I have mountains to climb, rivers to cross, and contributions to offer. I will continue onward and upward. I believe the best is yet to come for me and all who follow God. There is a special place in heaven for those who suffer and lay their burdens on the Lord. Life is for living and is good. God is good. May God bless us all and help us to be good and righteous, even in tragedy, especially in difficulty.

I remember a time when my mother was passing through a refiner's fire of monumental proportions. Someone had tried to give her a boost by commenting to her on the value and importance of her name—which happens to be Ella. My mother responded that this was rubbish. When I heard this, I understood that we often are quick to see the supposed negative attributes in ourselves, especially when circumstances are not what we wish they were, but it is usually more difficult to see the good. I wrote her a note saying the following:

> You are not rubbish. Remember the story of Cinderella. Her name was Ella. The cinder part of the name only came because of the cinders from the fire that impacted her when she was working hard to serve her ungrateful sisters and step-mother. It was intended as a term of derision, but in fact has become world renowned as indicating that she was, in fact, a diamond in the rough. She was beautiful—partially because of the fiery affliction she had passed through. This is really the whole point of the story. This applies to you too. We must always remember and never forget that the furnace of affliction enables people to become great—far greater than they would be without it. Rubbish is intended for the trash bin or the fire. What you are is someone passing through the fire to become shined, polished, and ready for glory. Cinderella went to the ball—after passing through the fire of affliction and not before it!

I relate this story to indicate how easy it is to be downcast and downtrodden as we face the constant challenges of a fallen world. Mortality is not an easy experience for anyone. However—and this is the critical point—we sometimes travel this mortal journey without a full awareness of the help and strength that are available to us through the Son of God. A little reflection on this doctrine can yield great insights, encouragement, and comfort.

CHRIST IS GREAT

"Listen to the voice of Jesus Christ, your Redeemer, the Great I AM, whose arm of mercy hath atoned for your sins" (Doctrine and Covenants 29:1–2). Christ is the Great I AM, not simply the "I was" or the "I will be." He is always present, ever ready, and continually available to help us. He is constantly able to bless, lift, strengthen, and guide us. As we draw close to Him, He will draw close to us. He will empower, inspire, encourage, motivate, and uphold us. We need to hear His words and follow His counsel—this is the path to true greatness. "Wherefore, men are free according to the flesh; and all things are given them which are expedient unto man. And they are free to choose liberty and eternal life, through the great Mediator of all men" (2 Nephi 2:27). This is powerful doctrine. Christ is a great person, a great example, a great Savior. He is a great advocate for us to have. There is none greater. We always have a choice between good and evil. Through the infinite power of Jesus the Christ we can always choose to live righteously, or having fallen, we can choose to repent. We must never underestimate this truth. We should never let the adversary convince us that worldly darkness is stronger than godly light. This is a marvelous certainty.

CHRIST IS MIGHTY

We have a mighty God who is relentlessly able to do His stunning work. When I am confronted by glaring inadequacy and transparent weakness in myself I find the following passage especially reassuring: "Yea, cry unto him for mercy; for he is mighty to save" (Alma 34:18–27). The Messiah is mighty to save—not weak to save, not incapable to save, not unable to save, and not reluctant to save. He is willing and eager to save us. It is useful to note that this salvation does not just concern itself with the eternities but is also very much concerned with the present and with all aspects of our lives. Does the Lord care about our health, relationships, careers, finances, or living conditions? The answer is an unmitigated yes. The Lord wants us to progress and prosper in every important area of our lives. I learned this lesson powerfully some years ago in a work assignment I faced. It was a particularly difficult matter to deal with. I tried every way I could conceive of to solve the issue and could not do so. I talked to others, and they were equally unable to suggest a workable solution. After failing to come up with a resolution, I asked the Lord to assist me. That very night He revealed to me a simple but effective solution to the issue that I had never even considered. I was greatly impressed by how simple and yet clever the solution was. I was able to apply the insight and solve the problem. I continued to use this "revelation" for yet other challenges I would face in work. The Lord is far more intelligent than I had given Him credit for. He is also far more willing to assist us than we might suppose. If a problem is important to us personally, then it is important to the Lord. He can and will help us in all important aspects of our lives. His power is practical and potent. We are truly sons and daughters of God. As children of a King we are inheritors of a precious promise—that our lives are of deep significance to God and that He is both willing and able to endow us with power. This power allows us to appreciate, envision, learn, grow, develop, contribute, bless, and serve. Remember that we are powerful through God's power. We are wonderful through God's wonder. We are capable through God's capability. We are mighty through God's might.

CHRIST IS STRONG

Do we suppose that Christ is any less interested in our welfare today or that He is any less capable of blessing us? Even if we have been casual about our commitments in the past or even hostile to the Lord, we can turn around and He will forgive us and bless us. He is truly magnanimous in mercy. I love the words of the prophet Isaiah concerning the power that God gives to those who trust in Him:

> Hast thou not known? hast thou not heard, that the everlasting God, the Lord, the Creator of the ends of the earth, fainteth not, neither is weary? there is no searching of his understanding. He giveth power to the faint; and to them that have no might he increaseth strength.
> Even the youths shall faint and be weary, and the young men shall utterly fall: But they that wait upon the Lord shall renew their strength; they shall mount up with wings as eagles; they shall run, and not be weary; and they shall walk, and not faint. (Isaiah 40:28–31)

This promise is sure and certain. As we keep His word, we will not be eternally disappointed. God is our power, strength, hope, and joy. He is not distant, asleep, tired, uninterested, uncaring, or dead. He is mighty, majestic, and marvelous. While strong humans have muscles that eventually become weak and sharp humans have minds that eventually lose their sharpness, while mortal status is temporary, while human achievements gradually are forgotten, while human fame and fortune are transitory, we can be confident that this cannot and will not happen to God. He lives, speaks, loves, and empowers. There is nothing truly needful that He cannot do. No matter how weak or strong we are, He is stronger than us. He is smarter, braver, wiser, and more powerful than us. He will heal us, help us, and hold us. We need to trust in Him deeply, daily, and desperately. God be thanked for His matchless goodness, patience, long-suffering, kindness, mercy, compassion, knowledge, and power. He is the endless supply of all that is good and beautiful. We can believe in Him now and forever.

"Yea, I know that I am nothing . . . , but I will boast of my God, for in his strength I can do all things; yea, behold, many mighty miracles we have wrought in this land, for which we will praise his name forever" (Alma 26:12). It is appropriate to boast of the goodness, greatness, and generosity of God. None of us can say too much about His astounding strength. God is the Master of miracles, both small and large; past and present; simple and profound; gentle and gigantic. He is the doer of good deeds, the bringer of blessings, and the saver of souls. His power is over all the earth, embracing each one of us and encompassing all of us. His strength will not falter or fail, and our praise for Him is as a fountain of water that will never run dry. "Have not I commanded thee? Be strong and of a good courage; be not afraid, neither be thou dismayed: for the Lord, thy God is with thee whithersoever thou goest" (Joshua 1:9). We can know the true source of our strength—God. He is the undiluted, overarching, and constant source of strength in our lives. He is with us as we trudge through troubles, wrestle with worries, face the fires, deal with difficulties, and surmount suffering. He abides with us in times of loneliness, fear, sadness, disappointment, hardships, and loss. He compensates us, consoles us, comforts us, encourages us, and cheers for us.

CHRIST IS SURE

> And now, my sons, remember, remember that it is upon the rock of our Redeemer, who is Christ, the Son of God, that ye must build your foundation; that when the devil shall send forth his mighty winds, yea, his shafts in the whirlwind, yea, when all his hail and his mighty storm shall beat upon you, it shall have no power over you to drag you down to the gulf of misery and endless wo, because of the rock upon which ye are built, which is a sure foundation, a foundation whereon if men build they cannot fall. (Helaman 5:12)

Christ is the rock of ages, the rock of our salvation. We must build our foundation of faith on the solid rock of Christ, the living Son of God. Our Messiah is the sure, steadfast, and certain Savior. He abides, stays, and is loyal, definite, resolute, dependable, everlasting, reliable, constant, able, unchanging, powerful, eternal, enduring and rock solid. His word is His bond. His gospel is eternal. We can have total confidence, absolute reliance, determined clarity, and complete surety in the Lord's restored work. We are to learn how to be faithful, loyal, and steadfast in Him—no matter what. He is the only sure foundation. We can take comfort from the truth that those who build on this rock and remain built on that rock cannot fall. Not that they might not fall, but that they cannot. That is true.

CHRIST IS POWERFUL

"And now, my beloved brethren, I would that ye should come unto Christ, who is the Holy One of Israel, and partake of his salvation, and the power of his redemption. Yea, come unto him, and offer your whole souls as an offering unto him, and continue in fasting and praying, and endure to the end; and as the Lord liveth ye will be saved" (Omni 1:26). We have need to come to terms with the power of the Lord. He has the power to save us from weakness, sin, error, mistakes, and tragedy. To come unto Christ is to come unto a new life, a changed way of seeing the world, a fresh perspective, and a radically transformed way of being. It is to give ourselves the best possible opportunity for meaningful success in this world and the next. The doctrine of Christ is true, powerful, and everlasting. He is the way, truth, and life. In fact, there is no other way to happiness than His way. There is no Messiah other than Him. There is no other doctrine that brings peace to the soul except His. To come to Him unreservedly, wholeheartedly, deeply, longingly, and lastingly is to rejoice forevermore. There simply is no better type of life, no deeper joy, no more transcendent meaning, and no more powerful purpose than to come to Him, stay with Him, love Him, and bring others to Him. He lives, loves, heals, blesses, and saves. This is the one true reality of life.

"And ye may know that he is, by the power of the Holy Ghost; wherefore I would exhort you that ye deny not the power of God; for he worketh by power, according to the faith of the children of men, the same today and tomorrow, and forever" (Moroni 10:7). God works by power, capacity, ability, and strength. It is by His divine power that we experience miracles. It is by His great power that we experience spiritual promptings. It is by His marvelous power that we are healed, renewed, strengthened, blessed, and guided. Through the strong power of the Holy Ghost we know that God lives, speaks, works, intervenes, transforms, and saves. Let us not begin to doubt this but choose to believe it now and always. The power of men is as a feather in the wind—temporary, transitory, and timebound. The power of God is as the Mighty Wind. God has not lost His power to bless, heal, love, speak, and save. He is mighty. He is strong. His strength is excellent above all. When we sense that He has power that we do not, that He has power over our sins and our death, then we will perceive his power personally and majestically.

"And Christ hath said: If ye will have faith in me ye shall have power to do whatsoever thing is expedient in me" (Moroni 7:33). This faith in Christ needs to be more than just a general acknowledgment that He lives. It is fundamental to know that He has the ability and capacity to accomplish all sorts of wonderful things through us. Whatever the Lord designs for us to do can be done—as we develop faith in His specific traits and power—we can come to see this truth in a whole new light. This is what happens as we learn the true character of Christ. "When I think of the Book of Mormon, I think of the word power. The truths of the Book of Mormon have the power to heal, comfort, restore, succor, strengthen, console and cheer our souls."[1] I too feel this way about the Book of Mormon. The reason it carries this power is it is loyal to the Prince of Power—Jesus Christ. It teaches His doctrine, sustains His character, reveals His purposes, is loyal to His name, and promotes His cause. It teaches that we come to Christ through covenants. It is a book of truth. Power comes from the truth and light in Christ.

> I marveled, for I understood that the Savior spent about three years in his ministry among the Jews and those of the house of Israel, endeavoring to teach them the everlasting gospel and call them unto repentance;
>
> And yet, notwithstanding his mighty works, and miracles, and proclamation of the truth, in great power and authority, there were but few who hearkened to his voice, and rejoiced in his presence, and received salvation at his hands. (Doctrine and Covenants 138:25–26)

We can see the Savior's power in a spiritual way. Some persons during His mortal ministry were looking for the Messiah to be a warrior, a king, or a man of fame or fortune. They were looking for someone with worldly power—power to impress, the power of status, power of station. However, the Lord did not utilize that kind of power in His life. His was the power of truth, the power of righteousness, the power to heal the sick, to help people see things they previously had not seen. He used His power to love, to forgive enemies, to encourage others to change, to perform miracles, to bring about a change of heart within. The miracles of preaching the word of God in spellbinding fashion, softening hearts, forgiving sins, cleansing lepers, and raising the dead are far more impressive that the powers of influence manifested by the worldly wise.

---

[1] Russell M. Nelson, "The Book of Mormon: What Would Your Life Be Like without It?" October 2017 general conference, churchofjesuschrist.org/study/ensign/2017/11/saturday-afternoon-session/the-book-of-mormon-what-would-your-life-be-like-without-it?lang=eng.

PERSONS OF POWER

The Lord Jesus Christ is not jealous and possessive of His power. He wants to bless us with power to be instruments in His hands in assisting in His work of salvation. He endows us with power to do His will. As we learn, live, and share doctrine, we become persons of power. This is how we learn, grow, develop, expand, increase, and enlarge our abilities, interests, and capacities. "And as sure as the Lord liveth, so sure as many as believed, or as many as were brought to the knowledge of the truth, through the preaching of Ammon and his brethren, according to the spirit of revelation and of prophecy, and the power of God working miracles in them—yea, I say unto you, as the Lord liveth, as many of the Lamanites as believed in their preaching, and were converted unto the Lord, never did fall away" (Alma 23:6). So it is that Ammon and the other sons of Mosiah became persons of power in the work of the Lord. This was the power to do good, to preach truth, receive revelation, make prophecies, and work miracles. This was through the power of God in their lives. These messengers of mercy had the mighty power of the Lamb bestowed upon them so that they could defend the flocks of the king, endure difficulty, and preach with convincing power to the conversion of many souls. Such righteous persons of power are powerful internally and externally. They are good within and they can do good works. They obtain the mind of Christ by learning His ways. They also evidence that they wear the armor of the Lord and can act in godliness. To become such persons of power we need to access the power of the Lamb of God. That power will wash over us, purify us, fill us with love, restore our goodness, renew our faith, forgive our sins, and help us endure to the end.

Indeed, the power of the Lamb will come upon the covenant disciples of the Lord in the last days. They will be armed with God's power in a glorious manner: "And it came to pass that I, Nephi, beheld the power of the Lamb of God, that it descended upon the saints of the church of the Lamb, and upon the covenant people of the Lord, who were scattered upon all the face of the earth; and they were armed with righteousness and with the power of God in great glory" (1 Nephi 14:14). This is the covenantal power of

Christ, and through it we will be empowered to resist evil, endure persecution, acquire knowledge, increase our faith, display courage under fire, show deep love to others, and accomplish and perform all godly labors, no matter how challenging they might be. It is significant to remember the power available to us through ordinances and covenants. We need to covenant consciously with God—all three members of the Godhead are involved in true worship. We can gain spiritual power through ordinances and covenant connection. This is more than will power—it is God's power. The Lord leads thirsty men and women to living waters, not empty wells. Loyalty to sacred covenants connects us to the power of God:

- Power to endure afflictions (Doctrine and Covenants 24:8)
- Power to overcome (Doctrine and Covenants 63:20, 47)
- Power to endure all things (Moroni 7:45)
- Power to be diligent (Moroni 8:26)
- Power to endure God's presence (Doctrine and Covenants 84: 24; Moses 1:2)

As we gain closeness to the Lord in our homes, stakes, and temples, we become the people of the Lord, ready to build the Zion of the Lord. We will have energy to impact, influence, bless, help, transform, and inform others. This dynamic power can be ours. If our motives are pure, then we can do wonders. We will be clothed in all the comprehensive and complete elements of the Lord's armor—truth (which combats falsehood), righteousness (which defeats sin), faith (which surmounts fear and doubt), peace (which trumps war), spirit (which gives life), and salvation (which provides redemption and joy). This is a holistic covering of all the important parts of the body. This represents a full commitment to God and a total protection from evil and temptation. We are then able to proceed with spiritual confidence and resolute determination in all aspects of life.

FACING DIFFICULTIES WITH DIVINE HELP

What is the best way to face apparently overpowering burdens? When the forces arrayed against us increase, then it is wise to increase our level of resolve. We also need to increase our access to strength. This is done by relying on the great source of our strength—God. "And it came to pass that I, Nephi, said unto my father: I will go and do the things which the Lord hath commanded, for I know that the Lord giveth no commandments unto the children of men, save he shall prepare a way for them that they may accomplish the thing which he commandeth them" (1 Nephi 3:7). This was a faith-filled Nephi, an obedient Nephi, a committed and dedicated Nephi, a testimony-bearing Nephi, and an exemplary Nephi. We can follow his example by showing persistent devotion to God, especially in challenging circumstances. The circumstances around getting the plates were not easy, and there was no way Nephi could get them without doing difficult things. But God always works in way that will allow us to succeed if we follow His direction. If extra access to divine help is required, He will provide such. As we trust in Him and do the works of righteousness, then great results will inevitably follow.

"Now when our hearts were depressed, and we were about to turn back, behold, the Lord comforted us, and said: Go amongst thy brethren, the Lamanites, and bear with patience thine afflictions, and I will give unto you success" (Alma 26:27). We all face times of discouragement, fear, and opposition. No one can avoid the ups and downs of difficult circumstances. Not one of us is immune to pain, sadness, or disappointment. However, we have a perfect source to turn to in such times. We need to look to Him who is powerful, pure, and peaceful. Our mighty Messiah not only can help us, but He will do so—if we let Him. His promises are sure. His commitment is total. His strength is unending. He will bless us, sustain us, uphold us, empower us, befriend us, heal us, and transform us. God is love. God is power. God is real. God is both willing and able to bestow upon us every needed assistance—no matter what the difficulty is. God lives. God loves. God lifts. Never forget that He is the eternal and never-failing source of our knowledge, power, and strength. He lives.

"And it came to pass in the thirty and fourth year, in the first month, on the fourth day of the month, there arose a great storm, such an one as never had been known in all the land."

(3 Nephi 8:5). The Book of Mormon is more than historical—it is also prophetic. The physical storms we face today have an unusual intensity and frequency to them. Similarly, the spiritual storms we face now in this world surpass anything in history. Hence, the deep need we all have for heeding the prophetic word to remember the true source of our power—God. A turning back to God allows us to go forward in faith—regardless of the storms of the moment.

> And if thou shouldst be cast into the pit, or into the hands of murderers, and the sentence of death passed upon thee; if thou be cast into the deep; if the billowing surge conspire against thee; if fierce winds become thine enemy; if the heavens gather blackness, and all the elements combine to hedge up the way; and above all, if the very jaws of hell shall gape open the mouth wide after thee, know thou, my son, that all these things shall give thee experience, and shall be for thy good. (Doctrine and Covenants 122:7)

To be opposed is to gain strength. To face Goliaths with faith is to gain knowledge that will stay with us. To return love for hatred is to obtain wisdom. To overcome dark dangers is to discover goodness within. As the Prophet Joseph Smith learned, we also find a newness of life as we rise above persecution, difficulty, tragedy, heartbreak, and loss. Our resolve to persist through affliction is to uncover greatness within our souls. God is the great source of our power in times of testing. He will not remove challenges from our way, but He will help us find courage, hope, peace, and determination. This will be to our temporary and everlasting benefit. God is indeed good. A life of challenge is a blessed life, a meaningful life and is a measure of the confidence and trust that God has in us.

"If trials make us turn to God, see life from a more eternal perspective, and help us to grow and conquer our own weaknesses, even the most serious challenges can become tools to refine us . . . they may actually benefit us."[2] Such wise words from an experienced man of God. Challenges are for growth. Difficulties are for progress. Tribulations and trials can be advantageous to us. If we are humble,

---

2   Dieter F. Uchtdorf, Thanksgiving Day devotional, Provo Utah MTC, November 22, 2018.

we will define adversity as an opportunity rather than an affliction. We are thus greatly blessed to be able to show courage in the face of adversity, to display faith in the face of doubt, to possess humility in the face of hubris. We can do this when God is our High Tower, our protector, our guide, our strength, and our constant help. He can develop in us the hope we need in times of despair, the love we need in times of hate, the compassion we need in times of indifference, and the fortitude we need in times of challenge. Jesus the Christ is indeed our loving Lord and mighty Messiah. As we come to know the true source of our power—God—we are enabled, empowered, enlightened, encouraged, and energized.

The First Presidency and the Quorum of the Twelve have encouraged us to continually teach correct doctrine and consistently receive revelation. Given the strong and pervasive influence of worldly philosophies impacting people of faith in our day, it is critically important that we learn and teach gospel doctrines and principles with clarity, power, and enthusiasm in order to strengthen faith and bolster testimony on a consistent basis. This will prove vitally pivotal in protecting and enhancing the spiritual understanding and commitment especially of youth, friends, and new converts, and will be a source of comfort and uplift for long-time members and Church leaders. We can regularly and deeply receive heaven-sent power in the last days. Our desire can be to enhance our capacity to know true doctrine, access priesthood power, experience the renewing and revitalizing help that comes through the Atonement of the Savior, learn more fully how to follow prophetic direction, and increase ability to receive and act on personal revelation. As we have been directed, it is wise and helpful to prepare ourselves for spiritual instruction by having carefully considered questions that will be answered by revelation through the Holy Ghost. We are fortified through divinely inspired edifying experiences. Divine assistance is always available to help us with life's opportunities, and we can encourage and empower individuals to more readily and frequently partake of these divine powers. As always, our true success will be measured by the positive difference we make in the lives of others—especially those who are facing difficulties and need encouragement and support. We can indeed draw on the powers of heaven in these latter days—and this can happen often. We can focus on those wonderful and precious resources we have in and through The Church of Jesus Christ of Latter-day Saints to empower, lift, strengthen, aid, and bless all the world. We have continual opportunities to be renewed in faith, rejuvenated in spirit, and encouraged in our discipleship. We can all move toward a higher, holier, and happier way of life. This can be accomplished in small, daily steps. Every one of us has the power to move from where we are to where we wish to be. The important thing is to start moving toward the good things that await us.

VALIANT IN THE NAME OF CHRIST

Given that we have taken upon ourselves the most dignified name of our Lord, the most precious name of our Savior and the most powerful name of our Redeemer, we need to honor, respect, reverence, and hold in high esteem that name. I am always impressed with the sons of Helaman. Consider the description of these young men:

> And they were all young men, and they were exceedingly valiant or courage, and also for strength and activity; but behold, this was not all—they were men who were true at all times in whatsoever thing they were entrusted.
>
> Yea, they were men of truth and soberness, for they had been taught to keep the commandments of God and to walk uprightly before him. (Alma 53:20–21)

That is to say that they were brave, strong, true, trustworthy, sober, and obedient. Why? Because they knew and honored the name by which they were called. They knew that Christ was their valiant Lord, and they sought to be likewise valiant. They desired to be valiant in the testimony of Christ. They fulfilled that desire. We likewise need to highly value the name we have covenanted to take upon us. Our consecration to that name is no small thing. To truly take upon us the name of Christ is to partake of His identity, character, substance, attributes, perspectives, and powers. The virtue of the Master distills upon us. The valor of the Lord emboldens me. The valiant behavior of the Savior encourages us. The victory of the Christ inspires me. The vigor of the God of Israel enables us. The vitality of our Redeemer empowers me.

BE NOT WEARY IN WELL DOING

Sometimes we can become burned out or worn out in gospel living and service if we feel we are getting nowhere or accomplishing nothing useful. We can pray for the continued desire to serve. The Lord can shape our desires. He can give us new desires. He can also help us make peace when frustrations, disappointments, and breached expectations are readily apparent. Sometimes we might feel that we are more of a burden than a blessing, that we are not making much of a difference, that there is little point to our service. I can very much understand and empathize with these sentiments. However, it is also important to remember that we never really know the good we do, the impact we make, and the people we help. Our service is pleasing to the Lord if we give Him ourselves (see Doctrine and Covenants 4). If we put our devotion into our service, then He sees that intentional effort. He sees the consecrated sacrifice. He sees the willing offering. It is something I have certainly faced personally with sometimes feeling I was not making a positive difference. Of course, it suits the adversary for us to feel this way because he loves it when we are discouraged. This is his modus operandi—to encourage us to feel hopeless, pointless, aimless, insignificant, small, unimportant, trivial, meaningless, and unnecessary. He is a man of misery and seeks our sadness also. He wants us to feel alone, isolated, estranged, worthless, useless, and invisible. I have certainly felt these emotions many times in my own life. I have had to confront them, and that has not been easy or automatic.

However, I do think there is a remedy to this difficulty, a solution to this problem, an answer to this question, an antidote to this poison, a redress for this imbalance. There is hope, help, and healing. God will be a source of strength to us in our weakness, a friend to protect us from foes, a shield from devilish darts, and an injection of encouragement in our darkness. Consider the following verse:

"Teach them to never be weary of good works, but to be meek and lowly in heart; for such shall find rest to their souls" (Alma 37:34). We are asked to continue to do good works and not lose heart, vision, or vigor. We are to remain humble and contrite. We will then find a spiritual rest to our bodies and spirits. This rest to our souls will be soothing, sweet, satisfying, and bring us solace. It will be a rest that no worldly endeavor could ever match.

> Wherefore, as ye are agents, ye are on the Lord's errand; and whatever ye do according to the will of the Lord is the Lord's business... And behold, I, the Lord, declare unto you, and my words are sure and shall not fail, that they shall obtain it.... Wherefore, be not weary in well-doing, for ye are laying the foundation of a great work. And out of small things proceedeth that which is great. Behold, the Lord requireth the heart and a willing mind; and the willing and obedient shall eat the good of the land of Zion in these last days. (Doctrine and Covenants 64:29–34)

When we are engaged in the Lord's work, we are His agents. He is invested in our work. He wants it to be successful. He wants us to grow in achievement and accomplishments. He is a participant in the work because it is His work. His words of encouragement to us are strong and reliable. We are to continue to serve and not become tired of that service—meaning not to give up and give in. Why? Because we are laying a sure foundation for great things to happen. Out of the efforts we make and the small results that we see happening, there is a great reward unfolding that may not be immediately obvious to us. The Lord wants us to give our desires over to Him, to lose ourselves in His plan, to submit our thoughts to His greater thoughts, to yield our faculties and energies to His plans and purposes.

> And again I say unto you, my friends, . . . that ye become even as my friends in days when I was with them, traveling to preach the gospel in my power; For I suffered them not to have purse or scrip, neither two coats. Behold, I send you out to prove the world, and the laborer is worthy of his hire.
> And any man that shall go and preach this gospel of the kingdom, and fail not to continue faithful in all

things, shall not be weary in mind, neither darkened, neither in body, limb, nor joint; . . . Therefore, let no man among you, for this commandment is unto all the faithful who are called of God in the church unto the ministry, . . . And whoso receiveth you, there I will be also, for I will go before your face. I will be on your right hand and on your left, and my Spirit shall be in your hearts, and mine angels round about you, to bear you up. (Doctrine and Covenants 84:77–88)

That is to say that we are worthy to receive wages from the Lord when we serve Him with devotion. We are promised that every person who engages in the ministry of the Lord and continues to serve with diligence will have power to endure, energy to persist, the will to keep going. We will have light from God to guide our way. We will feel that we are surrounded and supported by God, by His Spirit, and by His angels. We are told that we will be held up by divine power. That is no small promise.

> See that ye love one another; cease to be covetous; learn to impart one to another as the gospel requires. Cease to be idle; cease to be unclean; cease to find fault one with another; cease to sleep longer than is needful; retire to thy bed early, that ye may not be weary; arise early, that your bodies and your minds may be invigorated. And above all things, clothe yourselves with the bond of charity, as with a mantle, which is the bond of perfectness and peace. Pray always, that ye may not faint, until I come. Behold, and lo, I will come quickly, and receive you unto myself. Amen. (Doctrine and Covenants 88:123–126)

Thus, as we go forward to do God's good work we will have renewed minds and bodies. We will have strength, energy, and enthusiasm that is divinely given. We will wear divine love as a cloak, a covering to abide with us and protect us from throwing in the towel. As we continue to supplicate the Lord for His matchless help, we will not faint for as long as the Lord needs us to continue. What does this mean? It means, I think, that we will not lose our will to keep going, we will not become burned out by the journey, we will not be overcome by opposition or trounced by trouble. If we so endure, for a moment or for a lifetime, then the day will come when the Lord will receive us into His divine presence, His amazing kingdom, His loving embrace, His heavenly mansion.

> And all saints who remember to keep and do these sayings,walking in obedience to the commandments, shall receive health in their navel and marrow to their bones; And shall find wisdom and great treasures of knowledge, even hidden treasures; And shall run and not be weary, and shall walk and not faint.
>
> And I, the Lord, give unto them a promise, that the destroying angel shall pass by them, as the children of Israel, and not slay them. Amen. (Doctrine and Covenants 89:18–21)

I love this prophetic promise to the Saints of God. As we keep the Word of Wisdom and all other divinely revealed commandments, we will receive physical renewal, spiritual wisdom, and pearls of truth. We will be able to do hard things of small and large degree. We will be able to fight the good fight, maintain our resolve, keep our concentration, retain our focus, and perform our assignments. We will receive our daily bread of life and our daily water of sustenance. We will be able to run a spiritual marathon requiring longevity of persistence and power of will. We will not be weary in doing this. This does not mean that this will always be a walk in the park, although there are times when we will feel full of strength and alive with passion and purpose beyond what we had imagined. However, it does mean that we will be able to keep going even when it is challenging. Our tiredness will be swallowed up in the joy of Christ. We are also told that we will not be slayed. This clearly has reference to avoiding the spiritual and physical death that comes from sin. We will also be covered by the redemptive protection of the atoning blood of Jesus Christ. We will be passed over and be able to abide the day of trial, tribulation, trouble, and testing. God is good and can do His work. You are stronger than you think when you travel with Him. You are braver than you know when you work with Him. You are more capable than you realize when you allow Him to teach you who you are and what you can accomplish with His help. So, we can keep the faith. God will abide with us in sunshine and in rain.

ENDURING TO THE END

Many years of life and Church membership have taught me many key precepts of power. It is deeply important for us to know the deep purposes of mortality. Life is a great test—a test of character manifest in obedience to the voice of God. We need to learn to live based on divine revelation. One of the most difficult challenges we face is breached expectations—when things happen differently to what we thought they would. We learn things we did not know, have experiences we do not want, and face hurdles that we never anticipated. In these critically important times, it is vital for us to maintain faith and hope as our anchors—to trust in divine direction received. Even prophets are surprised by such challenges and tests. What matters is how they respond to the test. Greatness is not found in the absence of difficulty, but rather in meeting challenges head on and surmounting them through righteous character. Our response to unanticipated difficulties determines our result on the mortal test. It is truly vital to learn the importance of making pivotal decisions based on eternal laws. The laws of God are eternal, and spiritual wisdom is to live by those laws in the time of opposition, temptation, distraction, and shifting standards. We can strive to live with no spiritual regrets. Mortality is a small and precious moment not to be wasted on fruitless pursuits with no eternal value. "For behold, this life is the time for men to prepare to meet God; yea, behold the day of this life is the day for men to perform their labors" (Alma 34:32). Now is the time to choose to follow God. Today is the day to choose to get ready for what awaits us all. Procrastination is not good for anyone. This is especially true when we are talking about spiritual things. Now is the time to rise in righteousness, to choose to believe, to repent and to get our lives in order. Mortality is such a short time, and it is important to make precious use of our opportunities rather than squander them. This is a powerful lesson when we learn it.

This means to see with an eye of faith, to have a divine perspective, a godly vision, to begin with the end in mind, to take the long view. We are to learn to abide by celestial laws while living in telestial conditions. To endure in faith is to choose the vital instead of the pressing, popular, easy, comfortable, convenient demands of the moment. Immoral fads and unethical fashions are transitory. We can live based on eternal perspective grounded in correct and lasting principles. We need to focus on what is vital, crucial, critical, elemental, important—what is best and most valuable. We can think straight and learn to discern what is good, better, best, praiseworthy, pure, virtuous, and so on. It is vital to adopt a posture of spiritual attitudes and attributes. We can remember that greatness is born from righteous struggle. We are to show spiritual courage under fire. Be brave, valiant, true to God. Do what is right, worthy, righteous—rather than what is expedient, popular, and easy. Reframe challenges from hardship to compliments—we are ready to move to the next level of spirituality so God will give us new challenges to expand our souls. Focus on the good, holy, positive, and beneficial. Be thankful for what we have already achieved, hurdles we have overcome, and distances we have already traveled. We can regain our spiritual composure, balance, and equilibrium. We can find daily renewal and recharged healing. We will have joy in the journey—laugh, smile, sing, rejoice, be glad, be thankful, be cheerful, be hopeful. It is pivotal to regularly exercise our agency in faith in Christ. We do not need to give in to fears and doubts. There are no good substitutes for action taken now. Look at the prophets and apostles—they did not get to a position of devotion by consistently giving in to laziness and fear, taking shortcuts, or making excuses. They progressed by having faith and taking faithful action. They are thus happy. Their example of persistence has encouraged me to change for the better. When we exercise agency in faith, we develop power over ourselves—mastery, control, direction over self. I believe every person who wishes to do this can do it with divine help. None of us are doomed or destined to permanently fail by God. It is crucial to keep in mind the rewards of righteousness. Wonderful blessings always follow faithful endurance. We can be alive, lifted, blessed, guiltless, sin-remitted, sanctified, saved, partakers of glory, inheritors of eternal life, receivers of thrones, and exalted.

CONCLUSION

Jesus Christ is the great standard, the perfect ideal, the master ruler by which our lives are to be measured. The true success of our lives is seen in how much we have learned of Him, accepted Him, followed Him, served Him, become like Him, and revealed Him to the world. Can we ever become as He is? The answer is a definite yes. How will we measure our lives? By how closely we have endeavored to follow His perfect example. By how much our will has been swallowed up in doing the will of the Father. By how valiant we have been in keeping His commandments, teaching His doctrine, sharing His love, and abiding in His covenant. The more perfectly our lives conform to the divine standard, the better. This is especially vital when we are faced with deep difficulties such as doubts, disease, despair, discouragement, and death. As we endure trials well, develop our talents, acquire intelligence, render service, and learn lessons, we will become spiritually advanced. As we form and maintain important relationships, touch lives for good, and take worthwhile risks, we will achieve social and emotional success. As we discover and apply useful knowledge, we will gain mental wisdom. As we treat our bodies as a temple, we will know physical happiness. To become more like the Savior in how we think, perceive, feel, learn, act, and live will be the greatest success of all. We are able, capable, and strong because God is our power, might, and strength. Every person can go to the Father in prayer and receive pertinent and potent guidance. He knows us well. He is eager to bless us and strengthen us. I certainly know that those facing deep and difficult life-changing circumstances can approach Him, as I have been in this category more than once. He has never disappointed me. Rather, He has been a constant source of healing, guidance, and renewal. Our Father can help us face and surmount every single challenge. There simply are no exemptions from pain and suffering. However, we can find meaning and hope in even the darkest of days. We need to look to God and live. We start with a desire to believe and God will work His miracle. This is not simply good counsel—this is my personal experience. God lives, loves, and lifts. This is not just rhetoric—it is real. He does live. And He is powerful, merciful, strong, generous. This I know. Come to the Father, now and always. He will amaze you.

11

THE KING OF KINGS RETURNS

How would you feel if you were told that you were to be introduced into a royal court and ushered into the presence of a king? Would you prepare to bow in humble reverence and respect? You would want to prepare and be ready. You would want to be properly dressed and know the protocols. You would show respect and honor for the dignity of the position. You would listen carefully. You would perhaps want to make a petition for a loved one or to right some wrong or recompense some injustice. You would be excited, nervous, and expectant.

The day will come when we will be introduced into the presence of the King of Kings and Lord of Lords, Jesus the Christ. We have been instructed that there will be a second coming of Jesus Christ to the earth in a not-far-distant day. Prophets of all dispensations have prophesied of the coming day in which the Lamb of God will return to reclaim His earth and His people from the powers of darkness. Now is the time to prepare for that marvelous day. In fact, in our own day, the gospel has been restored through the Prophet Joseph Smith to prepare the entire world—on both sides of the veil—for the second advent of Christ.

His second coming is sure and certain. He will come in a day of great wickedness and great righteousness. The wicked will not abide the day because the elements will melt with fervent heat. However, the righteous will have a shield of protection so that they will not be harmed. We need to recognize the signs of the times and be prepared for the great and dreadful day of the Lord. The hastening of the work of salvation in our time indicates the time of preparation is running short. We must take the Holy Spirit as our constant guide to avoid deception, distraction, discouragement, and despair. When the Christ returns in glory, the entire earth will be transformed to abide His glorious presence. He will reign as King of Kings and Lord of Lords. That is to say that He will be Lord and King of the righteous, the great, the good, and the noble. He will reign, govern, preside, and lead His people in righteousness. He holds the keys of presidency and the keys of resurrection. He will bring treasures of knowledge and blessings of joy with Him. Every knee will bow in humble submission before Him, and every tongue will confess that He is the Christ. There will be none to escape hearing His message in preparation for His glorious appearance. When He comes, the words used to describe his names will be realized in a more full and complete manner:

- Emmanuel—God with us
- Wonderful—His wonders will fill the world
- Counselor—the one whose counsels are ever perfect
- The Mighty God—His might will cover all the earth
- The Everlasting Father—His children are saved through His name, the name of the family of Christ
- The Prince of Peace—He will bring an end to war and destruction and usher in a time of peace such as the world has never known

So, this opportunity to be ushered into the presence of royalty will be ours, if we are faithful now. In a coming day we will have the opportunity of opportunities, the privilege of privileges, and the honor of all honors. We will meet the Righteous Judge, the Chosen Redeemer, the Special Soul. We will greet in person that Lord that we have thought about so often, longed to be with so fervently, testified of in humility, and hoped for with sincere expectation. On that day we will not be disappointed. You and I will be amazed at His goodness, astonished by His love, moved by His compassion, strengthened by His smile, and humbled by His power. He is the living embodiment of all we long for, all we hope for, all we dream of. He is the perfect person, our unyielding friend, our loyal companion, and our loving Lord. I suspect that your tears will flow freely, your gratitude will rise to a new level of appreciation, and you will fall to your knees in reverent adoration. Your soul will surge with overpowering feelings that this is indeed Jesus of Nazareth, Savior and King. Perhaps you will be speechless, stunned into silence, enwrapped in joyful contemplation at what you are experiencing. I will feel likewise.

"And again, verily I say unto you that it is your privilege, and a promise I give unto you that have been ordained unto this ministry. . . . The veil shall be rent and you shall see me and know that I am" (Doctrine and Covenants 67:10). This verse gives us the assurance that seeing the Savior is an honor promised to the priesthood holders of this dispensation who have learned the principles of righteousness. Those brethren who have become humble and courageous in the Lord's work will see and experience first-hand the spiritual truths reserved for those who live according to the dictates of God's spirit. It is clearly not the case that no one has or can see the Lord face to face. It is only the case that those who live according to the precepts of the natural man—worldly, proud, selfish, and so on—do not get to enjoy the experience in mortality of seeing the Lord face to face. However, for righteous priesthood holders there are no such barriers. The veil between time and eternity is described in this verse as being rent, or torn asunder, so that spiritual manifestations such as these can be had.

"And again, verily I say unto you, my friends . . . ye shall call upon me while I am near—Draw near unto me and I will draw near unto you; seek me diligently and ye shall find me; ask, and ye shall receive; knock, and it shall be opened unto you" (Doctrine and Covenants 88:62–63). That is to say that the Lord wants His Latter-day Saints to reflect carefully on the reality that we are not only invited—but commanded—to draw close to Him. We are to seek Him, search for Him, long for Him, want to know Him, and reach toward Him. This effort will not be fruitless. In fact, we are instructed that this persistent searching will most certainly be rewarded with a closeness to the Savior, a discovering of Him, receiving from Him, and an opening of the door to His presence. I know enough about the spiritual life to know that this is no delusional dream, no mindless myth, no ignorant illusion. This will happen, as sure as day follows night. On that great day we will know the solace, peace, compensation, and reward for which we have so desperately wished for so long during times of trial, tribulation, torment, and testing. God's promises are not trivial or given in jest. He means to reveal Himself to us so that we may enjoy His companionship, teachings, trust, guidance, direction, mysteries, and love.

THE KNOWLEDGE OF CHRIST COVERS THE EARTH

"And moreover, I say unto you, that the time shall come when the knowledge of a Savior shall spread throughout every nation, kindred, tongue, and people" (Mosiah 3:20). The saving knowledge of the Savior is no small thing, no insignificant insight, no worthless pursuit. The Father is determined that the entire world and all of humanity learn of His special Son and His atoning work. This time is coming closer. The time when the saving knowledge of the Redeemer will fill the world as a mighty flood. The time when the revelation that Jesus of Nazareth is the literal living Son of the literal living Father will be widespread like the waters that cover the sea. The time when the reality of the infinite Atonement of Christ will be known, accepted, and understood in every nation and among all people. The time when priesthood power will be felt among people of every diverse tongue and unique language on the planet. The time when the testimony of the Prophet Joseph Smith concerning the Son of God will be borne in each country. This time will be one of tremendous rejoicing in every home and family where the good news is heard and believed.

A LITERAL RETURN TO EARTH

"For I say unto you . . . blessed is he who cometh in the name of the Lord, in the clouds of heaven, and all the holy angels with him" (JS—Matthew 1:1). Indeed, He will come again—in marvelous glory and transcendent power. How important it is that we play our part in preparation for this event by remaining focused on the things that matter most. Our task is to ensure that we are not overcome by the worldly distractions that are everywhere and to remain steadfast in our faith. This is our excellent duty and special privilege. "And then they shall look for me, and, behold, I will come; and they shall see me in the clouds of heaven, clothed with power and great glory" (Doctrine and Covenants 45:44–46). The Lord will come in splendor and supremacy, in might, in majesty, and in towering triumph. The faithful will abide the day, whether they are mortal or living in the spirit at that time. The Saints will ascend to be with Him and then descend to live with Him on earth. Those who await His promised return will not be disappointed, forgotten, or lost.

"For they that are wise and have received the truth, and have taken the Holy Spirit for their guide, and have not been deceived—verily I say unto you, they shall not be hewn down and cast into the fire, but shall abide the day . . . For the Lord shall be in their midst, and his glory shall be upon them, and he will be their king and their lawgiver" (Doctrine and Covenants 45:57–59). It is interesting to note the importance of our personal preparation for His glorious return. We need to wisely accept the truth of the restored everlasting Gospel, actively follow the revelations of the Holy Ghost, avoid distraction and deception whether they come in the form of wickedness or spiritual apathy. If we do this, then we will withstand the difficulties of the last days, whatever they may be. We will not be swept aside by storms, moved aside by falling mountains, or pushed aside by worldly powers. We will meekly inherit the earth as a promised land, we will grow in prosperity, and our children will know salvation. The Lord will be physically with us, we will partake of His glorious countenance and smiling approval, and He will be the one whom we honor, sustain, and revere as King and Lawgiver. We will look to Him as the perfect example of justice, judgment, equity, fairness, righteousness, power, authority, and royalty. His law will be one in which all men then living can place perfect trust and reliance.

"And with one heart and with one mind, gather up your riches that ye may purchase an inheritance which shall hereafter be appointed unto you. And it shall be called the New Jerusalem, a land of peace, a city of refuge, a place of safety for the saints of the Most High God" (Doctrine and Covenants 45:65–66). We will, in that blessed day, be unified in righteousness with the other Saints on the earth. We will enjoy spiritual riches in abundance and earthly treasures in plenty. We will be able to live the law of the Lord. Our abode will be one of sanctuary, protection, harmony, contentment, and love. "Yet a little while and ye shall see it, and know that I am, and that I will come and reign with my people" (Doctrine and Covenants 84:119–120). We will be known as the Lord's people. His power and influence will be over all the earth. We will know Him. We will see Him, hear Him, touch Him, embrace Him. We will have the personal experience of meeting the Lord we love. He will reign over the earth. He will preside, govern, direct, lead, and control the Saints of God and all people on the earth. Goodwill will abound. Knowledge will flow. His leadership will be pure and perfect.

"And . . . the face of the Lord shall be unveiled; And the saints that are upon the earth, who are alive, shall be quickened and be caught up to meet him. And they who have slept in their graves shall come forth, for their graves shall be opened; and they also shall be caught up to meet him in the midst of the pillar of heaven— They are Christ's, the first fruits" (Doctrine and Covenants 88:95–98). The Lord will not be hidden, obscured, kept covered, or mysterious to us. We will see Him as He is. His face will be before us in plain sight. His eyes will be upon us. His hands will bless us. His smiles will console us. His teachings will inspire us. His tears will move us. His character will astound us. We will be enlightened, moved, transformed, enabled, and empowered to do and be more than we now are. We will ascend into the sky. This will be miraculous, transcendent, comforting, and validating. This will be a divine convergence between heaven and earth.

REJOICINGS AT HIS COMING

"And it shall come to pass that the righteous shall be gathered out from among all nations, and shall come to Zion, singing with songs of everlasting joy" (Doctrine and Covenants 45:71). When He returns, we will be with others who are like minded and of a similar heart to us. We will meet with those of testimony and faith. We will sup with those who are humble, gentle, and generous. We will listen to those who are true and good. We will work with those who are prayerful and faithful. We will serve with those who are pure, virtuous, hardworking, kind, forgiving and merciful. We will learn from those who are eager to teach. We will teach those who are willing to be taught. We will smile, laugh, and worship together. At His coming we will be glad, happy, content, consoled and joyful. We will sing, glorify, rejoice, exult, and praise. This will be a worldwide conference of beauty, benevolence, beneficence, and blessings.

"Until all shall know me, who remain, even from the least unto the greatest, and shall be filled with the knowledge of the Lord, and shall see eye to eye, and shall lift up their voice, and with the voice together sing this new song, saying: . . . glory, and honor, and power, and might . . . forever and ever, Amen" (Doctrine and Covenants 84:98–102). This day will be the culmination of thousands of years of expectation. It will be a day of prophecy and power, a day of fulfillment and fortune, a day of blessing and bounty. Covenants will be brought to fruition. Promises will be realized. We shall know the Lord personally and powerfully. We shall see clearly. We will praise powerfully. We shall sing sublimely. The earth will be new and glorious. We will rejoice in God, worship Him, serve Him, praise Him, adore Him, and acknowledge Him.

CHANGES TO THE EARTH

"We believe . . . . the earth will be renewed and receive its paradisiacal glory" (Articles of Faith 1:10). Even as the Son of God has a renewing impact upon us as individuals, He also has the power to renew the earth. We know that at His coming, the earth itself will be restored to its pre-Fall status as a garden paradise. Hence, sin and death will be banished, and the earth will be healed, purified, and beautified. Given the level of pollution, natural disasters, and fragmentation on this planet, this magnificent alteration of the earth will be a phenomenal restoration to a state of resplendent glory brought about by the transformative capacity of the Son of God. As Christ brings new life to individuals, he also brings new life to families, nations, and all of creation. He has the power to give new life to the world. Consider this prophecy from Isaiah:

> The wilderness and the solitary place shall be glad for them; and the desert shall rejoice, and blossom as the rose. It shall blossom abundantly, and rejoice even with joy and singing: the glory of Lebanon shall be given unto it, the excellency . . . for in the wilderness shall waters break out, and streams in the desert. And the parched ground shall become a pool, and the thirsty land springs of water: in the habitation of dragons, where each lay, shall be grass with reeds and rushes. And an highway shall be there, and a way, and it shall be called The way of holiness. . . . No lion shall be there, nor any ravenous beast shall go up thereon, it shall not be found there; but the redeemed shall walk there: And the ransomed of the Lord shall return, and come to Zion with songs and everlasting joy upon their heads: they shall obtain joy and gladness, and sorrow and sighing shall flee away. (Isaiah 35:1–10)

What a marvelous message this is. This world is full of waste places, deserts, wilderness, scorched grounds, dead seas, icy wastes, and volcanoes. We are ravaged by cyclones, tsunamis, earthquakes, fires, floods, tempests, mudslides, and hurricanes. The world is awash with pollution, war, droughts, destruction, famines, diseases, poverty, and the like. The time will come when all of this will be no more. The deserts shall bloom and blossom. The previously parched land will then find abundance of life. Famines will be replaced by feasts. Droughts will give way to liquid healing. Fires will be quenched, the waste places will see life, animals will no longer threaten men, pollution will be replaced with purity. The righteous will walk in the holy way without obstruction. In modern revelation, this prophecy is again pronounced upon the world. We are told that the Lord will touch the earth and bring His healing, refining, renewing, cleansing, and saving powers upon the earth and upon the people: "For behold, he shall stand upon the mount of Olives, and upon the mighty ocean, even the great deep, and upon the islands of the sea, and upon the land of Zion. . . . And the land of Jerusalem and the land of Zion shall be turned back into their own place, and the earth shall be like as it was in the days before it was divided. . . . And in the barren deserts there shall come forth pools of living water; and the parched ground shall no longer be a thirsty land" (Doctrine and Covenants 133:20–33). Thus, Christ will bring to the world beauty for ashes. He will bring abundance, fruitfulness, life, water, bread, peace, plenty. The world will be one. It will be productive and harmonious. Humans will live in righteous unity and know the treasures of God's great bounty. In the scriptures the world is often expressed in such images as being in bondage, being lost, being starving, being hungry, being thirsty, being afflicted, being a stranger, and so on. However, in the gospel kingdom, the Lord Jesus Christ brings the opposite of this—He gives us food, water, deliverance, family, friends, feasts, rains, sunshine, and every other good thing. Indeed, all willing things are made alive in Christ in this sense of endless productivity and regeneration.

CONCLUSION

I have a lively and firm testimony that in a day that will soon arrive, He will certainly come again. He will rule in righteousness and reign in majesty. One day He will surely come with healing in his wings to set his people free. He who is the King of Kings and Lord of Lords. He who is the Bright and Morning Star. He who is the Light and the Life of our world. He who is the Hope of Israel and the hope of the whole world. What a glorious day that will be! Now is the time to prepare for that special event through diligent devotion to God and His ways.

12

GLORIOUS RESURRECTION

When I was a full-time missionary almost thirty years ago, on many occasions people would comment to me that no one has come back from the grave to tell us that there is life after death. I would respond by saying that heavenly messengers have come to the earth to show us that there is indeed life after death—and that it comes in the form of a physical life such as we have now—but that this new life would be more wondrous than what we know here. In fact, the central messages of the restored gospel teach of the Only Begotten Son of God and not only His literal Resurrection, but also that of all men and women. Consider the following verse:

"And righteousness will I send down out of heaven; and truth will I send forth out of the earth, to bear testimony of mine Only Begotten; his resurrection from the dead; yea, and also the resurrection of all men; and righteousness and truth will I cause to sweep the earth as with a flood, to gather out mine elect from the four quarters of the earth . . . and it shall be called Zion, a New Jerusalem" (Moses 7:62). This righteousness sent down from heaven is a clear reference to the visits of heavenly beings such as the Father and the Son, Moroni, John the Baptist, Peter, James, John, Elias, Moses, Elijah, and others. The truth sent forth out of the earth refers to the Book of Mormon. Both the evidence of these divine visitors and the witness of the Book of Mormon is that resurrection is not an idle dream, a fictional fantasy, or a mysterious conundrum. We are instructed also in modern revelation unique to our day that all human beings will come forth in the literal bodily resurrection: "Speaking of the resurrection of the dead, concerning those who shall hear the voice of the Son of Man: And shall come forth; they who have done good in the resurrection of the just; and they who have done evil, in the resurrection of the unjust" (Doctrine and Covenants 76:16–17). This indicates that the coming forth in the resurrection is clearly because of a call from the Lord. The Savior holds the power of resurrection, and He will govern and direct it. It is also evident that those who have lived a just life will be resurrected, as will those who have lived an unjust life. Our obedience to the commandments of God will therefore have a significant impact on both when we come forth in the resurrection and what type of resurrection we will experience.

Let us consider what the resurrection of the just entails:

> And again we bear record—for we saw and heard, and this is the testimony of the gospel of Christ concerning them who shall come forth in the resurrection of the just . . .
>
> That by keeping the commandments they might be washed and cleansed from all their sins, and receive the Holy Spirit by the laying on of the hands of him who is ordained and sealed unto this power;
>
> And who overcome by faith, and are sealed by the Holy Spirit of promise, which the Father sheds forth upon all those who are just and true.
>
> They are they who are the church of the Firstborn.
>
> They are they into whose hands the Father has given all things—
>
> They are they who are priests and kings, who have received of his fulness, and of his glory;
>
> And are priests of the Most High, after the order of Melchizedek, which was after the order of Enoch, which was after the order of the Only Begotten Son.

Wherefore, as it is written, they are gods, even the sons of God—

Wherefore, all things are theirs, whether life or death, or things present, or things to come, all are theirs and they are Christ's, and Christ is God's.

And they shall overcome all things.

Wherefore, let no man glory in man, but rather let him glory in God, who shall subdue all enemies under his feet.

These shall dwell in the presence of God and his Christ forever and ever.

These are they whom he shall bring with him, when he shall come in the clouds of heaven to reign on the earth over his people.

These are they who shall have part in the first resurrection. . . .

These are they who are come unto Mount Zion, and unto the city of the living God, the heavenly place, the holiest of all.

These are they who have come to an innumerable company of angels, to the general assembly and church of Enoch, and of the Firstborn.

These are they whose names are written in heaven, where God and Christ are the judge of all.

These are they who are just men made perfect through Jesus the mediator of the new covenant, who wrought out this perfect atonement through the shedding of his own blood.

These are they whose bodies are celestial, whose glory is that of the sun, even the glory of God, the highest of all, whose glory the sun of the firmament is written of as being typical. (Doctrine and Covenants 76:50–70)

So, we are discussing those who receive a witness from the Holy Ghost of the Lord Jesus Christ, believe in Him, are baptized by immersion by proper authority, keep the commandments to the removal of their sins, receive the Holy Ghost by the laying on of hands, overcome the tendencies of the natural man or worldly woman, are promised salvation, belong to the true Church of Christ on earth (or the spirit world) and in heaven, receive all blessings, honor the royal birthright, receive the full glory of God, possess all things, live with God eternally, abide with Christ, come forth in the first resurrection, dwell in celestial Zion, live with Saints of all ages, have their names written in the Lamb's Book of Life, become perfect through the infinite Atonement of the Lord, and receive a tangible, celestial body in the eternities.

We are instructed that our redemption from the fall of man—which brought spiritual and physical death into the world—comes through the bodily resurrection:

"Now, verily I say unto you, that through the redemption which is made for you is brought to pass the resurrection from the dead. And the spirit and the body are the soul of man. And the resurrection from the dead is the redemption of the soul. And the redemption of the soul is through him that quickeneth all things" (Doctrine and Covenants 88:14–17). Thus, the spirit and body combined constitute the soul of man. Hence, the resurrection of the body is not simply the culmination of spiritual cleansing from sin and the healing of the body from death. Rather, body and spirit united make the soul, and the resurrection saves the soul. In this sense the resurrection is the overturning of the effects of Adam's Fall. This redemption, this saving, this resurrection is only possible through Christ. He quickens us, resurrects us. I love the idea of quickening. It is a hastening, a surge, an enlivening, a renewal. The resurrection involves a newness of life for all eternity. How amazing. The poor and meek of the earth will therefore inherit a new physical earth in their new physical body.

> As I pondered over these things which are written, the eyes of my understanding were opened, and the Spirit of the Lord rested upon me, and I saw the hosts of the dead, both small and great.
>
> And there were gathered together in one place an innumerable company of the spirits of the just, who had been faithful in the testimony of Jesus while they lived in mortality. . . .
>
> All these had departed the mortal life, firm in the hope of a glorious resurrection, through the grace of God the Father and his Only Begotten Son, Jesus Christ.
>
> I beheld that they were filled with joy and gladness, and were rejoicing together because the day of their deliverance was at hand.

They were assembled awaiting the advent of the Son of God into the spirit world, to declare their redemption from the bands of death.

Their sleeping dust was to be restored unto its perfect frame, bone to his bone, and the sinews and the flesh upon them, the spirit and the body to be united never again to be divided, that they might receive a fulness of joy.

While this vast multitude waited and conversed, rejoicing in the hour of their deliverance from the chains of death, the Son of God appeared, declaring liberty to the captives who had been faithful;

And there he preached to them the everlasting gospel, the doctrine of the resurrection and the redemption of mankind from the fall, and from individual sins on conditions of repentance. (Doctrine and Covenants 138:11–19)

From this revelation to a prophet, it is evident that the righteous Saints in the spirit world who had been faithful in the testimony of the Lord in mortality had lived and died with an expectation of a resurrection that would be glorious in due course. They were gathered as Saints and were glad because they would soon see the Lord and receive release from their bondage of physical death. They fully expected to receive their body back, except now it would be perfect and no longer subject to disease, decay, and dissolution like it had been in mortality. In this resurrected state, they would be able to obtain all the joy which the children of God are able to receive. The Lord appeared to them after His success in the atoning sacrifice and taught them that their time of captivity was at an end. He preached the reality of resurrection to them. We are further told, "But among the righteous there was peace; And the saints rejoiced in their redemption, and bowed the knee and acknowledged the Son of God as their Redeemer and Deliverer from death and the chains of hell. Their countenances shone, and the radiance from the presence of the Lord rested upon them, and they sang praises unto his holy name" (Doctrine and Covenants 138:22–24). The Saints of all ages had peace and rejoiced that death and hell had been overcome for them by their Lord.

It is abundantly clear that these valiant prophets and dedicated disciples had viewed their disembodied state as a form of entrapment: "For the dead had looked upon the long absence of their spirits from their bodies as a bondage. These the Lord taught, and gave them power to come forth, after his resurrection from the dead, to enter into his Father's kingdom, there to be crowned with immortality and eternal life" (Doctrine and Covenants 138:43, 49–51).

So, they had longed for this redemption from death to come to them. They wanted their physical bodies back. The body is no prison, no confinement, no curse. Rather, it is a great treasure to us in time and eternity. These faithful Saints looked forward to getting their bodies back—in perfect condition—and to the immortality and eternal life that would inevitably follow this righteous resurrection of the just. All this abundance of new life was to be given to them by the Lord of Life, the giver of all good things, their rescuer, recovery expert, and Redeemer. Likewise, the Savior will grant us a literal bodily resurrection. It is a permanent union of body and spirit in a perfected form, a joyful restoration with our temporal tabernacle in glory, a continual blessing of health, youth, and radiance. Can anyone imagine the glory of such a supernal gift?

RESURRECTION AS THE POTENTIAL ULTIMATE HEALING

Consider the healing influence of the Lord as mentioned in Mosiah 3:5–6. It is evident that this passage refers to the mortal ministry of Christ as it specifically says He will do this while dwelling in a tabernacle of clay (a mortal body subject to corruption). What is remarkable about this is that while He Himself was subject to the aging and decaying influence of mortal dust, He would nevertheless have the power to heal the sick. Obviously, He would have power over mortal ailments and would rebuke these on many occasions. Given the reference to casting out devils, I think it is fair to say that His influence clearly includes the capacity to heal the spiritually sick in addition to the physically sick. Forgiving sins is an example of this. However, we are also instructed that Christ will "rise from the dead, with healing in his wings" (2 Nephi 25:13–14).

GLORIOUS RESURRECTION

This is most interesting. This passage clearly relates to the resurrected Christ because it is centered on crucifixion and burial. I note that in the resurrection the Lord would rise from the dead "with healing in his wings." The obvious question is what this means. He already had the power to heal others as a mortal. I understand that this means a continuation of His ability to heal, and even more so, this seems to relate to a greater capacity to heal because the healing is in His wings. I understand this to mean ability to influence, capacity to make your power felt widely. Wings mean power, might, ability, extension. So here we have the Messiah with healing in His wings. His capacity to heal seems to be increased due to the Atonement and resurrection. Given the burden He had faced, the compassion He felt, and the victory He won, this is probably no surprise. It never quite hit me in this way before. Interestingly, we are told in the same passage that after His resurrection He showed Himself to the righteous who believed on His name. That is wonderfully important. Doctrine and Covenants 138 tells us He did not visit the wicked in prison. From the gospel accounts it is evident He did not visit the wicked in Jerusalem either. That is to say that He arose with healing in His wings AND His ministry was then to the righteous on earth and in the spirit world. It strikes me that this is not coincidental. We are told in 3 Nephi 9 that He offered the people who survived the destruction the opportunity to turn to Him, be converted, and be healed.

"O all ye that are spared because ye were more righteous than they, will ye not now return unto me, and repent of your sins, and be converted, that I may heal you?" (3 Nephi 9:13–14). So it is that the more righteous part of the people still needed to return to Him, repent, and be converted so that they could be healed. This healing clearly goes far beyond healing of the body into the realm of spiritual healing. We are told that those who came to Him at that time would have eternal life. Those surviving people would then be received by Him. Think of that. The somewhat righteous would find a sure salvation in this manner.

We are then told in 3 Nephi 17 that He very much fulfilled this promise. He taught them the gospel and then healed them of their bodily afflictions. I understand that to mean that they were healed spiritually and then healed physically. "And he said unto them: Behold, my bowels are filled with compassion towards you. Have ye any that are sick among you? Bring them hither. Have ye any that are lame, or blind, or halt, or maimed, or leprous, or that are withered, or that are deaf, or that are afflicted in any manner? Bring them hither and I will heal them, for I have compassion upon you; my bowels are filled with mercy" (3 Nephi 17:5–10). We are also told that those cleansed every whit from iniquity can perform miracles for others (see 3 Nephi 8:1). We are informed that the gift of healing among the Book of Mormon peoples only ceased because of iniquity and unbelief. Indeed, denial of the gift of healing and other gifts reflects not knowing or misunderstanding the gospel (see Mormon 1:13–14).

> And again I speak unto you who deny the revelations of God, and say that they are done away, that there are no revelations, nor prophecies, nor gifts, nor healing, nor speaking with tongues, and the interpretation of tongues;
> Behold I say unto you, he that denieth these things knoweth not the gospel of Christ; yea, he has not read the scriptures; if so, he does not understand them. (Mormon 9:7–8)

We know in this modern dispensation that the gift of healing is a part of our faith "and to another, exceedingly great faith; and to another, the gifts of healing by the same Spirit" (Moroni 10:11). We are also told that the only miracles we should require are those the Lord commands. However, the gift of healing is exempted from this injunction. Rather, healing—if required by desiring and believing persons—is something that the Lord's ministers can appropriately perform. "We believe in the gift of tongues, prophecy, revelation, visions, healing, interpretation of tongues, and so forth" (Articles of Faith 1:7) and "require not miracles, except I shall command you, except casting out devils, healing the sick, and against poisonous serpents, and against deadly poisons; And these things ye shall not do, except it be required of you by them who desire it" (Doctrine and Covenants 24:13–14). We are also significantly told that in the last days the world will burn like an oven and the wicked be consumed. However, we are then told that those who believe in the name of the Christ shall be visited by the Son of God, who will come with healing in His wings. Here we have this phrase again. I only recently noticed the significance of this. We have already clarified that there is a special type of healing reserved for those who come to Christ willingly. He manifests this full healing influence only toward those who are humble and repentant. It strikes me that these survivors at Bountiful escaped physical destruction. However, perhaps at least some of them suffered ailments and needed spiritual reassurance and perhaps bodily healing. This may have consisted of both pre-existing afflictions/medical conditions AND injuries/sorrows acquired during the natural disasters. By logical extrapolation to the last days we might conclude that the need for the Savior's special healing will likewise arise during and after the destruction pertaining to the last days.

"For behold, the day cometh that shall burn as an oven; and all the proud, yea, and all that do wickedly, shall be stubble; and the day that cometh shall burn them up, saith the Lord of Hosts, that it shall leave them neither root nor branch. But unto you that fear my name, shall the Son of Righteousness arise with healing in his wings" (3 Nephi 25:1–2). Perhaps this might mean that even the righteous who survive the latter-day destruction may have afflictions of various kinds. Is it possible that some of them might be burned, scarred, hurt, wounded, scalded, and so on in these latter-day commotions of fires and earthquakes? Is it further possible that as He did with Shadrach, Meshach, and Abednego, the Son of God will appear to them to protect them from the fire, or perhaps to heal their burns? Will He be like aloe vera to the skin of these wounded soldiers? Will He calm the fire and soothe the aches of these righteous believers? I believe there may be something here to consider. Christ will arise with healing in His wings to save those who believe on His name. This healing will be full and complete in due course and will represent more than temporary or partial healing. This will not be simply giving sight to the blind but giving new sight to those who can already see.

This will be giving new ears to those who already hear, new hearts to those who are already soft hearted. This will be a new life, a new mind, a new heart, a new spirit, a new body. This celestial resurrection will represent the ultimate healing of the body and spirit. How great is our Master healer, our suffering servant, our anointed deliverer, and our rescuing Redeemer. He is truly the Christ. I rejoice in his healing influence in my life. Through Him, my soul takes flight.

13

THE GREATEST OF ALL GIFTS

THE MEANING OF GIFTS

Often, the gifts we receive and give can bring us and others temporary pleasure and satisfaction. There are, of course, great gifts in this life that can be a wonderful source of joy and rejoicing to us. At special times such as birthdays, wedding anniversaries, Easter, Thanksgiving, and Christmas we can reflect on the most important gifts in mortality. For example, the gifts of Christmas can be truly profound. Beyond the obvious material gifts, we are grateful, for there are the gifts of deeper worth and value. We have much to celebrate when we consider faith, family, and friends. We have the gifts of time, music, and love. We have the gift to start over, change our lives for the better, and be grateful. We have gifts of reflection, contemplation, and pondering on the powerful truths of existence. As we see with grateful eyes, we can come to see existing gifts in a new light, with a deeper appreciation for their abundance and meaning.

THE NATURE OF THE NEW LIFE, ETERNAL LIFE

However, the greatest gift of all lies for us in the future. It is the gift of eternal life. This gift is defined as enjoying eternally not only the presence of God and loved ones but also sharing in the type of life that God possesses. To try to put into perspective what eternal life will be like, we might consider a few critical questions such as the following:

- Can you imagine receiving this gift you have desired, worked for, prayed for, hoped for, and longed for during an entire lifetime?
- What would this gift look like and feel like?
- What opportunities will be available to us on reception of this gift?

Let us turn to the revelations for hope-filled answers: "The mysteries of his kingdom which he showed unto us, which surpass all understanding in glory, and in might, and in dominion" (Doctrine and Covenants 76:114). Thus, God's great works and marvelous mysteries are beyond what we can presently fathom in terms of their beauty, power, strength, and influence. "For whoso is faithful unto the obtaining these two priesthoods of which I have spoken, and the magnifying their calling, are sanctified by the Spirit unto the renewing of their bodies. . . . And he that receiveth my Father receiveth my Father's kingdom; therefore all that my Father hath shall be given unto him" (Doctrine and Covenants 84:33–38).

As I read these promises, there is no power or influence that will be withheld in the eternities from those who obtain and magnify their calling from the Lord. They will be sanctified and renewed in body. They will receive all the glorious privileges that God can give to His faithful children. Their eternal life will be never-ending in duration. Their eternal life will be qualitatively superb and glorious. Their eternal life will be a state of joyfulness, ability, and opportunity. I love Doctrine and Covenants 88:40–41 because these verses indicate to me that if we love light, then we will cleave to light and it will cleave to us. If we value wisdom, then we will find a friend in wisdom. If we pursue intelligence, then we will find a companion in intelligence. If we know mercy, then mercy will relate to us. We become what we gravitate toward. We accentuate what we desire. We learn to mirror what we focus on. And if this principle is true for us in this mortal probation, then it will be true in the eternities, only greatly magnified. We will become what we long for, cling to, associate with, and connect with. If we long to be with God and to be like Him, then that is what will happen. We will be attracted to beauty, truth, goodness, mercy, courage, and diligence. We will become the living embodiment of the values we espouse, the thoughts we think, the aspirations we give voice to. The ultimate new life in Christ is the life that loves what He loves and shares in His redeeming graces.

THE REQUIREMENTS TO OBTAIN ETERNAL LIFE

Eternal life is the potential reward for each child of God that seeks it with full purpose of heart. While we do not, strictly speaking, earn eternal life by our own merits, it is true that we need to meet certain criteria of our own volition to be candidates for this ultimate blessing. The requirements are presented to us plainly and frequently throughout the scriptural word of God. Consider Alma 13:13, which talks about entering the rest of the Lord. We need to humble ourselves before God, recognizing Him as the source of our salvation. Humility inexorably leads to our turning to God with genuine contrition and a desire to put off the natural man through sincere repentance. Such repentance is deep inner transition toward God and His laws. Humility leads to real and lasting change. It leads to profound peace, gentle assurance, and confident gratitude. To place ourselves in the trust of our Father in Heaven and His bounteous plan will take us to a place of inward serenity, quiet contentment, and beloved hope. Humility is always beneficial, necessary, and rewarding. The rest that God promises is one of certain resolve and patient determination. It is a relief from the carnality of our own fallen nature. It is a departure from the conflict, confusion, contention, and consternation that comes with sin. To receive and believe in the Lord Jesus Christ is to obtain the power of eternal life from Him (see Doctrine and Covenants 45:8). So it is that we need to receive the Son of God. We need to accept Him for who and what He declares Himself to be. We must believe on His name, which is to say His authority, identity, character, mission, power, and atoning sacrifice. His name is powerful. As we rely on His name and the principles and powers that are inherent in His name, we find power to lay hold on every good thing. This is essential if we are to eventually obtain the kind and quality of life that He already possesses. We can only obtain eternal life if we learn to give exacting heed to the words of God (see Doctrine and Covenants 84:43–44). We need to learn His word with conscientious devotion and live His word with ongoing attention to detail. This expanding exact obedience is vital preparation if we are to attain the capacity to comply with all the terms and conditions of His gospel. Obedience to each and all laws of God is our goal and will provide us with the fulness of gospel blessings in the eternities to come.

THE GIVER OF ALL GOOD GIFTS

God is the provider of every good thing we can experience. There is no wonderful opportunity that He has not devised, no privilege that He has not catered for. Whether we are talking about temporal or spiritual blessings, it is God who has conceived of them and made them available for one and all. The music we love to listen to, the books we love to read, the friends we love to greet, the places we love to go, the truths we love to learn, and much more have been provided for us as part of God's eternal plan of happiness. Consider what eternal wonders God has in store for those who come unto Him with full purpose of heart (see Doctrine and Covenants 76:5–10). God will show us mercy, grace, and honor. He will bless us with great glory. He will uncover hidden truths to us. He will teach us of eternal principles. He will give us a wisdom greater than that of Solomon and a comprehension that is divine in scope and scale. He will show us spiritual things that transcend what we have seen, heard, and felt before. I think it is reasonable to assume that such blessings clearly go far beyond what we might envisage for ourselves. We do not presently comprehend all that this involves, given that much of it will be new to us. It is evident that God has in store for the faithful high rewards and marvelous messages. No doubt these experiences will allow us to discern the character of God and His abilities, powers, works, and purposes more clearly. He truly is a good father who wants to bestow upon His children all that He knows, loves, and experiences. He will not withhold any blessings from those who love Him. This is truly astounding when we try to contemplate what this involves.

Several powerful verses of scripture are found in Doctrine and Covenants 45:3–5. The idea that the Savior Himself is deeply invested in representing us as an advocate is stunning. Due to the tremendous goodness of the Lord in performing His atoning sacrifice for our benefit, He is in a position where He can ask the Father that we be spared from damnation. We can have the privilege of enjoying a life that is everlasting because of the greatness of our generous God. I think that means everlasting not simply in the sense of lasting forever but also in the sense of being abundant, rich, bountiful, special, and wonderful. The life that God gives is both quantitatively and qualitatively superb, precious, and enduring. Indeed, all the superlatives we can employ are shallow when we consider the rich depth and texture of what everlasting life will consist of. It is a life in full living color, with a richness to it that obviously transcends our mortal expectation and present understanding. We know the riches of this world are extensive. The abundance of property on this earth is spectacular. It is apparent that all land, jewels, precious metals, money, and so on all belong to God. He owns all the things we can see. Of course, the God of heaven has far more than just earthly treasures in His possession. His treasures are those also of knowledge, power, might, dominion, principalities, thrones, power, and so on (see Doctrine and Covenants 67:2). He plans to bless His faithful children with a rich endowment of treasures, with a mighty legacy of blessings. Clearly, the treasures of eternity by their very nature far exceed treasures of the earth in both magnitude and splendor. No doubt we will be surprised to discover what He has at His disposal to give to us.

GENEROUS GIFTS FROM A GRACIOUS GOD

Without wishing to be too personal, I would like to refer briefly to some of the spiritual experiences God has blessed me with. My purpose in doing this is to indicate how generous God has been in blessing me. I have no doubt He seeks to likewise bless all His children to the extent possible. When I was fifteen years of age, I received my patriarchal blessing. I wrote the following in my life history about this event:

> I felt like the veil was transcended. The spirit in the room was tangible and powerful. I felt precious to God and known by him. The words and promises and blessings seemed so amazing to me. I felt important and valued. One of the most spiritual experiences of my entire life. I felt like I was floating on air. I was in the world but not of the world. I was so in awe and amazed that I got the wrong bus home. I eventually realized and then had to run most of the way home due to the lateness of the hour and the fact that I had no way of communicating with my mother to let her know the situation and I was concerned that she would be worried about me. I got home quite late. This experience has taught me that God has given, does give, and will yet give us, great gifts that are a source of comfort, consolation and confidence to us.

When I turned eighteen, I received my mission call, as well as my temple endowment in Frankfurt, Germany. I recorded the following many years later: "I was honestly shocked by the experience. I was transfixed and overwhelmed. I was struck by the magnanimous nature of God and what he had in store for me and all mankind. Our potential as Children of God is truly phenomenal. I was on a spiritual high the entire week. The blessings and opportunities offered in the Temple are great and amazing. The experience was life changing when I thought of what God was offering to me."

I will never forget dating Veronica, the girl who became my wife. She had returned from her mission and was radiating both spiritual light and physical beauty. It was a thrilling experience filled with exciting romance and spiritual feelings. We progressed through very pronounced opposition, and at the sealing there was a palpable sense of love. It really was a sacred and sweet experience. The priesthood power of the sealing ordinance was prevalent. The difference between temporal weddings and celestial ones is profound and pronounced. We were happy and had a glimpse of eternal life. We knelt on holy ground and heaven was close. God is love, really and truly, and He certainly can make our marriages eternal if we allow Him to do so. Of course, temple marriage is only the beginning to that blissful possibility. It is so easy to say "I do" or "yes" on the day of marriage, but that resolve is tested deeply and consistently after.

About the birth of my son, I wrote the following:

> I will always remember the birth of our only Son. To see my literal Son. My flesh and blood. The creation of a new person. One moment there was a void and next there was life in its glorious and penetrating simplicity. What wonder and love I felt! This is the power of God in a smaller degree. We called him Thomas David Holton. How beautiful he was to me. How perfect. How amazing! This was not accident, chance, or luck. This was a new soul—body and spirit joined for holy and sacred purposes. It was a life changing moment! It was a majestic miracle to see new life come into this world. I was touched deeply to see new life. We felt the presence of many angels bringing our son to us. This was divine design in action. A heavenly bestowal of unique significance and everlasting proportions and meaning! To see our Son, learn and grow and help him in that process has been a joy and an experience of inestimable worth. To share all the ups and downs of life with him. To read to him and dance with him and laugh and play and hug and cry and a thousand other things has made more richness out of life than I ever really comprehended. To teach him the gospel and see him learn the important lessons of life is a vitally important experience. I think that in this way, like no other, I have come to see how God feels about His precious children and the tremendous lengths He will go to in blessing and leading them. The joy of parenthood is the joy of God Himself and especially when done in the light of the everlasting Gospel as our sure guide. It is a spiritual privilege and honor to be treated with the deepest respect and the most profound sense of responsibility. Each child is a gift of God precious beyond price. Being a parent radically changed my perspective.

THE NATURE OF JOY

We experience a measure of joy on this earth. Happiness, peace, contentment, elation, wonder, surprise, hope, and generosity all come our way and give us a welcome relief from the burdens of mortality. The joy that comes to us in overcoming the weaknesses of our lives, achieving hard things, seeing loved ones learn and grow, and in progressing toward the fulfillment of our divine destiny are all precious parts of mortal joy. The greatest joy in mortality comes from sharing the gospel with others with pure intent and seeing people receive the word with enduring gladness. Of course, this joy will be greatly magnified and amplified in the kingdom of God. In the eternities we will know a fulness of joy. This will consist of joy in the Lord, joy with the Lord, joy of the Lord, joyful music, joyful song, joyful feelings, joyful thoughts, joyful work, and joyful relationships. Our joy will be both deep and permanent. It will last always as it will be built upon the eternal foundation of God. The journey we take in the eternities will itself be a joyful journey.

CONCLUSION

May each one of us come to know the great and good givers of all good gifts—our Eternal Father and His beloved Son.

14

TESTIFYING OF THIS GREAT IMPORTANT TRUTH

It is my conviction that the message of new life through Christ is to be shared with all the world. In 2 Nephi 26:23–28 we are clearly taught that God works in the light. He reveals Himself in the light. He works plainly and manifests His purposes and ways without deceit, trickery, treachery, hidden motives, and agendas. His purpose is to save the world. We are instructed that all of His plans and actions are intended to bless and help us. His love is manifest in His deeds. Christ offered His own life as a sacrifice to show forth His devotion to us. We are told that the desire of the Savior is to draw all men unto him. That is most instructive. His restored gospel is to go to the ends of the earth, to all nations, tongues, kindreds, and peoples. He has not excluded any from His plan. Every individual will have the opportunity to hear His word. Whether black or white, male or female, rich or poor, famous or unknown. Whether they live in Anchorage, Alaska, or Cancun, Mexico. Whether they were born to rich stockbrokers or poor farmers. Whether they are shepherds in Mongolia or actors in Australia. Whether they were born in the Dark Ages or in the twenty-first century. Each person—on both sides of the veil—must be given the opportunity to learn this truth. His salvation is available to all. In fact, the entire ends of the earth—all countries and clans—are invited to come to Him. He will provide each of us with gospel milk and gospel honey—nutritious, delicious, and soul-satisfying. This is not food and drink we can buy with human money. It comes because of His infinite and eternal Atonement. He paid the price for us. The cost to Him was deeply expensive. His intention is that all should come to know Him. He has not excluded the Celts or the Aboriginals or the native American Indians from receiving His redemptive reward. We are not required to atone in His place—indeed we cannot do so. We cannot afford to pay for eternal life. We do not have the means to buy this. However, He can provide it for us—on conditions of our humble repentance.

He has not cast us out of the temple. He cast the money to the floor, but He wants us to attend His house of prayer—in our own homes, in His chapels, and in His temple. Those who have embraced His word are invited to come to Him. Those who have wandered are invited to come back. Those whose membership is withdrawn are invited to return. Those not yet of the fold are invited to come, see, hear, do, and partake. He has instructed His servants that they are to persuade all men to repent. We are to ask, invite, entice, encourage, entreat, convince, and persuade all to come unto Christ. We are to persuade the rich, the poor, the simple, the proud, the learned, the unlearned, the casual, the sick, the weary, the forgotten, the abandoned, the lonely, the forsaken, the downtrodden, the guilty, the embarrassed, the nervous, the shy, the stubborn, and the eager to come to Him. We are to speak up, stand up, lift, and call men and women to repentance everywhere we find them—whether in Toronto, Tipperary, or Tel Aviv. He wants the people of the world to know Him, hear Him, love Him, serve Him, and trust Him. He wants them to partake of His goodness, to know of His love, to rejoice in His name, to remember His promises, to rely on His strength, and to feel of His joy. None are commanded to go away. The only ones who do not partake of His goodness are those who refuse to do so. He wants them to partake of His salvation, learn His laws, keep His commandments, follow His ways, receive His blessings, and live with Him forever.

We are told that all men have this equal privilege. The gospel is the great leveler. Receiving the gospel does not require us to be rich, handsome, famous, well educated, of royal lineage, or to travel in the right social circles. It does not demand that we hail from certain countries or possess a certain pedigree. All individuals can come to God and experience His blessings first-hand. They can have direct experience with the senses of His great goodness. This message is for all the world. We are to give inspired invitations to all to come to Him. As men and women come to His covenant, they will become His people, the elect of God, the house of Israel, the Church of the Firstborn. How blessed we are to have the Book of Mormon, revealed to us through Joseph Smith, a seer, prophet, and revelator. This restored gospel will go to every person. There is nowhere to hide, none to escape. No tradition, background, heritage, or status can prevent us from being found by God and offered—through His servants in these latter days—an opportunity to hear and hearken. Each of us must make our own decision when backed up to the wall of faith. This is where we must make our stand. We must choose whether we will accept Jesus as the Christ, the Only Begotten of the Father, the Word made Flesh, the Divine Son, the Author and Finisher of the Only Faith that can save men and women with an everlasting salvation in the Kingdom of God. There is no other way, no other message, no other means, and no other Messiah. As we go forward to share His message with the world, we can remember that the Lord works with us in His cause (see Doctrine and Covenants 84:88). The Lord labors with us in the vineyard. His effect upon us is one of lifting us up, lightening our load, lengthening our stride, and lauding our efforts.

PERSUASIVE POWER

The Book of Mormon invites us to be a persuasive people. There are several key things that disciples are to endeavor to persuade all people to do, which revolve around a covenant relationship with Christ. "I persuade my brethren, that they might be faithful in keeping the commandments of God" (1 Nephi 3:21) and "he hath commanded his people that they should persuade all men to repentance" (2 Nephi 26:27). Also: "And I would that I could persuade all ye ends of the earth to repent and prepare to stand before the judgment–seat of Christ" (Mormon 3:22) and "For the fulness of mine intent is that I may persuade men to come unto the God of Abraham, . . . and be saved" (1 Nephi 6:4). Further: "Perhaps I might persuade them that they would remember the Lord their Redeemer" (1 Nephi 19:18) and "I might more fully persuade them to believe in the Lord their Redeemer" (1 Nephi 19:23). Likewise: "To persuade our children, and also our brethren, to believe in Christ, and to be reconciled to God" (2 Nephi 25:23) and "we might persuade them to come unto Christ, and partake of the goodness of God, that they might enter into his rest. . . . We could persuade all men not to rebel against God, to provoke him to anger, but that all men would believe in Christ" (Jacob 1:7-8). Finally: "to persuade to believe in Christ" (Moroni 7:16).

So, we are to invite, persuade, entice, convince, plead, encourage, inspire, and move people to be obedient to God's commandments, to repent of their sins through the reconciliation of the Lord, to believe in the Savior and draw close to Him, to remember our Redeemer and to prepare for the inevitable judgment that awaits us all. We need to use the powerful doctrines of Christ in the scriptures, especially the Book of Mormon, to propel men, women, and children to do these things. We should use our abilities to help others both inside and outside the Church to learn and act on these truths. This persuasion is not manipulation, coercion, emotional blackmail, or guilt-tripping. Rather, it is using our full faculties, complete energies, total wills, and holistic abilities to encourage and convince all that the Living Christ is the master of giving us all a new life.

A VITALLY IMPORTANT NEED

There is a tremendously important need to teach and testify of the glorious truth associated with the new life offered through the Son of God. This can be done in purity and power. Having found this new life ourselves, we are moved with compassion and passion to share this with others so that they might find that newness of life which surpasses understanding. The scriptures declare that those who believe in the Son of God not only find a new type and kind of life themselves, but that they are also empowered to share those blessings with others willing to hear and partake of these marvelous blessings. Consider the wonderful works performed by God through His servants in this mortal life (see Doctrine and Covenants 84:65–72). That is to say that this new life through Christ is not an isolated blessing—it is contagious and powerfully influential.

WHAT THINK YE OF CHRIST?

I hope that my views, thoughts, and feelings about Jesus Christ have permeated this work with clarity. In case that has not been so obvious, I would now like to share my perspective on Him. Jesus Christ is truly the living Son of the living God. He is the Great I AM, the strong Savior of our souls. Christ is the Creator of heaven and earth. He is the living water, the bread of life. He is the spiritual Father of those who are born again. He is the healer of body and spirit. He is the forgiver of sins and the bestower of resurrection of our bodies. I love being a disciple of Jesus Christ. It is an honor to be associated with His powerful name, His marvelous life, His astonishing character, His tremendous work, and His mighty ministry. To believe in Him is to value goodness at the highest level. It is a precious privilege to learn of Him, to follow Him, to love Him, to serve Him, and to strive to emulate His amazing example. How wonderful is our Messiah! God is so good to us. His mercy is such a pervasive influence in my life. His generosity is beyond compare. We are well advised to remember Him more frequently, know Him more deeply, and love Him more fully. Heaven on earth is a life touched by God's marvelous greatness. I will gladly boast of Him all day long.

How crucially important is it to teach and testify of His atoning sacrifice to save the world? Consider His great intercessory love and power in 2 Nephi 2:6–10. No person can return to God's presence without the redemption of the Savior. That includes the prophets, apostles, and saints. That includes those who serve and sacrifice in good causes, charitable endeavors, and acts of love. It includes all children who die before reaching the age of eight years. It includes all the people we admire, look up to, love, and care about. No matter how good we are or how much good we have done, we could not be reconciled to the Father without the merits of the Son. This does not mean we should not do any good works. I believe that the more we understand the virtue of the infinite Atonement, the more inspired we will be to waste and wear out our lives in service. We know that our decision to accept the Savior gives us an endowment of His power to cross every bridge, perform every duty, withstand ever storm, surmount every obstacle, learn every lesson, and develop every characteristic we need to inherit eternal blessings. The people on earth need to know that the salvation through Christ is the only salvation available in time and eternity, for all people. According to the first article of faith, we believe in the Godhead. *We believe.* These simple words carry majestic meaning. Belief is powerful. It stirs the soul to righteous action. It moves mountains of difficulty, helps us transcend mediocrity, and elevates us to a higher place. A living, active, vital faith in the God of glory, His beloved Son, and in the Comforter is life transforming and soul sanctifying. In a world awash with doubts, cynicism, and despair, it is illuminating and invigorating to believe in, hope in, trust in, and rely on God. I believe! Sharing this faith in a world that has become a battle ground over just about everything requires us to have divine power to aid us and assist us so that we do not miss the mark. We do not contend in sharing the good word of God. We share in love and confidence, and the power of spiritual truth is manifest to all who choose to believe our words.

We are to sing to the praise of God (see Alma 26:8). No amount of gratitude would ever be too much when it comes to thanking God for His excellent goodness, His perfect love, His astounding plan, His sublime inspiration, and His never-ending guidance. Singing, speaking, praying, loving, serving, and blessing others are all good things we can do to show our deep and lasting gratitude to Him. Our gratitude to God will be pervasive. It will enable us to face the difficulty we sometimes encounter in sharing the revealed word with others. God intends to invite each of His children using the restored gospel message (see Doctrine and Covenants 1:2). To the worldly this seems impossible. To God, it is His plan and purpose and cannot be prevented. All will get to see God's influence, all will get to hear God's word, and all will be touched in the heart with God's message. We can be a part of this unfolding. In this day of widespread doubt, we can hear the voice of the Lord. In fact, the time will come when all will hear the voice of the Lord through the voice of His servants. His great desire is to bless us and lead us back to Him. There is therefore no good reason to doubt Him or His goodness. He lives to connect with us and to bind us back to Him. How great it is when we share this truth and people come to sense it, feel it, experience it, and rejoice in it. They hear His voice and know His words. Their lives are changed by Him through us.

We are to "glory in God" (Doctrine and Covenants 76:61). God is great, generous, gentle, and glad. We can be grateful for His gracious goodness. We are blessed with blessings large and small by God. We are guided in important decisions, warned of dangerous paths, protected from evil, comforted amidst affliction, and strengthened in times of need by believing in Christ, following Him, learning about Him, loving Him, and serving Him. What enemies will He subdue? The enemies of sin, the enemies of death, the enemies of confusion, doubt, and meaninglessness. He will overcome every argument arrayed against His existence, every railing accusation that He is uncaring, every misunderstanding of Him and His purposes, every misdirected assault on His character. He is the source of light, life, and love. What a world this will be when more and more of His children come to know of His goodness, feel of His love, understand His ways, and see the wisdom of His workings. The restoration is a "voice of gladness" and "glad tidings of great joy" (Doctrine and Covenants 128:19). The restored gospel of Jesus Christ is a message of peace, reassurance, rejoicing, hope, and celebration. It builds faith, strengthens resolve, imparts knowledge, provides comfort, offers blessings, grants tender mercies, and bestows joy. This applies to individuals and families on both sides of the veil. We are richly blessed to know of God's plans, purposes, and priorities. Rejoice and be glad. Sing praises to your Heavenly

King. Let His love lift you. We can be glad about the good news. This enthusiastic rejoicing will be contagious to others who do not yet know of these things but who will learn them as we open our mouths, shine our light, and invite all to come to God and live.

PUBLISH PEACE AND JOY

In this time of uncertainty, we have a clear message for the world. In the day of commotion, ours is the voice of calm. Although some are filled with fear, we abound with courage. In times of darkness, we speak of light. When doubt is pervasive, we teach of faith. When hatred is rampant, we preach of divine love. Peace promoters of the last days preach news of beautiful joy in the form of a kingdom of Zion (see 1 Nephi 13:37). So, we are called to bring to light the Zion of Christ in these last days. Those who do so shall be blessed with divine assistance in doing this phenomenal work. They shall receive the power of the Holy Ghost—power to teach and testify of truth, power to comfort and console others. If these preachers endure faithfully, then they shall be taken up to heaven in due course and saved with a salvation that endures forever. Those who publish the restored gospel of peace and joy in these latter days are teaching a vital message. This word overcomes conflict, confusion, consternation. It transcends the temporary, trivial, and transitory. It rises above the rash, raucous, and riotous. It is more powerful than fads, fashions, fame, and fortune. It pushes away pain. We are told that those who preach this message of truth will be made beautiful, radiant, and lovely, and will find place on the high mountain—this is the Mountain of the Lord, His holy place.

PREACH THE WORD BY THE WAY

I love the description the Lord gives the elders of this dispensation of how they should do their work: "Let them go two by two, and thus let them preach by the way in every congregation, baptizing by water, and the laying on of the hands by the water's side" (Doctrine and Covenants 52:9–10). They are to preach by the way. That is simply to say wherever they find the people, they preach the truth to them. Whether in the homes, on the hills, in the valleys, in the streets, on the mountains, in the synagogues. Or as it could be said in these days, on Facebook, Twitter, WhatsApp, Skype, Zoom, the telephone, or anywhere else. The elders and sisters are to talk to the people on the way—never knowing exactly or beforehand who might hear them or where they might be located. They might be hidden in the holes, the rocks, the caves. Or, in other words, we seek them out, go looking for them, hunt for them, fish for them. We go to where they are to find them.

It also instructs that the missionaries are to say the things the prophets have written AND those things the Holy Ghost teaches them (the elders) through the prayer of faith. That is to say that not only do the elders teach the written word of God, but also the oral word that comes from divine sources. This is the word that comes through the Holy Comforter to heal the wounded soul, uplift the downtrodden, encourage the weary, reclaim the lost, inspire the seeking, and educate the willing. The Holy Ghost knows what the people need to hear to attract them to God's word. He knows the questions of the soul, the hidden sorrows of the heart, the deep longings of the honest in spirit. So, we must be in tune to give the needed portion. The elders or sisters are to go two by two—companions in the doctrine of Christ, as two witnesses to the word of God, to bear sure and certain testimony of the validity of this great latter-day work. Again, they are to preach by the way in every congregation. That is just to say they are to preach to the people that they come across, to give all an opportunity to hear, whether poor, rich, lost, lonely, or in whatever circumstances they find them. In congregations large and small, on the internet or in physical buildings, in groups of hundreds or gatherings of just one soul, they are to preach God's word to all. Those who listen and obey are to be immersed in water. The beautiful, clean, pure, refreshing waters of baptismal cleansing and renewal. Then the elders are to lay their hands on them by the water's side and give them the Holy Ghost. How like John the Baptist. Baptized in water and baptized in spirit—right at the water. In the way. How marvelous. Of course, in these times the confirmations are not usually done by the water's side immediately. However, they are still done in the spirit of righteousness and renewal. In the attitude of love and rejoicing, in the fellowship of faith and the brotherhood of blessings. The missionaries of the Lord are to teach, testify, and baptize all who will come to the waters of life. How wonderful is this imagery! In this time of challenge and difficulty we are to raise the voice of gladness, to proclaim the good news, to share hope, help, and healing with a lost and tired world. The Lord knows His sheep. He knows where they can be found. He knows what they need to hear. He knows how to lift them to a higher place, a greater vision, a nobler destiny. We are to seek them, knock on their doors, find them, and ask them to come unto Christ. We will go where they are and bring them back to Him, who is the good Shepherd of the entire flock. There they will find pasture, peace, plenty, and perfection in Him.

MY TESTIMONY

I return to where I began. The testimony of the Living Christ is the bedrock of my life. This testimony has been forged in the furnace of experience. I have read the Book of Mormon and the other standard works sincerely. I have attended Church searchingly. I have prayed in the revealed pattern seeking light. I have sought to undermine the natural man within. I have listened intently to the servants of the Lord endowed with power in this day and age. I have heard the prophetic voice. I have experienced the spiritual power of ordinances—baptism, confirmation, priesthood bestowal, temple endowment and sealing, and the sacrament. I have served in many callings. I have felt of the Holy Ghost surging through me. I have learned to keep the commandments of God. Through all of this, I have stood on holy ground, I have knelt on sacred ground, and I have experienced the transforming power of this latter-day work. I have come to know that Jesus Christ is revealed to us, in clear ways and in profound revelatory ways, by means of the restoration of His everlasting gospel through the Prophet Joseph Smith and his successors in these latter days. So, it is the Christ, as revealed to us through the channel of actual revelation, that has become an anchor to my soul. This personal revelation is deep, powerful, and transformative. It has permitted me to sense the truth, power, reality, and validity of this final dispensation through all the opposition, vicissitudes, darkness, conflicts, and circumstances of my life.

It is my witness that these ideas are not fictional fantasies, mad myths, idle illusions, or foolish falsities. They are true—pure, undiluted, and significant. I know with a solid, unshakable certainty that there is no good life of any kind or degree whatsoever without Christ. He is the Bright and Morning Star, the center of our lives, the bringer of every good gift. He is the rock-solid Messiah, the King of heaven and earth, the being of majesty and beauty, and the source of every wonder worth experiencing. Through the triumphant Only Begotten Son of God—who has revealed himself in glory in these latter days to His precious Prophet Joseph Smith—we come to a marvelous and wonderful new understanding and life. Let us celebrate the Light and Life of the World. He is the Living Christ that shines in darkness. He is the speaking, caring, teaching, and courageous Master. He is the rock-solid stone of Israel, the never-failing healer of our souls. My witness of Him is sure and certain. He is our Righteous Redeemer and our Strong Shepherd. He lives. He loves. He saves. As we come to Him completely and with a devotion that can become everlasting, He will bestow power upon us to overcome all things. He is truly mighty to save. May we always remember Him. "Pray always, that ye may not faint, until I come. Behold, and lo, I will come quickly, and receive you unto myself. Amen" (Doctrine and Covenants 88:126).

15

AN EYE SINGLE TO GOD'S GLORY

How pivotally crucial it is to see that all gospel principles are part of one great mosaic of meaning. They are not isolated or fragmented but unified into one great overarching plan. All the foregoing doctrines and devotions converge into one overall whole—this is how we connect all the truths together so that they are one in our hands and lives. Having an eye single to the glory of God is the scriptural terminology for coming to this singular perspective where we combine all spiritual elements into one. Our loyalty to God becomes not a passing phase or a transitory trek, but rather it becomes the sum and substance of our lives. I conclude in this chapter by bringing all these preceding principles together to show that God's plan is truly a holistic one. It is one of harmony, unity, oneness, completeness, and perfection. As the Father, Son, and Holy Ghost are at one when it comes to these truths, then we likewise can be one with them. To have an eye single to God's glory is to reach that point of purity, devotion, dedication, determination, and consecrated commitment that evidences we are unshakably on the Lord's side, no matter what the cost or difficulties associated with that. This is obviously no small achievement, but it is both possible and powerful.

A LIFE GIVEN TO GOD

Consider this inspiring statement: "Men and women who turn their lives over to God will discover that He can make a lot more out of their lives than they can. He will deepen their joys, expand their vision, quicken their minds, strengthen their muscles, lift their spirits, multiply their blessings, increase their opportunities, comfort their souls, raise up friends, and pour out peace. Whoever will lose his life in the service of God will find eternal life."[1]

I believe this with all my heart. Think about the rich range of this promise. God is interested in what we can see, think, feel, learn, do, and become. He will aid us in using all our faculties and will develop our capacity to a greater extent and degree than we possibly could unaided. This is a most marvelous reward from a God who loves to see His children become greater than what they presently are. I also note that these are comforting, consoling blessings—deepening, strengthening, and so on. Who is not in need of the reassurance of heaven during these times of challenge across the world? These are not idle promises. Who else could possibly present such an array of developmental and experiential opportunity to us? Only God can and only God will, if we turn to Him sincerely. My feeling is that He can make us men and women of might, mercy, miracles, and majesty. This is potent and poignant.

How central is having an eye single to the glory of God? The Lord said: "And faith, hope, charity and love, with an eye single to the glory of God, qualify him for the work" (Doctrine and Covenants 4:5). That is to say that along with having faith, hope, and charity (very important characteristics in their own right), we need to have an eye single to God's glory to be a missionary and indeed to be an effective servant in His latter-day kingdom. There is no valid substitute for developing this core value and disposition. These attributes make us able to do the Lord's work, and without them we cannot truly succeed in the way He desires. An eye single to God's glory does not come about automatically or in one attempt. It is

---

1 President Ezra Taft Benson, Jesus Christ—Gifts and Expectations," *Ensign*, December 1988, 4.

a prolonged effort over time that allows for this ability to develop within us: "Nevertheless they did fast and pray oft, and did wax stronger and stronger in their humility, and firmer and firmer in the faith of Christ, unto the filling their souls with joy and consolation, yea, even to the purifying and the sanctification of their hearts, which sanctification cometh because of their yielding their hearts unto God" (Helaman 3:35).

The Book of Mormon Saints fasted regularly, prayed frequently, exercised their humility consistently, and developed their faith continually. This allowed them to have true happiness and consolation from God in their afflictions. This also led to them having pure hearts, hearts that were becoming more and more set on things divine. This spiritual sanctification—or holiness of heart, meaning purity of purpose, focus of intent—came to them because they gave way in their desires to wanting what God wanted, to seeking what He sought, to doing what He would have them do. If we have submissive hearts, then our service will be sanctified. An eye single to God means that our will is swallowed up in wanting and doing the will of God, not on our own agendas, desires, ambitions, intentions, and aims. This is no easy task and requires attention to detail and regularly examining our motives. We need to strip away pretense and level with the Lord. We divest ourselves of desires for acclaim, position, power, or influence for impure motives. What the will of God is becomes the driving force for our internal questions and outward efforts.

> And if your eye be single to my glory, your whole bodies shall be filled with light, and there shall be no darkness in you; and that body which is filled with light comprehendeth all things.
>
> Therefore, sanctify yourselves that your minds become single to God, and the days will come that you shall see him; for he will unveil his face unto you, and it shall be in his own time, and in his own way, and according to his own will. (Doctrine and Covenants 88:67–68)

Those with eyes single to God are filled with light—divine light—so that they see clearly, discern wisely, and view appropriately.

They understand spiritual realities better than they did when clouded by sin, confusion, distraction, or selfish ambition. This light fills them with clarity of purpose and long reaching vision. Eventually, when they are sufficiently ready, they can see the Lord because of His revealing Himself to them. They are spiritually mature enough to cope with the implications of such sacred and special disclosure.

> I pray for them: I pray not for the world, but for them which thou hast given me; for they are thine.
> And all mine are thine, and thine are mine; and I am glorified in them. . . .
> And for their sakes I sanctify myself, that they also might be sanctified through the truth.
> Neither pray I for these alone, but for them also which shall believe on me through their word;
> That they all may be one; as thou, Father, *art* in me, and I in thee, that they also may be one in us: that the world may believe that thou hast sent me.
> And the glory which thou gavest me I have given them; that they may be one, even as we are one:
> I in them, and thou in me, that they may be made perfect in one; and that the world may know that thou hast sent me, and hast loved them, as thou hast loved me.
> Father, I will that they also, whom thou hast given me, be with me where I am; that they may behold my glory, which thou hast given me: for thou lovedst me before the foundation of the world.
> O righteous Father, the world hath not known thee: but I have known thee, and these have known that thou hast sent me. (John 17:9–26)

This great Intercessory Prayer evidences the oneness in purpose that the Father and the Son enjoy. It is the purpose of Christ to make us one with Him. To make this possible, the Messiah lived a sanctified life so that we might also become sanctified through the truth of Christ. Also, those who hear the words of Christ from the servants of God will also become sanctified by believing and incorporating the word of Christ into their lives, their very souls. Hence,

Christ has an eye single to the glory of the Father and so will those who hear the voice of Christ directly or from His servants and hearken diligently to that sanctifying word. This is the only way we can become truly, deeply, and permanently one with God. As Christ has a fulness of life, so will we as we become like him.

ATTITUDES

In our endeavoring to establish an eye single to God's glory, we are to yield our ambitions to the will of God. We are to bend our will to His, knowing that having our wills swallowed up in His will give us a newness of life. We seek to become a more useful servant, not a more praised or well-known servant. We do not seek the limelight, spotlight, or praise of others. Of course, we do not seek to hide away from service or to shy away from responsibility. We will strive to step out of our personal comfort zones, show pure love for others, and develop an attitude of consecrated discipleship. We are to face toward God, heaven, and the temple—this is a posture of inclination towards the things of eternity. We will use our talents, knowledge, abilities, and gifts for the positive and constructive building of God's kingdom. We will work for the benefit and blessings of others, asking such questions as, what is best for the kingdom? Will this decision bless the lives of the people? Will these actions guide, bless, and help others? Will these efforts build faith and strengthen testimony? Will my example inspire others to rise to the potential greatness latent within themselves? Such essential motivation is obtainable for all who seek it and it is impressive to see this in others.

CHARACTERISTICS

Eradicating selfishness, eliminating impure ambition, abolishing self-interest, and jettisoning pride is like pulling the overgrown weeds from a garden—it is necessary to pave the way to grow beautiful flowers. These beautiful flowers are the qualities of the soul that need to be cultivated if we are to find a life that is productive, useful, fruitful, abundant, and resplendent. I believe there is intrinsic greatness in developing a godlike character—this involves acquiring the virtues of integrity, reverence, purity, humility, hard work, self-sacrifice, honor, duty, love, diligence, patience, kindness, and so on. These attributes are never outdated or outmoded. They are perennially valuable and desirable. To learn to live and serve out of an inner motive of pure love for God, others, and oneself is the work of a lifetime and is something that takes time, effort, and ongoing divine help. Our characteristics make up our character. It is what we are in the depths of our being. There will be deep joy in our souls as we learn to incorporate the ultimate characteristic of having a singular focus on doing the will of God for the right reason, in the right way, at the right time. A new life in Christ must involve the creation or renewal of a godly character within us. Character carries us through the most challenging currents of life.

CONNECTION WITH GOD

We are to become one with God, unified with Him in His purposes. We become partakers of the divine nature. We are to be essentially connected with Him as a tree branch draws sustenance from the roots—we draw power and life from the source of our strength, our living God. He is the vine and we are the branches:

> I AM the true vine, and my Father is the husbandman. . . .
> Abide in me, and I in you. As the branch cannot bear fruit of itself, except it abide in the vine; no more can ye, except ye abide in me.
> I am the vine, ye *are* the branches: He that abideth in me, and I in him, the same bringeth forth much fruit: for without me ye can do nothing. . . .
> If ye abide in me, and my words abide in you, ye shall ask what ye will, and it shall be done unto you. (John 15:1–7)

Therefore, when we as branches of the Savior bear fruit (in other words, when we produce good tasting and nutritious results by doing good works that are delicious and beneficial because they bless lives), then our Father in Heaven will purge us—test, polish, cleanse, refine, purify, sanctify us—so that we can bring forth more fruit. We can do more good, bless more lives, be more productive in the work of saving souls. How do we receive this purging? Through hearing and hearkening to the word of God. We are to abide in the Savior and He in us. What does this mean? To abide is to stay, keep company with, be able to associate with, be able to partake with, linger with. To abide in Christ is to be connected to Him, loyal to Him, devoted to Him, happy with Him, comfortable with Him. It is to enjoy Him and His character, to resonate with His projects, to find agreement with His plans. He likewise likes to link with us, find company with us, spend time together, and find joy in the same purposes. So, we are to find fellowship in His person. We are to be friends, traveling companions, pilgrims on the same journey, seekers on the same path, wanderers with the same destination. As we stay in this covenant connection with Him, we are nourished, strengthened, nurtured, and given life through and from Him. Our partnership becomes one of living power. Then, we become capable of bringing forth much fruit—of doing much good and blessing many lives. This reminds me of Jacob 5, the allegory of the olive tree, where we are told that the Lord of the vineyard labors along with the servant. We are further told that without the Lord we can do nothing. What happens to the branch of a tree that is cut off from the tree? It dies. For the branch to live, it must be connected to the tree. The branch must be connected to the vine to survive and thrive and bring forth fruit. The analogy is clear. Without our Savior we are akin to the branch cut off from the tree. We cannot possibly even live under such conditions, never mind grow and develop and produce fruit. To disconnect from Christ is to lose the link to the source of our life, power, and fruit bearing capacity.

PROPHETIC EXAMPLES

In my mind, the prophets are great examples of showing an eye single to the glory of God and how this essentially involves being alive in Christ. Think of Abraham being willing to sacrifice Isaac. This was obviously not something Abraham found easy to do. It was phenomenally difficult. He knew that God had commanded this offering, and He knew that God had the power to fulfill His promises, even if such appeared impossible to the natural man. He determined to do what God had asked of Him. While this is partially a story about doing's God will, even if it is deeply heart-wrenching and counterintuitive, there is another side to it. Abraham received a posterity as numerous as the sands on the seashore and as glorious as the stars in the sky. This was a fulfillment of his deepest desires—that he would be a father of many righteous nations. So, God brought life where there was an expectation of death. I believe the symbolism is rich in this example. Through the sacrifice of the Father and death of the Son Jesus Christ, we come to a newness of unexpected and unmatched life, albeit in the initial face of both spiritual and physical death. We all face types of Abrahamic tests in our own lives. No doubt they always involve loss, sacrifice, death, and so on in some form. But they always lead to a newness of life through God. We can pass these tests well if we will, and they will always lead us to remember that the rich blessings of life here and hereafter come to us through the death and suffering of God's Only Begotten Son in the flesh.

I think of the Prophet Joseph Smith, who went into the grove wanting to simply find salvation for himself and to know which Church to join. He had no anticipation of being confronted by the phenomenal adversity he faced for the rest of his life. He had no awareness of being called as a prophet. He had no notion that he was going to be appointed to carry a very heavy responsibility that would come to define the very nature of his life. Joseph was called upon to do things that would stretch even the most capable of souls. He became, over time, completely aligned with God's will. This was no easy task, even for someone as great as he was. It was an extremely difficult mountain to climb. I think of the time he reproved the guards when he was locked in chains as a time reflecting his commitment to the Lord. This was a moment of powerful majesty. He could have lived a much easier life if he had decided that what God asked was too hard. He could have opted out of his difficult calling. Thankfully, he did not do so. God bestowed on him great power to do a great work. He had an eye single to God's glory and was given a life that was rich in revelation, deep in faith, sound in doctrine, and abundant in the opportunity to benefit others. A life following

God is not an easy life, but it is a deeply blessed and rewarding life.

Consider the prophet Nephi. He is extremely easy to admire:

> And it came to pass that I, Nephi, returned from speaking with the Lord, to the tent of my father.
>
> And it came to pass that he spake unto me, saying: Behold I have dreamed a dream, in the which the Lord hath commanded me that thou and thy brethren shall return to Jerusalem . . .
>
> Wherefore, the Lord hath commanded me that thou and thy brothers should go unto the house of Laban, and seek the records, and bring them down hither into the wilderness.
>
> And now, behold thy brothers murmur, saying it is a hard thing which I have required of them; but behold I have not required it of them, but it is a commandment of the Lord.
>
> Therefore go, my son, and thou shalt be favored of the Lord, because thou hast not murmured.
>
> And it came to pass that I, Nephi, said unto my father: I will go and do the things which the Lord hath commanded, for I know that the Lord giveth no commandments unto the children of men, save he shall prepare a way for them that they may accomplish the thing which he commandeth them.
>
> And it came to pass that when my father had heard these words he was exceedingly glad, for he knew that I had been blessed of the Lord.
>
> And I, Nephi, and my brethren took our journey in the wilderness, with our tents, to go up to the land of Jerusalem. (1 Nephi 3:1–9)

The significance of this event is important to note. Nephi was already speaking with the Lord before this incident happened. He was in the posture of discipleship. Then his father told him that he needed to return to Jerusalem to get the brass plates. This was the very place they had already been commanded to leave. This was a dangerous place where their lives were in jeopardy. Nephi was told his brothers had already been informed of this commandment and had complained. How is that for a context for receiving a calling? Your bishop tells you the last person interviewed for the difficult calling moaned about it and now you are asked to do it, and to work with the very person who moaned. Not a very enticing offer, is it? Lehi said that the commandment came from the Lord, not from a man. He was the messenger, not the commander. Nephi was told that he would be favored of the Lord because he did not complain about the call.

I believe we can all be favored of the Lord. We are in the driving seat on this issue. It is our approach that determines whether we become favored or not. The Lord asked Nephi's older brethren to take on the assignment first. The Lord gave them an opportunity to become favored of Him. Nephi gave the classic response known so well: I will go and do. He essentially bore his testimony to his father. He said that he knew the Lord always prepares a way when He asks us to do something. How did he know this? I believe it was because he had witnessed it already and had discerned the lesson involved. Notice that he said that the Lord prepares the way, but the children of men still need to perform and accomplish the task. The Lord does not come down and do it Himself. What purpose would that serve? The Lord wants developing disciples, not dependent subjects. Lehi, on hearing this testimonial, was happy because he knew that Nephi had caught the vision of the work, without being nagged into it, compelled into it, or spoon fed continually. Then we are told that Nephi and his brethren simply took their journey into the wilderness. No delay, no procrastinating, no second guessing, no changing of minds. I am so impressed by Nephi.

It is very insightful what Nephi said and what he did not say in this account. He did not say, "Why did no one think to get the plates before we left? What kind of a hair brained idea is this? What is in it for me? Why me? Why this? Why now? Ask someone else, ask Laman or Lemuel—they are older, they are in charge, they are responsible. It is too hard. I cannot do it; I am not able for this. I will not do it."

He did say, "I will go and do. I trust, I believe, I accept. I will show faith and courage. God will help me." Nephi was true to his word. He refused to go back to his father without the plates, despite not knowing exactly how to accomplish the task, despite being cast out and threatened by Laban, despite being attacked by his brothers for failure, despite being robbed of the family treasures, and despite having to take the life of Laban, which was a deeply difficult thing for him to do. He made sure he accomplished the task. This is commitment to the Lord that is worthy of emulation. Nephi continued to show resilience under pressure and courage under fire again and again and again. His humility, tenacity, and persistent devotion are an inspiration to me. His ability to forgive his brothers and learn how to do hard things are examples of what the Lord can do with someone who is spiritually pliable. His was an eye single to the glory of God, a life of resolve and determination to do what was right under extremely uncomfortable circumstances.

THE MIGHTY MESSIAH

What of the Son of God? Any praise we offer seems like a poor reflection in a darkened pool. His life and submission are remarkable by any standard and are astonishing to the thoughtful observer. He was fully spiritually submissive, never altering from the covenant path even when He stood drenched in blood before the soldiers who were mere men—this was Towering Majesty in visual form. When Pilate said the words *Ecce Homo* (Behold the Man), I think we are well advised to look at the man who stands before us all. His manhood is without fault, He is the marvelous manifestation of what it means to surrender to the divine will when faced with the worst possible evil imaginable. His ascendancy over darkness is a stunning example of His capacity, commitment, and consecration. My admiration for Him knows no bounds. And He has a life that is glorious beyond description because of that.

ALL THAT WE HAVE AND ARE

So, what is involved in this gaining an eye single to God's glory? It is to learn to give all that we have and are to the Lord, without reservation, hesitation, reluctance, or rebellion. I think of the following words as core to this: yield, submit, humble, penitent, contrite, soft-hearted. Full, total, complete, entire, absolute. Resolute, determined, resilient, committed, persistent. I ponder the following phrases which are central to this: last full measure of devotion. Singularity of purpose. Single-minded devotion. Purity of intent.

Sincerity of heart. Full purpose of heart. A pure heart. I think this involves all our senses—sight, hearing, touch, taste, and feeling. It includes our heart, might, mind and strength. It involves our thoughts, feelings, spirit, and body. It requires a change of heart, an alteration of state, a transformation in disposition, a newness of perspective, a shift in thinking, a move to a higher way of living.

THE MEASURE OF GREATNESS AND SUCCESS

When it comes to things divine, the ultimate test of greatness and success is not how popular we are, how rich we are, or how famous we are. It is not the status we have achieved, the honors we have been awarded, the accolades from others. It is not about how we compare to others or whether we are faster, stronger, smarter, or more visible than others. The ultimate test is found in whether God has become the first great priority of our lives. The true measure of success is a life of devotion to God and His children. If God is the core central focus of our lives and we seek to cherish our spouse, love our children, and serve others for God's glory and their benefit, then we have achieved eternal success from the perspective of our Father in Heaven and His Son, Jesus Christ. That does not mean that riches, honors, looks, intelligence, fame, and so on are bad or undesirable. It means that they are not the standard of judgment we should employ. Our greatness is determined by the degree to which we have surrendered our will to God, by how completely and enduringly we have focused on keeping the commandments of God as the vital and critical driving force in our lives. This is a station to which all can arrive if they choose to. This choice to submit our agency to God will lead to a fulness of life, which is clearly beyond the capacity of any mortal to fully appreciate. Only those who come to know such submission from the inside will come to eventually see the amazing and eternal rewards of such a stance of dignity, power, and might.

REMEMBER THE COVENANTAL PROMISES OF THE LORD

God is a being of perfect reliability and power. His word is His bond. His character is sure. His strength is unfailing. His devotion is unwavering. His character is flawless. He is the ultimate man of integrity (see Mormon 8:26). He is a being of moral rectitude, integrity, honor, uprightness, virtue, loyalty to principle, abiding faithfulness, moderation, and temperance. Scripture shows that God always remembers and fulfills His oaths, promises, vows, declarations, and covenants (see Mormon 9:25). God's entire plan reflects His deep and ongoing devotion to us. His covenants are unbreakable. His covenants shall be fulfilled. The Lord remembers His covenant to the house of Israel (see Mormon 9:37). All His pronouncements shall be fulfilled. "For the eternal purposes of the Lord shall roll on, until all his promises shall be fulfilled" (Mormon 8:22). Thus, our God is a being of covenantal promises. "Behold, I say unto you that whoso believeth in Christ, doubting nothing, whatsoever he shall ask the Father in the name of Christ it shall be granted him; and this promise is unto all, even unto the ends of the earth" (Mormon 9:21). Christ's deep dedication to His role was not spoken in jest, triviality, or pretense. He was serious, devoted, and dedicated. He kept His word and was loyal to His promise. He said "nevertheless," despite terrible suffering. This commitment to His covenant made before the foundation of the world facilitated Him in proceeding to win the victory over sin and death. Men may sleep, tire, forget, neglect, break promises—but God will not. His promises will be fulfilled and achieved (see 2 Nephi 10:17; Doctrine and Covenants 45:16). No power on earth or hell can stop Him or His work. He promises to heal us, teach us, guide us, bless us, reassure us, resurrect us, exalt us, and abide with us if we are true and faithful. His promises are sure and certain. He will remember His promises to all and keep them. His judgments are just, discerning, wise, merciful, generous, righteous, good, and perfect. We can rejoice with hope that we are not forgotten, abandoned, lost, or cast off (see Moroni 10:4). Indeed, I have been struck by how often the Lord uses such words as "will, must, surely, shall, sworn" in the revelations. His wording is not tentative. Rather, it is decisive, definitive, declarative, and destined: "For this, the waters of Noah unto me, for as I have sworn that the waters of Noah should no more go over the earth, so have I sworn that I would not be wroth with thee. For the mountains shall depart and the hills be removed, but my kindness shall not depart from thee, neither shall the covenant of my peace be removed, saith the Lord that hath mercy on thee" (3 Nephi 22:9—10).

PROMISES TO THE FATHERS

"The order of this priesthood was confirmed to be handed down from father to son, and rightly belongs to the literal descendants of the chosen seed, to whom the promises were made" (Doctrine and Covenants 107:40). Therefore, the priesthood was given from Adam to his sons and by his sons to their sons. This was the divine order. It was a family government. Adam was the first covenant disciple (along with his wife, Eve) and was promised that the priesthood, which administers the blessings of salvation, would be transmitted in a family setting from father to son. From the very outset, the priesthood plan has been centered on the idea of life, family, creation, posterity. Obviously, this could not happen unless Adam and Eve were both personally involved in the promises and made partakers thereof. This enriches our understanding of what it means to be alive in Christ. The life we are discussing does not just impact us directly but also our children, down through the generations. This is an intergenerational life in Christ. Salvation, in the full and true sense, involves not just individuals but husbands and wives and their children. This is what the promise entails. What promises has God made to the fathers that are being fulfilled in the latter days? Consider these words that Jehovah spoke to Father Abraham:

> And I will make of thee a great nation, and I will bless thee above measure, and make thy name great among all nations, and thou shalt be a blessing unto thy seed after thee, that in their hands they shall bear this ministry and priesthood unto all nations;
>
> And I will bless them through thy name; for as many as receive this Gospel shall be called after thy name, and shall be accounted thy seed, and shall rise up and bless thee, as their father;
>
> And I will bless them that bless thee, and curse them that curse thee; and in thee (that is, in thy priesthood) and in thy

seed (that is, thy priesthood), for I give unto thee a promise that this right shall continue in thee, and in thy seed after thee (that is to say, the literal seed, or the seed of the body) shall all the families of the earth be blessed, even with the blessings of the gospel, which are the blessings of salvation, even of life eternal. (Abraham 2:9–11)

We are taught that Abraham would be blessed to have a great and good posterity that would hold the priesthood and minister to the entire world with the gospel covenant. All who would receive the gospel after Abraham at the hands of his children would then be counted as if they were Abraham's covenant children. By this means, all individuals and families would be offered the blessings of eternal life. So, essentially, this promise is one of a great life, a blessed life, a saved life, an everlasting life to those who are of the righteous covenant family of the Lord through Abraham. Properly understood, this is a fulfillment of the promises originally made to Adam and other righteous patriarchs down through the ages. They all focused on the family covenant. Life is in the family. Life in Christ is in the family, now and eternally. Think of the saved family of God in the eternities and how this will be a glorious unity of righteousness both numerically and in terms of the quality of this endless joyful life.

God has promised that the seed of Joseph (great-grandson of Abraham) should always exist on the face of the earth and that through Manasseh (son of Joseph), the Book of Mormon would likewise be preserved through time: "Wherefore, for this cause hath the Lord God promised unto me that these things which I write shall be kept and preserved, and handed down unto my seed, from generation to generation, that the promise may be fulfilled unto Joseph, that his seed should never perish as long as the earth should stand" (2 Nephi 25:21). It is interesting to me that the promise of the Lord in this context is centrally bound up with the preservation of the spiritual and temporal life of the covenant family.

We have, in 1823, a revelation from the Lord that explains the vital link between prophets in ancient times and prophets today:

> Behold, I will reveal unto you the priesthood, by the hand of Elijah the prophet, before the coming of the great and dreadful day of the Lord.
>
> And he shall plant in the hearts of the children the promises made to the fathers, and the hearts of the children shall turn to their fathers.
>
> If it were not so, the whole earth would be utterly wasted at his coming. (Doctrine and Covenants 2:1–3)

This means that Elijah, an Old Testament prophet, would restore the sealing power of the priesthood in our day. The significance of this is profound. Elijah would plant in the hearts of the latter-day children the sacred promises that were made to their fathers. The wording is important. Think of Alma's discourse on planting the seed of the word of God within us and helping it grow into a full tree (see Alma 32). The symbolism is useful. The heart is the place of our deepest desires, our most profound longings. To place something in your heart is to have it lodged there, and it becomes a part of your very nature. The heart is the soil. A soft heart receives and loves the word of God. A seed grows into a tree only when it is planted in good soil and nourished continually. So, in the family garden, each seed is cultivated, every tree is nourished, and all trees are to be together in a united collective. To have the promises planted within us is to become a participant in the great family drama. We are to discover and live the covenantal promises made to our fathers Adam, Enoch, Noah, Abraham, Moses, and Peter. We are to partake in the patriarchal promises of the priesthood and the ministry. By so doing, we become living trees of life in the garden of the Lord. Our hearts turn to them with love and devotion. The family breach is repaired. No wonder Elijah appeared in person to confer this power. The family is a personal institution. It is a place of belonging, connection, meaning, and purpose. To prevent the world from being a waste of space and to stop it from being obliterated at the Second Coming, there needs to be a righteous covenant family which is intergenerational in nature.

The Lord instructed Joseph Smith in 1830 that the priesthood promises made to the ancient patriarch Abraham and renewed upon his sons were still in play in the latter days and were applicable to

Joseph Smith as the seed of Abraham: "And also with Joseph and Jacob, and Isaac, and Abraham, your fathers, by whom the promises remain;" (Doctrine and Covenants 27:10). The Lord later goes on to say to Joseph Smith:

> Abraham received promises concerning his seed, and of the fruit of his loins—from whose loins ye are, namely, my servant Joseph—which were to continue so long as they were in the world; and as touching Abraham and his seed, out of the world they should continue; both in the world and out of the world should they continue as innumerable as the stars; or, if ye were to count the sand upon the seashore ye could not number them.
>
> This promise is yours also, because ye are of Abraham, and the promise was made unto Abraham; and by this law is the continuation of the works of my Father, wherein he glorifieth himself.
>
> Go ye, therefore, and do the works of Abraham; enter ye into my law and ye shall be saved.
>
> But if ye enter not into my law ye cannot receive the promise of my Father, which he made unto Abraham. (Doctrine and Covenants 132:30–33)

This is wonderfully instructive. The Prophet Joseph Smith was of the seed of Abraham. The promises made to Abraham concerned not simply blessings to his posterity in this life but also in the worlds to come. Abraham would have seed that would be countless in number and that would radiate with light as the stars would. Both large numbers and spiritual might would be involved. Joseph Smith also receives this same promise—on the basis, of him being of Abraham AND accepting the gospel covenant. Notice again how the promises always revolve around the idea of the quality and quantity of the lives of the children of God being impacted. The foregoing explains why the Lord has set his hand to gather the house of Israel in the latter days to their lands of inheritance by covenant and promise:

> Nevertheless, when that day cometh, saith the prophet, that they no more turn aside their hearts against the Holy One of Israel, then will he remember the covenants which he made to their fathers.

> Yea, then will he remember the isles of the sea; yea, and all the people who are of the house of Israel, will I gather in, saith the Lord, according to the words of the prophet Zenos, from the four quarters of the earth.
>
> Yea, and all the earth shall see the salvation of the Lord, saith the prophet; every nation, kindred, tongue and people shall be blessed. (1 Nephi 19:15–17)

The Lord is gathering scattered Israel to fulfill the divine promises He made to the ancient righteous men and women who were so concerned about their family forever. All will know that the Lord is serious about His family promises. That is why we do missionary work. It is to bring the family back together again, in unity and love and salvation. All must be invited to partake of the family promises of rich life now and eternal life in the eternities. There is no power on earth or in hell that can stop the redemption of each and all who seek to be in God's eternal family.

PROMISES TO THE RIGHTEOUS

So, what are the promises the Lord has made to those who become and remain devoted covenant disciples?

They are promised that they will receive the gift of the Holy Ghost if they are baptized by immersion by proper authority (see 2 Nephi 31:18).

That is amazing to me. To receive the companionship of the Holy Ghost is a blessing beyond words. He is a pure and holy friend, a cleanser, a testifier, a revelator, a comforter, and a guide through all types of experiences. In the trials, troubles, tribulations, tests, temptations, and terrors we face in this life, the Holy Ghost will be with us. His help will be as an oasis in a desert, a covert from the storm, a light in the darkness. I note that through His precious and godly companionship we are given new life while in mortality and prepared for a glorious life in the world beyond this one.

They are promised that under inspiration from the Holy Ghost, they shall speak revelatory words, which will be borne in the spirit of divine testimony (see Doctrine and Covenants 100:5–8).

So it is that they will be given, based on need, powerful words which will meet the critical needs of the situation.

They are promised that a multitude of blessings will come to them as they are married according to the law of the Lord (see 4 Nephi 1:11).

What are these blessings? The gifts of a helpmeet to walk the road of life with in times of trial and triumph, the privilege of having children and raising them up in righteousness, the opportunity to experience family life and all the educational development that comes with that. We cannot find a fulness of life alone. We need to belong to a family to find the many wonderful opportunities God has in store for his children.

They are promised that through the Son of God, their blindness will be turned to sight, their tears to joy, their sickness to health, their deafness to hearing, their corruption to perfection and their death to life (see 3 Nephi 17:5–7).

This sermon happened in a place call Bountiful. How appropriate. Indeed, God will mourn with those who mourn, comfort the afflicted, feed the hungry and clothe the naked, and strengthen the weak. He will abide with us in every time of trouble, and one day He will compensate us for all our troubles. He will save us with a mighty salvation. The meek shall inherit the earth and the fulness thereof.

They are promised that their observance of the Word of Wisdom, in conjunction with all other commandments, will provide them with protection from death accruing to those who believe in the blood of the Lamb Jesus Christ (see Doctrine and Covenants 89:3, 21).

They are promised peace in mortality and eternal life in the eternities (see Doctrine and Covenants 59:23).

How marvelous. The blessing of peace in this life is a rare commodity, a precious possession. Given the turmoil, tumult, and travail of so many in this world of war and strife, whether within individuals, between people, inside nations, or across boundaries, the reward of peace—peace of conscience, peace of feeling, peace of mind—is a truly remarkable blessing. Of course, the peace we can feel now is but a prelude to what lies ahead in the world of peace that is God's kingdom of peace where the Prince of Peace lives.

They are promised that they will have hope through Christ's Atonement and resurrection to be raised to eternal life (see Moroni 7:41).

This is a hope worth having, a hope that transcends the temporary and transitory, a hope that gives meaning to our days and purpose to our lives, a hope that sees us through many mists of darkness. This lively hope is not in vain. It will be rewarded with a life of loving longevity.

They are promised that they will see the Lord in this life, in the next, or in both (see Doctrine and Covenants 67:10; 88:68–69; 93:1).

This is a promised privilege. It is the word of the Lord, and He does not lie or play games. The Lord is interested in His people. He loves them personally. He wants them to see Him, know Him, and love Him. So, those who are sufficiently humble will see beyond the veil that separates this world from the next. This veil is to be pierced, transcended, peered through. That is, they will break the barrier of worldliness and see the face of the Lord. Also, they shall know it is the Lord they see—there will be no confusion about who it is. To those who are spiritually ready, this guarantee is a most welcome invitation and declaration. Those faithful who do not see the face of the Lord in this life will nonetheless see Him in the next world. This is sure and certain.

They are promised a second Comforter to attend them and stay with them. This is the sure promise of being cleansed and sanctified so that they can dwell in celestial glory (see Doctrine and Covenants 88:3–4, 75).

This is a promise worth preparing for and living for. The promise of being clean before the Lord, of being spotless through His grace so that we might be holy and be qualified to enter the presence of the Lord for all eternity. This promise will rest in their hearts and minds and fortify their souls through all the vicissitudes of life.

They are promised that either they will not taste of death or that their death will be sweet, if they die in the Lord (see Ether 12:17; Doctrine and Covenants 42:46).

They are promised that they will be raised to live with God forever, in a condition of happiness that will endure everlastingly (see Alma 28:12).

In times of darkness and turmoil, we need to know the source of our salvation. We can rejoice that our troubles are for a moment, but our joy will have an infinite duration. God is our hope in darkness and daylight, in strength and weakness, in love and loss.

They are promised that the things that will be revealed to them in time and eternity will be the meaningful things of God, which will surpass what they have heard, seen, and felt before (see 1 Corinthians 2:9–10).

I believe that God will give the righteous such wonderful experiences of sight, sound, touch, taste, and feeling that they will cause wonder, amazement, astonishment, surprise, rejoicing, and happiness beyond compare.

PROMISES TO THE CHURCH

God has promised that faithful covenant Church members will be armed with righteousness and power in the latter days (see 1 Nephi 14:14). We can trust in His help, gain strength from His loyalty, and receive power at His hand. God's power will be upon us as we are loyal to our covenants. This will be a very real shield and protection to us against danger, temptation, and distraction.

PROMISES TO THE WORLD

We are promised that Christ will return in a day not far distant and reign in righteousness on the earth. The earth will be renewed and abound with treasures of knowledge and material plenty. We will experience a paradise of beauty. Wickedness, war, worldliness, waste, and weariness will be conquered, and the world will experience a season of peace and prosperity never known before.

OUR PROMISES TO HIM

It is important that we make and keep promises to God. We must go and do (see 1 Nephi 3:7). He will prepare the way, and we must desire, work, commit, focus, and endure. There will be difficulties and tests, but we can accomplish if we persevere in righteousness. Our strategy should be to do likewise—be men and women of promise. We are to stand fast and be steadfast. Our determination can be sure. The strait and narrow way is the path of promise. As we faithfully follow this covenant path the blessings are certain—in the Lord's own time and way. Our promise is to live up to the godly likeness inherent within us. We can receive His image in our countenances, His character in our souls, His attributes in our example, and His might in our devotion (see Alma 5). We are what we love, what we focus on, devote ourselves to, align ourselves with, spend our time on, and dedicate our energies to.

I love the description given to us in the Book of Mormon about how we are to nourish the gospel seed:

> And behold, as the tree beginneth to grow, ye will say: Let us nourish it with great care. . . . But if ye will nourish the word, yea, nourish the tree as it beginneth to grow, by your faith with

great diligence, and with patience, looking forward to the fruit thereof, it shall take root; and behold it shall be a tree springing up unto everlasting life. . . . By and by ye shall pluck the fruit thereof, which is most precious, which is sweet above all that is sweet, and which is white above all that is white, yea, and pure above all that is pure; and ye shall feast upon this fruit even until ye are filled, that ye hunger not, neither shall ye thirst.

Then, my brethren, ye shall reap the rewards of your faith, and your diligence, and patience, and long-suffering, waiting for the tree to bring forth fruit unto you. (Alma 32:37–43)

I note that the nourishing we are to do of the word of God planted within us is to be done with **great** care. We are to look forward in faith to the outcome of eternal life, we are to nourish the tree also with **great** diligence, patience, vision, faith, and long-suffering. If we take this approach, then eventually we will see the full flowering as manifest in the complete tree. Essentially, we must do more than receive the gospel initially. We must continually work at helping the seed grow, develop, expand, and increase. We need to continue to do this on a long-term, lifelong basis. So, what is our promise to the Lord? It is a promise of lifelong effort and loyalty until the task is complete.

"Come unto the Lord with all your heart, and work out your own salvation with fear and trembling before him" (Mormon 9:27). As God shows no deviation and fickleness in His promises to us, so likewise we are to learn to listen to Him, believe in Him, come to Him, and work with Him. The idea of doing this amidst our own fear and trembling suggests that we will have to face some fears and overcome some obstacles in this process. Thus, our standing before Him will be steadfast. We will continue to fulfill our promises to Him, come what may. We are to rely on, lean on, depend upon, and trust in Him. In this way He will be able to trust that our word is our bond. "I, the Lord, am bound when ye do what I say; but when ye do not what I say, ye have no promise" (Doctrine and Covenants 82:10). The Lord must bless us when we act in accordance with His direction. It is an eternal law. He is bound by His own promise to reward us in righteousness. Therefore, we need to **remember,**

reflect, and renew our faith in God and His promises. This will help us to stand firm in times of difficulty, holding on to our hope that his word will not fall to the ground.

CONCLUSION

We may be in the middle of "a mountain height, a stormy sea, the battle's front, the dark and rugged way, a lowly place" (see Hymn no. 270). We may be facing a lion's den, a furnace of affliction, a deep pit, a dark abyss. However, we do not face this lion alone or trudge this rugged way unaided. We have access to the matchless power of God. He has granted us power, knowledge, strength, capacity, and might. He has walked with us, watched over us, welcomed us into His circle of love, and washed over us with His spirit. He is mindful of us. In the strength of the Lord we can be helped, healed, and held. Many times, I have struggled. I faced much darkness of the soul, midnight moments, self-doubts, emotional turbulence, fear, and worries. Fear of people, of situations, of conflict, of failure. I had many inadequacies and weaknesses. The Lord helped me many times to endure. I needed His help deeply, daily, and desperately. And of course, such challenges have also been a feature of my life since then—in so many ways, in diverse circumstances, and numerous times. But God is faithful, able, strong, and powerful. He has consoled and comforted me. He has lifted and inspired me. He has nourished and embraced me. His hand has been upon me. His light has been my guide. His power has reinvigorated me. His purity has cleansed me. I have walked through the valley of the shadow of death many times. I have wept and wearied the Lord with my pleadings. I have gone to my Father in Heaven in fervent prayer in search of divine help. God has not failed me but has been a never-failing strength in times of terrible trouble.

Those who trust in God, though they be hurt, afflicted, downtrodden, rejected, sick, downcast, humiliated, or broken will find that He will bless them with a power far beyond their own, with a resolve that is astonishing, with ability far in excess of what they naturally possess. I believe these great and precious promises with all my soul, for I have felt them. I am a witness. I know that God is our high tower, our strength, our salvation. He is amazing. Jesus Christ is supremely intelligent, energetic, and alive. He is powerful, strong, and mighty. He shares His power with mortal man when we bow before God in humble penitence. He will lift the tired, bless the afflicted, give hope to the despairing, and strengthen the weak. He will quiet the storms, restore the sick, and save the downtrodden when we come unto Him. These are not idle promises but are certain realities. I believe, and am sure, that He is the Christ, the living Son of the living God. I know this personally and deeply. He is my Lord and my God. He is my redeeming Savior, my hope, my joy, my all. Without reservation I declare that He lives—with all that this declaration means. He listens, loves, and lifts. He is mighty beyond compare. He is the Only Begotten of the Father—full of grace, equity, mercy, and truth. Nothing can conquer Him or His power. He has derailed death, smashed sin, and hurled hell away from us.

I rejoice in God's marvelous goodness. His plan is one of life, abundance, and beauty. He will likewise help you during your darkness. He will lighten your burdens or strengthen your soul so that you can carry your cross. He will raise you up to dwell with Him in glory. In the strength of the Lord you can do all things. I pray the blessings of this good, generous, and great God upon you now and forever. We do well to always remember that our loving Lord is able to light our lives. I therefore conclude in remembrance of the miraculous majesty of the Light and Life of the World—the Lord Jesus Christ. He is truly the light that never darkens, the helper that never tires, and the joy that never fades. There is no other way to true joy but His way. There is no other Messiah except Jesus of Nazareth. There is no other path to happiness except for the one He has revealed through His living servants. There is no true church other than the one He leads and directs. There is no light or life except that which comes from Him. This is certain. This is sure. This is the foundation upon which an eternal house of faith must be built if it is to survive the storms of life. I rejoice in His character, goodness, love, and perfection. Life is truly and deeply meaningful because of Him. The Son of God descended beneath all things for us—all sadness, all sickness, all sin, all suffering. Then He ascended above all things—all worldliness, all weakness, all weariness, all wastefulness. The restored gospel teaches this powerfully, clearly, and consistently. He is truly the King of Kings, the Great Emmanuel, the Bright and Morning Star who atoned for the world. May we each find the remarkable new life that can be ours through Him.

ABOUT THE AUTHOR

Thomas Holton lives in the Emerald Isle. He achieved degrees in taxation, social science, and international relations and two years toward a professional financial planning diploma. His career has been in insurance, tax advice, and as a manager in the civil service. His Church service includes a mission to England, Sunday School teacher four times, branch/district/stake Sunday School president, bishop's counselor, elders quorum president twice, branch president (for ten years), stake high councilor, and Church history specialist for the island of Ireland. He survived two major surgeries and loves to share his faith in Jesus Christ. He and his wife, Veronica, are the grateful parents of one son.

PERSONAL NOTES

You've dreamed of accomplishing your publishing goal for ages—holding *that* book in your hands. We want to partner with you in bringing this dream to light.

Whether you're an aspiring author looking to publish your first book or a seasoned author who's been published before, we want to hear from you. Please submit your manuscript to

CEDARFORT.SUBMITTABLE.COM/SUBMIT

CEDAR FORT HAS PUBLISHED BOOKS IN THE FOLLOWING GENRES

- LDS Nonfiction
- Fiction
- Juvenile & YA
- Biographies
- Regency Romances
- Cozy Mysteries
- General Nonfiction
- Cookbooks
- Children's Books
- Self-Help
- Comic & Activity books
- Children's books with customizable character illustrations